SAA

Series on International Arbitration

Volume 9

Selected Papers on International Arbitration

Series on International Arbitration

SAA

SWISS
ARBITRATION
ACADEMY

Volume 9

Selected Papers on International Arbitration

Stämpfli Publishers

Bibliographic information published by the Deutsche Nationalbibliothek
Bibliographic information published by the German National Library
The German National Library lists this publication in the German National Bibliography; detailed bibliographic data are available on the Internet at http://dnb.d-nb.de.

ISBN 978-3-7272-2630-4

In our online bookshop www.staempflirecht.ch
the following edition is available:

E-Book ISBN 978-3-7272-2423-2

For questions regarding product safety
Producer: Stämpfli Publishers Ltd., Wölflistrasse 1, CH-3001 Bern,
verlag@staempfli.ch, www.staempflirecht.ch
EU Importer: Brockhaus Commission GmbH, Kreidlerstrasse 9,
DE-70806 Kornwestheim, gpsr@brocom.de, www.brocom.de

Der Schreiber steht für unseren Anspruch, gemeinsam mit unseren Autorinnen und Autoren relevante und herausragende Inhalte zu produzieren.

Note from the Editors

The Swiss Arbitration Academy (SAA) Series on International Arbitration presents a curated selection of outstanding research papers by participants who have successfully completed the SAA postgraduate program in international arbitration, offered in cooperation with the Universities of Lucerne and Neuchâtel. In addition to meeting rigorous academic standards, only papers that achieved distinction in the Certificate of Advanced Studies (CAS) and demonstrate clear relevance to the law and practice of international arbitration are considered for publication. All contributions have been supervised by members of the SAA Academic Council.

This ninth volume brings together four studies addressing distinct and timely dimensions of international arbitration. Alex Alvise Corti analyses the intersection of international commercial arbitration and third-party litigation funding, with particular emphasis on conflicts of interest and disclosure obligations. Samantha Regenthal examines investment treaty arbitration and access to medicines, focusing on post-pandemic developments. Mehmet Tank reassesses procedural safeguards by considering the implications of artificial intelligence for the right to be heard in international arbitration. Finally, Lauri Markus Heiskanen investigates consent beyond signature, addressing the extension of arbitration agreements under Finnish and Swedish law.

The Swiss Arbitration Academy offers an intensive program in international arbitration for lawyers, in-house counsel, graduate students and other professionals seeking advanced education in international dispute resolution. The Certificate of Advanced Studies is a joint degree of the University of Lucerne and the University of Neuchâtel, delivered in collaboration with the SAA, and is conferred upon participants who successfully complete four modules and pass an oral examination. The program provides comprehensive treatment of the fundamentals of international arbitration, as well as the practice and procedures of major arbitral institutions, including the Swiss Arbitration Centre, ICC, SIAC, HKIAC, DIS and VIAC, among others. It also addresses the specific features of ad hoc arbitration. Further information is available at: http://cas-arbitration.ch/

The editors thank the authors for their valuable contributions and are pleased to present their work to the arbitration community. We also extend our gratitude to the Director of Studies, Anna Ptitsina, for her invaluable support throughout the editorial process. This publication has been made possible through the continued support of Stämpfli Verlag AG.

November 2025

Daniel Girsberger and Christoph Müller Professors at the Universities of Lucerne and Neuchâtel

Table of Contends

ALEX ALVISE CORTI

International Commercial Arbitration & Third – Party Litigation Funding: Conflicts of interest and Disclosure

LAURI MARKUS HEISKANEN

Consent Beyond Signature: Extending Arbitration Agreements in Finnish and Swedish Law

List of Abbreviations

¶/¶¶	Paragraph(s)
AAA	The American Arbitration Association
AAA-ICDR Principles	The American Arbitration Association's International Centre for Dispute Resolution Principles
ADHD	Attention Deficit Hyperactivity Disorder
ADR	Alternative Dispute Resolution
AG	Aktiengesellschaft – Swiss joint-stock company
ANDA	Abbreviated New Drug Application
AI	Artificial Intelligence
AIDR	AI-assisted dispute resolution
art./arts.	Article/articles
ASA	Association Suisse de l'Arbitrage (Swiss Arbitration Association)
ATF	Arrêts du Tribunal fédéral (French)
BGE	Bundesgerichtsentscheid – Published decision of the Swiss Federal Supreme Court
BGH	Bundesgerichtshof (Federal Court of Justice, Germany)
BGer	Bundesgericht – Not published decisions in the Swiss Federal Supreme Court
BGFA	Bundesgesetz über die Freizügigkeit der Anwältinnen und Anwälte – Federal Act on the Freedom of Movement of Lawyers
BIT	Bilateral Investment Treaty
CAGR	Compound Annual Growth Rate
CAS	Certificate of Advanced Studies
CEPEC	Commission européenne pour l'efficacité de la justice (European Commission for the Efficiency of Justice)
CIArb	Chartered Institute of Arbitrators
CIArb Guideline	The Chartered Institute of Arbitrators Guideline on the Use of AI in Arbitration

consid.	Considering, paragraph
COVID-19	Corona VIrus Disease – 2019
CPR	Conflict Prevention & Resolution
DISCO	DISCO E-Discovery Platform
DSC	Decision of the Swiss Federal Supreme Court
eds.	Editors
Ed.	Edited
et al.	Et alii / aliae (and others)
et seq.	Following pages/paragraphs
et seqq.	Et sequentia (following pages)
e.g.	exempli gratia – for example
EU	European Union
EU AI Act	European Union's Artificial Intelligence Act
EU Ethics Guidelines	EU Independent High-Level Expert Group on Artificial Intelligence Ethics Guidelines for Trustworthy AI
f./ff.	Following page(s)
FAI	Finland Arbitration Institute
FCTC	Framework Convention on Tobacco Control
FET	Fair and Equitable Treatment
ff.	following
FINMA	Eidgenössische Finanzmarktaufsicht – Swiss Financial Market Supervisory Authority
fn.	Footnote
FPS	Full Protection and Security
FS	Festschrift
FTA	Free Trade Agreement
GAR	Global Arbitration Review
GATT	General Agreement on Tariffs and Trade

GDPR	General Data Protection Regulation
GPT	Generative Pre-trained Transformer
HKIAC	Hong Kong International Arbitration Centre
IBA	International Bar Association
ICC	International Chamber of Commerce
ICC Rules	International Rules of the International Chamber of Commerce
ICCA	International Council for Commercial Arbitration
ICDR	International Centre for Dispute Resolution
ICSID	International Center for Settlement of Investment Disputes
IIA	International Investment Agreement
ILFA	International Legal Finance Association
Infra	Cited below
IP	Intellectual Property
JAMS	Judicial Arbitration and Mediation Services
JFT	Juridiska Föreningens Tidskrift
KKO	Korkein oikeus (Supreme Court of Finland)
LCIA	London Court of International Arbitration
LLM(s)	Large Language Model(s)
Ltd	Limited
MFN	Most Favoured Nation
MoH	Ministry of Health
NAFTA	North American Free Trade Agreement
NJA	Nytt juridiskt arkiv (Supreme Court of Sweden case reports)
N./n.	number
NLP	Natural Language Processing
NYC	New York Convention (Convention on the Recognition and Enforcement of Foreign Arbitral Awards, 1958)

OECD	Organisation for Economic Co-operation and Development
OCR	Optical Character Recognition
OGH	Oberster Gerichtshof (Austrian Supreme Court)
OR	Obligationenrecht – Swiss Code of Obligations
p.	Page
Para. (s)	Paragraph (s)
PhD	Philosophiae Doctor
PILA	Swiss Federal Act on Private International Law
R&D	Research & Development
SAA	Swiss Arbitration Academy
SAC	Swiss Arbitration Centre
SCAI	Swiss Chambers' Arbitration Institution
SCC	Arbitration Institute of the Stockholm Chamber of Commerce
SIAC	Singapore International Arbitration Centre
SPILA	Swiss Private International Law Act
SSRN	Social Science Research Network
Swiss Rules	Swiss Rules of International Arbitration
SVAMC	Silicon Valley Arbitration & Mediation Center
SVAMC Guidelines	SVAMC, Guidelines on the Use of Artificial Intelligence in ArbitrationSupra
SvJT	Svensk Juristtidning
TIP	Treaty with Investment Provisions
TPLF	Third Party Litigation Funding
TRIPS	WTO Agreement on Trade-Related Aspects of Intellectual Property Rights
UK	United Kingdom
UKHL	United Kingdom House of Lords (Judicial Committee)

UNCTAD	United Nations Trade and Development
UNCITRAL	United Nations Commission on International Trade Law
UNCITRAL Model Law	UNCITRL Model Law on International Commercial Arbitration
UNESCO	United Nations Educational, Scientific and Cultural Organization
USP(s)	Unique Selling Proposition(s)
US	United States
VAG	Versicherungsaufsichtsgesetz – Insurance Supervision Act
v.	Versus
VIAC	Vienna International Arbitral Centre
Vol.	Volume
WHO	World Health Organization
WIPO	World Intellectual Property Organization
ZGB	Zivilgesetzbuch – Swiss Civil Code
ZPO	Zivilprozessordnung – Swiss Civil Procedure Code

International Commercial Arbitration & Third – Party Litigation Funding: Conflicts of interest and Disclosure

ALEX ALVISE CORTI

Table of Contents

I. Summary

Third-party litigation funding (hereinafter TPLF) refers to an arrangement where a non-contracting entity provides financial or other material support to help a disputing party pursue a dispute resolution proceeding. While this mechanism offers significant benefits, such as enhancing access to justice, experts have raised concerns about the potential risks it entails, chief among them being conflicts of interest. Conflicts of interest primarily arise between arbitrators and disputing parties. As more funders enter the picture, the web of relationships grows, increasing the likelihood for such conflicts to occur. If a conflict of interest remains undiscovered, the integrity and legitimacy of the arbitration process are put at risk. This can compromise the impartiality of the tribunal and even the validity of an award. Delays in proceedings may arise when a conflict is detected late, but the greater danger lies in conflicts that go unnoticed, leading to wasted time, resources, and ultimately undermining trust in the arbitral system.

The TPLF market has experienced rapid growth in recent years, particularly in the field of international arbitration as it will be shown in the following. Its benefits as well as the potential risks it may carry, have drawn significant attention from arbitral institutions and arbitrators. On a global level, the TPLF market size is estimated at 17.5 billion in 2024. It is awaited to reach USD 67.2 Billion by the end of 2037, with an estimated growth of 11.1 % Compound Annual Growth Rate (also CAGR).[1] TPLF has become a topic of growing interest among the legal community, especially for the lack of proper regulation. In Switzerland, many funders are active on the market. Most participants based in Switzerland appear to concentrate primarily on state court litigation, particularly, in cases involving civil liability, intellectual property, and inheritance disputes.[2] Other areas of law with funded cases include general contract and corporate law, such as matters related to the liability of directors and officers.[3] Compared to the global market, the Swiss is still rela-

[1] For more details on the market growth see: PartResearch Nester Report on forecast period 2025 – 2037 available at https://www.researchnester.com/reports/litigation-funding-investment-market/2800#market-trends, last visited on August 26, 2025.

[2] As a general indication, funders focus on Bankruptcy, Real Estate, Divorce and Inheritance, Commercial dispute. See also at https://www.swisslegalfinance.ch/qualifying, last visited on August 26, 2025.

[3] See WEGMÜLLER M., Prozessfinanzierung in der Schweiz: Bestandesaufnahme und Ausblick, in: HAVE 2013 235 et seqq., p. 240 et seq.; DÄHLER P., Juristische, ökonomische und soziale Aspekte der Prozessfinanzierung, Presentation at the Europa Institut Zürich on 27 January 2012, Section 8.

tively small. Swiss funders ordinarily require a minimum amount in dispute, ranging from 250,000 to 7 million Swiss francs.[4]

Because very little information or guidance is provided on the topic of disclosure, conflicts of interest could arise.[5] Although arbitral institutions emphasize and enforce the necessity of an arbitrator's independence and impartiality,[6] they provide limited guidance on third-party TPLF agreements and their potential impact on an arbitrator's impartiality or independence in the event of a conflict.

II. Introduction

TPLF refers to an arrangement where an entity from outside the contractual relationship provides financial or material support to help a disputing party pursue a dispute resolution proceeding. Despite its seemingly simple definition, TPLF is a multifaceted concept. Its economic implications, and the benefits it provides to funded parties, have gradually prompted regulatory changes worldwide. Institutional rules require their arbitrators to be and to stay independent and impartial. Where impartiality refers to the aim of the arbitrator and independency refers to the personal relationship between the arbitrator and the involved parties, TPLF included.[7]

The rise of third-party funding agreements has allowed parties to pursue arbitration, but it also introduces a considerable risk of conflicts of interest. among the involved parties. Attorneys involved must take care to avoid such conflicts, ensuring their professional duties to their clients are upheld.[8] The

4 As a rule, minimum requirements are 250,000 francs (Profina), 1.5 million francs (Swiss LegalFinance) and 7 million francs (Nivalion), see http://www.profina.ch/eignung.html, last visited on January 26, 2025; https://www.swisslegalfinance.ch/qualifying, last visited on August 26, 2026; https://nivalion.com/en/what-we-do/direct-funding, last visited on January 26, 2026).

5 GARIMELLA S. R., Third Party Funding in International Arbitration – Issues and Challenges in: Asian Jurisdictions, AALCO Journal of International Law, 2014, Vol. 3, Issue 1, pp. 45-60, at par. 47. Available at SSRN: https://ssrn.com/abstract=2520393, last visited on August 26, 2025.

6 ICC Rules of Arbitration art. 11.1 – ICDR International Arbitration Rules art. 14 – LCIA Arbitration Rules art. 5.3. – UNCITRAL Arbitration Rules art. 12.1 – Swiss PILA Art. 12.

7 GARIMELLA S.R, Third Party Funding in International Arbitration – Issues and Challenges in: Asian Jurisdictions, AALCO Journal of International Law, 2014, Vol. 3, Issue 1, pp. 45-60, at par. 47. Available at SSRN: https://ssrn.com/abstract=2520393, last visited on August 26, 2025.

8 See Section IV.

arbitral community is relatively small, with arbitrators frequently being reappointed, counsel representing multiple parties, and funders exerting influence over financial decisions. It happens that a lawyer caught between the interests of the client and those of the funder may find themselves in a precarious role, because as counsel he/she has to serve multiple tasks. This dynamic strikingly echoes the predicament portrayed in Carlo Goldoni's celebrated comedy *"The Servant of Two Masters"*. In the play, the cunning protagonist *"Truffaldino"* attempts to serve two employers at once, deftly navigating their conflicting demands while concealing his divided loyalties. Likewise, in the context of third-party litigation funding. The constant tension between these competing obligations creates fertile ground for conflicts of interest, threatening both professional integrity and procedural fairness.

The purpose of this research is to define the potential conflicts of interest, which may arise between the parties, with particular attention to arbitrators, TPLFs, and investors.

At Section III the research begins with a definition of TPLF and its market mechanism. It then progresses towards a practical definition, exploring various application models tailored to the needs of different stakeholders, both claimants and private interests. The research then discusses the potential effects of conflicts of interest related to TPLF on the arbitration process and clarify the situations in which such conflicts may arise.

Following this premises, the paper examines the Swiss market and its regulation of TPLFs, considering both the legislative framework and evolution with its practical implications. The analysis will also explore the practical structure of a Swiss Agreement on TPLF.

Moreover, Section IV addresses the issue of conflicts of interest and the obligation of disclosure. The chapter begins by defining what constitutes a conflict of interest, identifying the parties involved (arbitrators, TPLFs and investors). It then explores the key aspects of disclosure, what should be disclosed, how, and when. From the perspective of impartiality and independence of arbitrators, this Part examines various systems designed to prevent conflicts of interest, concluding with recommendations on the disclosure obligation and consequences of a violation.

Section V revisits the disclosure obligation, emphasizing its positive impact on both the arbitration process and the subsequent award. The section highlights how proper disclosure contributes to the potential international recognition of the award, ensuring transparency and fairness throughout the process.

Finally, in the Section VI, the research will summarize the key points discussed throughout the research and reflect on the main findings, while also suggesting possible future directions or areas for improvement.

III. Third – Party Litigation Fundings

The TPLF financing system for cases related to international arbitration law has become predominant, making it comparable to any other investment instrument. Not surprisingly, doubts and concerns have been raised about this system's legitimacy. Chief among them, at least, is the potential confusion between the role of the arbitrator and the role of the legal representative,[9] as well as situations where the funder exerts such influence over the proceedings that they effectively become a party to the case; therefore, allowing them to participate in the selection and appointment of arbitrators.[10] It was in 2013 when Chief Justice Sundaresh Menon first expressed concern over these developments, and since then, many states and international arbitration institutions have felt the need to regulate or to, at least, establish rules for this investment system. However, critical issues remain, particularly concerning conflicts of interest and the obligation of disclosure for the parties involved.

A. Market Overview on TPLF

In the economic landscape, there is a continuous development of new financing systems to better meet market demands. A critical observer may have noticed TPLF and wondered whether they represent an investment vehicle or rather serve the legal proceeding. Without retracing the history of TPLF, which has already been extensively covered in the literature, it is sufficient to say, despite initial skepticism,[11] they have gradually established themselves in the market.

---

9 In this example the author refers to the possible situation where a funder funds multiple different claims, in which the same person has been appointed as an arbitrator in one claim and act as a legal representative in another.

10 SUNDARESH M., Some cautionary notes for an age of opportunity, Keynote Address, Chartered Institute of Arbitrators International Arbitration Conference, Penang, 22 August 2013, p. 6.

11 The High Court of Australia was to first to rule on the legitimacy of TPLF. In 2006 the High Court ruled on the *Fostif Case* establishing its legitimacy under the Australian law. It is not against public policy for a funder to finance and control litigation for profit. Litigation funded on this basis is not considered an abuse of the court's pro-

As expressively codified in many jurisdictions[12], the party initiating or defending a lawsuit is responsible for covering the costs and bearing the risks associated with litigation. For those lacking the financial means to pursue legal proceedings, modern legal systems offer various degrees of legal aid through public funds based on the individual's financial situation to help manage legal fees and court expenses. Limited economic resources, and the resulting inability to afford legal costs or assume litigation risks,[13] constitute the fundamental premise and the primary obstacles to accessing justice and resolving disputes.[14] The principle of access to justice is conceived as a natural right and codified in modern constitutions. It is now widely recognized that affirmative state action is essential to guarantee universal access to these fundamental social rights.[15] The rising costs and challenges of litigation, along with the financial capacity are making it harder to resolve disputes, even for those with enough resources.[16] In this climate of uncertainty and limited resources, legal entities have emerged, offering to cover the costs and risks of litigation in exchange for a percentage of the recovery, but only if the case is successful, sometimes even taking over the claim itself. This growing business practice, known as TPLF,[17] is often linked to the expanding litigation market.[18] On this basis, it should come as no surprise various actors with

cess. On the contrary, the minority in the High Court saw third parties as alien in the controversy before the court aimed to make money by creating disputes and assuming the control of the legal strategy in order to manipulate the procedure and obtain the maximal profit. Among the issues raised during the process, some ethical concerns were about the TPLF taking control of the litigation, possible conflicts of interests and breach of the confidentiality principle. In other words, an abuse of the administration of justice by "trafficking" disputes and, not least, a decline in the lawyer's independency and fiduciary duties towards the funded client.

12 Switzerland under artt. 98 and 106 of the Swiss Civil Procedure Code (RS 272); United Kingdom (Civil Procedure Rules, Part. 44, Rule 44.2.a) and Unites States of America (Federal Rules of Civil Procedure, Rule 54 on Judgement and Costs) follow the same principle where the losing party bears the costs of the litigation; Germany under art. 91 and following under the German Civil Procedure Code.

13 Such as legal costs, adverse costs in case of loss, damages and penalties.

14 For more details see CAPPELLETTI M. / GARTH B., Access to Justice: The Newest Wave in the Worldwide Movement to Make Rights Effective, Buffalo Law Review 181, 1978, Vol. 27, p. 186 ff.

15 Ibidem.

16 CROFT J., Litigation Finance Follows Credit Crunch, January 27, 2010, available at https://www.thejudgeglobal.com/litigation-finance-follows-credit-crunch/, last visited on August 26, 2025.

17 For further details about the definition of this term see Section B.1.

18 ABRAMS D. / CHEN DL., A Market for Justice: A First Empirical Look at Third Party Litigation Funding, University of Pennsylvania Journal of Business Law, 2013, Vol 15, p. 1075. Third-party litigation funding is growing fast, with more high – value

a primarily economic focus have been able to respond to market demand. In other words, private entities – third parties – interested in intervening with the prospect of profit from a variable investment and willing to take on the associated risks. In doing so, the door is effectively opened to speculative avenues,[19] allowing hedge funds, private equity funds, or sovereign wealth funds to invest and even directly interfere in the dispute, potentially controlling its progress.[20]

In contrast to the past, property rights have evolved significantly, and the law now recognizes various forms to accommodate different needs. In this context, a party holds property rights in a claim, which include the rights to possess and transfer it. By selling all or part of the claim, the party can effectively transfer these rights and eliminate the associated risks of litigation. A rational claimholder will try to get the maximum value from the case, keeping the rights they consider most important and selling or transferring the others to those who value them more. For example, they could sell their claim to an assignee or transfer part of the interest in the outcome of the case to an investor, thus transferring all or part of their legal rights. Also, since many people are risk-averse, they might be willing to pay to reduce the risks related to the case, thereby increasing the overall value of the claim.[21]

At the core, the involvement of TPLF in legal disputes creates a system with multiple economic actors, whose entities are not always distinctly defined,

---

cases like IP disputes and class actions pushing the market toward $67.2 billion by 2037. There are more legal cases happening across different areas, adding to this growth. Easier access to funding also means more people and smaller businesses can now afford to take legal action. See COLEMAN J., 5 Trends in litigation funding for 2025: key insights for investors, available at https://www.haysmewscapital.com/news/litigation-funding-trends#:~:text=What's%20driving%20this%20market%20expansion,their%20slice%20of%20the%20pie, last visited on August 26, 2025.

19 As more private actors enter the market for purely economic purposes, despite the high uncertainty and risk, it blurs the line between strategic funding and opportunistic interference in legal disputes.

20 See also U.S. Chamber of Commerce, Setting the Record Straight on Third-Party Litigation Funding, October 15, 2024, available at https://www.uschamber.com/lawsuits/setting-the-record-straight-on-third-party-litigation-funding, last visited on August 26, 2025.

21 The claimholder could seek the support of TPLF, who cover the legal costs in exchange for a portion of the profits from a successful outcome of the case. This allows the claimholder to reduce financial risk, as they will not have to bear all the costs alone. DE MORPURGO M., A Comparative Legal and Economic Approach to Third-Party Litigation Funding, in: Cardozo Journal of International & Comparative Law (eds.), 2011, Vol. 19, p. 350, available at http://biblioteca.cejamericas.org/bitstream/handle/2015/260/Morpurgo.pdf?sequence=1&isAllowed=y, last visited on August 26, 2025.

and in which interests unrelated to the dispute become part of the proceedings. In practice, this forms a phenomenon better known as "legal finance",[22] whose apparent goal is to facilitate access to justice, ensuring a level playing field and mitigating the risks associated with loss. Nevertheless, one must question why investors are willing to assume the risk. The obvious answer lies within the realm of high-risk financial instruments, where the investor, aware of the potential profit in case of victory, is willing to invest a sum of money in anticipation of future success. This behavior is manifestly speculative, raising concerns about how to protect the legal process from the private interests of investors who aim only to maximize their return on investment. What is known as arbitration finance is now a branch of corporate finance.[23] It focuses on treating arbitration claims as assets, capable of being leveraged to finance entire portfolios of cases, as well as individual disputes.[24] As well as the claim can be valued, the possible form of financing is endless giving the financial investment the structure of derivatives.[25]

---

22 As stated from the International Legal Finance Association (ILFA): Commercial legal finance serves individuals who are unable to take on the financial risks of seeking redress against more powerful opponents, those unwilling to shoulder the material financial burdens inherent in obtaining such redress, or those in search of rational capital solutions for their litigation challenges. In an imbalanced litigation system, well-financed repeat defendants have secured an undue advantage, which they are eager to maintain. By levelling the playing field, commercial legal finance threatens this advantage, prompting a global campaign of disinformation aimed at discrediting both the concept and its providers. As a globally constituted trade association, ILFA is committed to countering these misleading narratives through worldwide advocacy and data-driven information, ensuring that access to justice is fairly transformed. See also https://www.ilfa.com/#best-practice, last visited on August 26, 2025.

23 There is a lack of comprehensive information on TPLF in commercial litigation, and even less regarding investor state arbitration. In these areas, commercial TPLF providers often operate discreetly within small, niche markets (VAN BOOM WILLEM H., Third-Party Financing in International Investment Arbitration, 2011, p. 30 available at SSRN: http://ssrn.com/abstract=2027114 or http://dx.doi.org/10.2139/ssrn.2027114). Many funders view TPLF as an all-encompassing investment product, rather than merely a contract for legal services (Ibidem). Hedge funds and certain investment banking traders have long found litigation risks appealing because these risks are uncorrelated with traditional financial markets (Ibidem). Since the outcome of a lawsuit is independent of stock or bond market fluctuations, hedge funds aiming for diversified portfolios have increasingly turned to litigation financing (Ibidem).

24 See also BURFORD CAPITAL, Financing international arbitration, available at https://www.burfordcapital.com/media/pk0lub05/international-arbitration-financing-us.pdf, last visited on August 26, 2025.

25 Imagine the situation where a hedge fund invests in a portfolio of pending lawsuits without caring about the merits. After a due diligence, it bets that a few big wins will exceed the losses. Multiple legal claims bundled into portfolios and used to attract risk

B. Definitions and Organisation

1. Definitions

At first glance, the definition of *"Third-Party Litigation Funding"* may seem firmly established as it is the most widely used term; however, it is not the only term employed to refer to this phenomenon in legal finance. On the contrary, *"the nomenclature to describe this kind of third-party capital investment in arbitration or litigation claims is all over the map and woefully undescriptive"*.[26] It has been referred to as *"third-party funding"*, *"third-party litigation funding or financing"*, or most commonly *"alternative litigation funding or financing"*.[27] Focusing exclusively on the United States, it has been suggested to use the term *"Alternative Litigation Financing"* to characterize the practice of providing capital from non-traditional sources to civil plaintiffs, defendants, or their lawyers for litigation-related activities. Specifically, this refers to entities other than the plaintiffs, defendants, their lawyers, or the defendants' insurers.[28] Regardless of the terminology used, it appears to be merely a stylistic debate. What matters is understanding the functioning of the financing model itself. Therefore, for the purposes of this paper, the various nomenclatures employed should be regarded as referring to the same phenomenon, regardless of any strictly theoretical considerations. TPLF, within the field of legal finance, is a litigation financing instrument enabling law firms and their clients to pursue their claims by leveraging capital from

- based investments. Like in the structured debt investment, TPLF don't own the legal claim and speculate on the outcome without being directly involved. SUNDARESH M., Some cautionary notes for an age of opportunity, Keynote Address, Chartered Institute of Arbitrators International Arbitration Conference, Penang, 22 August 2013, p. 9 with reference to Rebecca Lowe, "Speculate and Arbitrate to Accumulate", IBA Global Insight April/May 2013.

26 DE STEFANO BEARDSLEE M., Non-Lawyers Influencing Lawyers: Too Many Cooks in the Kitchen or Stone Soup, 2012, in Fordham Law Review (eds.), Vol 80, Issue 6, Article 16, 2791, p. 2796, footnote 22. See also ABA Common Ethics 20/20, White Paper on Alternative Litigation Finance 1 & nn.1–4 (draft Oct. 19, 2011), available at http://www.americanbar.org/content/dam/aba/administrative/ethics_2020/20111019_draft_alf_white_paper_posting.authcheckdam.pdf, last visited on August 28, 2025.

27 Ibidem.

28 GARBER S., Alternative Litigation Financing in the United States: Issues, Knowns and Unknowns, 2010, Rand Corporation occasional paper, 1, p. 1. Available at http://www.rand.org/content/dam/rand/pubs/occasional_papers/2010/RAND_OP306.pdf, last visited on August 28, 2025.

the venture capital market. In this sense, TPLF has been defined[29] as a contractual arrangement in which a non-disputing third party provides funds or equivalent support to a disputing party (whether involved in litigation or arbitration) to cover legal fees or dispute-related costs. In return, the funder receives a reimbursement, remuneration, or share of the proceeds that is wholly or partially contingent on the success of the case or the outcome of the arbitration.[30] In other words, TPLF is a financing strategy where a third party - not directly involved in the dispute, covers a party's legal fees or settles an order, award, or judgment against the party, or both.[31] Apart from the semantic debates surrounding its proper terminology, TPLF remains a highly relevant financial model, playing a predominant role in both arbitration finance and public debate. In fact, this financial tool allows disputing parties to access essential financial resources without having to bear the full risk of litigation. However, although the definition attempts to qualify this system of third-party financing in some way, it says little about the potential implications of such external involvement. Indeed, as is easily deducible, by introducing third parties into a process in which they are not strictly involved, one must ask what their interest might be. This point is clarified in the TPLF definition, which states these parties aim to *"maximize their investment"*. But under what conditions? At a purely theoretical level, one might naively assume these entities are passive; however, as analogous investment systems, such as private equity funds demonstrate,[32] one is to assume that external interests easily intrude into the process to secure their own investment.

---

29 DERAINS Y., 'Foreword' in: Bernardo Cremades Sanz-Pastor and Antonias Dimolitsa (eds), Third-Party Funding in International Arbitration (ICC Dossier), International Council for Commercial Arbitration, n. 1, 50, Kluwer Law International 2013, p. 5.

30 ROWLES-DAVIES N., Third Party Litigation Funding, 2014, at 4. See also MENDEZ C., Welcome to the Party: Creating a Responsible Third-Party Litigation Finance Industry to Increase Access and Options for Plaintiff, n. 39, 1, Mississippi College Law Review, 2021, pp. 102-23 in International Council for Commercial Arbitration, n. 1, 50; DERAINS Y., Foreword in BERNARDO CREMADES SANZ-PASTOR / ANTONIAS DIMOLITSA, Third-Party Funding in International Arbitration (ICC Dossier), Kluwer Law International, 2013, p. 5; European Parliamentary Research Service, n 23, p. 45: The funder's compensation is determined by factors such as the likelihood of success, the presumed duration of the civil proceedings, and the value of the claim.

31 STEINITZ M., Whose Claim Is This Anyway? Third-Party Litigation Funding, 95 Minnesota Law Review, 2011, pp. 1275-1276.

32 I refer by analogy to certain forms of corporate governance involving a third-party investor who acquires a significant stake in a company, thereby, gaining the ability to exert considerable influence over its management. The behavioural model adopted by the professional investor, whether grounded in agency theory, stewardship theory, or typical of angel investing, determines the extent of the investor's involvement in shaping the company's strategic direction. In this context, these economic theories serve as

2. *Financial and Jurisdictional Perspectives*

TPLF involves a non-disputing entity covering all the costs associated with arbitral proceedings for one of the disputing parties. In return, the funder is entitled to receive a predetermined percentage of the final compensation awarded.[33] If the claim fails, the financing third party will typically receive no compensation and may still be responsible for the claimant's attorney fees and adverse costs, unless the applicable law provides otherwise.[34] This chapter offers an overview of the diverse types of funders. From institutional investors to specialized litigation finance providers, it explores how various legal landscapes approach TPLF.

a) Funding the legal frontier

aa) Attorney

There are various ways in which legal representation can fall within the scope of TPLF, and as we will see, they are partially interdependent. The first system is pro bono legal representation, in which a lawyer provides services to an indigent individual or someone unable to afford the costs of arbitration proceedings without expecting or having any guarantee of reimbursement. This is a unique concept and is not universally regarded as a form of TPLF. However, it is essential to consider who bears the financial burden and risk: the attorney.[35]

Similarly, under a contingency fee arrangement, the attorney assumes the risk of litigation by entering into an agreement with the client, whereby the lawyer will receive a percentage of the award as compensation for their legal services in the event of a successful outcome.[36] In the case of a loss, the same princi-

useful tools for assessing the potential risks associated with third-party influence on decision-making processes.

33 VAN BOOM W. H., Third-Party Financing in International Investment Arbitration 25, 2011, available at SSRN: http://ssrn.com/abstract=2027114 or http://dx.doi.org/10.2139/ssrn.2027114, last visited on August 28, 2025.

34 DE BRABANDERE E. / LEPELTAK J., Third Party Funding in International Investment Arbitration, ICSID Reviews, Vol. 27, No. 2, 379-38, 2012, p. 25.

35 NIEUWVELD L. B. / SHANNON V., Third-Party Funding in International Arbitration, Kluwer Law International, 2012, p. 6.

36 *"these arrangements are only entered into by lawyers where a claim is considered to be sufficiently strong and a sufficient recovery is contemplated to offset the risk to the lawyer of non – payment."*, BOWMAN C. / HURFORD K. / KHOURI S., Third party funding in international commercial and treaty arbitration - a panacea or a plague? A discussion of the risks and benefits of third-party funding", TDM 4, 2011, available at

ple applies as with pro bono representation, as the attorney receives no payment[37]. A similar model is the conditional fee arrangement, in which the lawyer applies a discounted rate to their fees, with the provision the fee increases in the event of a successful outcome.[38] The key difference lies in how the risk is distributed between the attorney and the client.

In any case, it is important to emphasize the claimant maintains overall authority over the direction of the proceedings, including key decisions such as the legal strategy to pursue, whether to negotiate a settlement, or to proceed with appeals. Nevertheless, the lawyer remains faithful to their function as advocate for the client's interests, acting merely as counselor and executor of the client's instructions. For instance, a settlement offers advantageous to the lawyer, due to a conditional fee arrangement, may be legitimately rejected by the client.

bb) Loans

It can be obtained from a lawyer or a law firm, as well as requested from a financial institution.[39] While this system offers a practical solution, it is not without risks: on the one hand, the borrower benefits from maintaining full control over the direction and coordination of the proceedings; on the other hand, they bear the entire risk of an unfavorable outcome. Regardless of whether the award is positive or negative, the loan must still be repaid.

cc) Insurance

Another well-known TPLF instrument, is insurance.[40] Numerous insurance institutions offer policies that cover legal expenses.[41] The terms of the agree-

---

www.transnational-dispute-management.com/article.asp?key=1747, last visited on August 28, 2025.

37 STEINITZ M., Whose Claim is This Anyway? Third-Party Litigation Funding, 95 Minnesota Law Review, pp.1292-1293.

38 NIEUWVELD L. B. / SHANNON V, Third-Party Funding in International Arbitration, Kluwer Law International, 2012, p. 7.

39 RICHMOND / DOUGLAS R., Other People's Money: The Ethics of Litigation Funding, 2005, in Mercer Law Review, Vol. 56, No. 2, Article 4, available at https://digitalcommons.law.mercer.edu/jour_mlr/vol56/iss2/4, last visited on February 22, 2025, pp. 650 – 651.

40 In Switzerland, when it comes to regulation, the court made it clear: the third-party litigation funding can't be considered a form of insurance under the Swiss Insurance Supervision Act (ISA), mainly because it doesn't involve paying a premium to cover

ment vary depending on the extent and type of coverage (whether for the claimant or the defendant).[42] It is important to highlight, unlike other more flexible forms of financing, these contracts involve a high degree of intervention in the dispute. This can range from the right to request information to influencing strategic decisions in the proceedings.[43] Consequently, the actual rights holder must relinquish full control and management of their case in favor of the insurance company.[44]

dd) Assigning contractual rights

Throughout a corporation's life, events such as mergers, acquisitions, asset sales, and liquidation can lead to significant structural changes. As a result, contractual rights may be transferred to third parties under general contract law. Unless restricted by law or specific contract terms, parties are usually free to assign their contractual rights to third parties.[45] On one hand, the transferring creditor receives immediate payment and can consider their claim settled. On the other hand, the third-party purchaser assumes the burden of enforcing the claim, including the risk of never recovering the full amount.[46]

---

a potential future risk (Swiss Federal Court' decision BGE 131 I 223 consid. 4.7 of December 10, 2004).

41 As seen in the following Section C, the TPLF institution in order to be characterized as insurance agreement, needs to include: Risk or hazard, the insured's contribution (premium), the insurer's obligation, the autonomy of the operation (not just a subsidiary agreement), and a structured business model (risk balancing based on statistical principles). See WEY R., Kommerzielle Prozessfinanzierung - ein Überblick über Angebot und Rechtsfragen, in: FELLMANN/WEBER (eds.), Haftpflichtprozess 2008, p. 69.

42 STEINITZ M., Whose Claim is This Anyway? Third-Party Litigation Funding, 95 Minnesota Law Review, pp. 1295-1296; While legal protection insurance is designed solely to cover the costs of future disputes, litigation funding allows for the transfer of legal cost risks even after a dispute has already arisen. Additionally, legal expense coverage is limited to the maximum insured amount. As a result, there remains a significant gap not covered by legal protection insurance, creating room for litigation funding to step in. WEY R., Kommerzielle Prozessfinanzierung - ein Überblick über Angebot und Rechtsfragen, in: FELLMANN / WEBER (eds.), Haftpflichtprozess 2008, p. 58.

43 NIEUWVELD L. B. / SHANNON V., Third-Party Funding in International Arbitration, Kluwer Law International, 2012, p. 6;

44 Ibidem.

45 Art. 164 and following of the Swiss Code of Obligations. STEINITZ M., Whose Claim is This Anyway? Third-Party Litigation Funding, 95 Minnesota Law Review, pp. 1296-1299.

46 Ibidem.

ee) Institutional litigation funding

Non-recourse financing with repayment contingent on success is a classic method of TPLF, closely resembling the contingency fee agreement previously discussed, except in this case, the funder is an institutional entity external to the dispute, such as a bank or financial institution.[47] As such, they are not bound by ethical codes and have greater flexibility in determining their financial objectives.[48] Moreover, some jurisdictions allow a certain degree of involvement in the day-to-day management of the case.[49] Nevertheless, the level of control exercised by these entities is generally lower than that exerted by insurance institutions, as previously discussed.[50]

b) Legal landscapes

Companies are becoming increasingly cautious about the costs of litigation. Additionally, recent global instability and uncertainty[51] have driven hedge funds, banks, and financial investors to identify investments uncorrelated with volatile financial markets[52]. The economic slowdown has also pushed companies facing bankruptcy to secure funding for claims capable of generating cash flow.[53] At the same time, the imminent global recession[54] is accelerating

---

47 VELJANOVSKI C., Third Party Litigation Funding in Europe, 8 J.L.Econ. & Pli'y 405, 2012, pp. 408-410.

48 Ibidem.

49 STEINITZ M., Whose Claim is This Anyway? Third-Party Litigation Funding, 95 Minnesota Law Review, p. 1294.

50 Their involvement is typically governed by sophisticated funding agreements managing risk, control, and return on investment. NIEUWVELD L. B. / SHANNON V., Third-Party Funding in International Arbitration, Kluwer Law International, 2012, p. 8.

51 For businesses, understanding the economic risks caused by uncertainty, trade disruptions, and the dynamics affecting investor confidence is crucial for strategic planning, risk management, and investment decisions. See Top Geopolitical Risks of 2025, https://www.spglobal.com/en/research-insights/market-insights/geopolitical-risk, last visited on August 28, 2025.

52 STEINITZ M., Whose Claim is This Anyway? Third-Party Litigation Funding, 95 Minnesota Law Review , p. 1294.

53 JONES D., Third-Party Funding of Arbitration, paper given at Hot Topics in International Arbitration at SJ Berwin, London, Sep. 22, 2008, p. 7.

54 According to the UN Trade and Development (UNCTAD) 2025 Report, the global growth is expected to slow to 2.3 % in 2025, putting the world economy on a recessionary path essentially determined by an escalating trade tension and uncertainty for the economic market (see TRADE AND DEVELOPMENT FORESIGHTS 2025, Under Pressure: Uncertainty reshapes global economic prospects, UNCTAD/GDS/INF/2025/1, 2025). The International Monetary Fund project the global growth at 3.0 % for 2025

the demand for alternative fee structures as a replacement for traditional billable hours in law firms[55]. International arbitration offers funders a lucrative investment avenue with high profitability, swift proceedings, predictable outcomes, and expert arbitrators. Nevertheless, this enthusiasm is not shared at the jurisdictional level, where, as will be seen, the legal landscape is not always favorable to this type of investment.[56] Returning to the initial theme of the right to access justice, not all jurisdictions are supportive of this alternative funding method to ensure this right, especially in light of the potential risks associated with the involvement of a third party in the dispute.

The regulation of TPLF varies significantly across jurisdictions, reflecting different perspectives on the balance between access to justice and the risks posed by external financial interests in legal proceedings. Some jurisdictions take a prohibitive approach, while others implement strict, moderate, or self-regulatory frameworks. In some cases, a completely free-market approach is adopted, relying on contractual freedom with minimal state intervention.[57] One of the most restrictive approaches is based on the doctrine of champerty, also known as pactum de quota litis. In these jurisdictions,[58] TPLF is strictly

and 0.1 % higher for the 2026 (see World economic outlook update, Global Economy: Tenuous Resilience amid Persistent Uncertainty, July 2025). In a more optimistic point of view, the World Bank Group set the global frowth at 2.5 % over the years 2026 – 27 (see World Bank. 2025. Global Economic Prospects, June 2025. Washington, DC: World Bank. doi: 10.1596/978-1-4648-2193-6. License: Creative Commons Attribution CC BY 3.0 IGO). In this field, litigation finance offers a valid solution offering *"the prospect of higher returns than traditional asset classes and returns that are truly uncorrelated to equity markets, which is particularly attractive during times of financial crisis, market downturn and volatility"* ROHNER P., Litigation Finance: A recession-proof asset class, Katch Investment Group CIO on 05/08/2022 in Insights, available at https://katchinvest.com/litigation-finance-a-recession-proofassetclass/#:~:text=Litigation%20finance%20offers%20the %20prospect,has%20its%20roots%20in %20antiquity, last visited on August 28, 2025.

55 GLATER J. D., Billable Hours Giving Ground at Law Firms, N.Y. Times, Jan. 30. 2009, at A1, available at 2009 WLNR 1784153 ("Clients are more concerned about the budgets than a year or two years ago").

56 EUROPEAN COMMISSION DG JUSTICE AND CONSUMERS, Mapping Third Party Litigation Funding in the European Union, JUST/2023/PR/JCOO/CIVI/0016, 2025.

57 EUROPEAN COMMISSION DG JUSTICE AND CONSUMERS, Mapping Third Party Litigation Funding in the European Union, JUST/2023/PR/JCOO/CIVI/0016, 2025, p. 9 and 55. BAJAI G., YANG E., CHAN Q., Third-party funding in the Asia-Pacific region, The Asian – Pacific Arbitration Review, Global Arbitration Review 2021, 2024.

58 Among EU Member State there is not a specific regulation nor prohibition. Ireland constitutes an exception on the grounds of TPLF representing maintenance and champerty. Similarly, many common law Countries in the past like Canada and United Kingdom or Singapore as well, prohibited TPLF on the grounds of maintenance and champerty. EUROPEAN COMMISSION DG JUSTICE AND CONSUMERS, Mapping Third

prohibited on the grounds that it allows third parties with no direct interest in the case to profit from litigation, potentially distorting the judicial process. The primary concern is, such financial arrangements could commodify the legal system, prioritizing economic gain over the fair administration of justice. This prohibition is meant to safeguard the moral integrity of litigation and prevent undue influence from funders who might manipulate legal strategies to maximize their returns. [59]

Recognizing the inevitability of TPLF and seeking to regulate it rather than ban it outright, some jurisdictions have opted for strict regulatory frameworks. A key example is the European Parliament's initiative to introduce oversight mechanisms through the Report with Recommendations to the Commission on Responsible Private Funding of Litigation, also known as the Voss Report.[60]

This report identifies significant risks associated with TPLF,[61] particularly the concern is funders may act primarily in their own economic interest rather than in the interest of claimants, which could compromise the fairness of legal proceedings.[62] The report stresses the need for robust regulation[63] to ensure

---

Party Litigation Funding in the European Union, JUST/2023/PR/JCOO/CIVI/0016, 2025, p. 9 and 55. BAJAI G., YANG E., CHAN Q., Third-party funding in the Asia-Pacific region, The Asian – Pacific Arbitration Review, Global Arbitration Review 2021, 2024.

59 See Case Fraser vs. Buckle Costello J. (1996-WJSC-SC 1113, 5-3-96): *"The reasons why the common law condemns champerty is because of the abuses to which it may give rise. The common law fears that the champertous maintainer might be tempted, for his own personal gain, to inflame the damages, to supress evidence, or even to suborn witnesses. These fears may be exaggerated; but, be that so or not, the law for centuries had declared champerty to be unlawful and we can- not do otherwise than enforce the law".*

60 European Parliament Draft Report with recommendations to the Commission on Responsible Private Funding of Litigation 2020/2130 (INL), Committee on Legal Affairs, Rapporteur: Axel Voss (Initiative – Rule 47 of the Rules of Procedure) (Voss-Report).

61 See European Parliament resolution of 13 September 2022 with recommendations to the Commission on responsible private funding of litigation (2020/2130(INL)). The EP's resolution includes in an Annex a Proposal for a Directive on the regulation of third-party litigation funding ('Draft EP Directive').

62 Legal proceedings face the risk of corruption due to TPLF's willingness to prioritize profit over justice, by sacrificing the integrity of the legal system in favor of investment interests. US Chamber of Commerce, Institute for Legal Reform, What You Need To Know About Third Party Litigation Funding, June 7, 2024, available at https://instituteforlegalreform.com/what-you-need-to-know-about-third-party-litigation-funding/, last visited on August 28, 2025. In Alan Bates & Others v Post Office Limited 555 sub-postmasters joined a group litigation order (GLO) against the

litigation funding enhances access to justice without undermining the integrity of the judicial system. By filling the legislative gap in this area, such regulations aim to protect litigants while maintaining in and accountability in funding agreements. On this point, it should also be noted how an excessive regulation, even if aimed at protecting consumers, may produce a negative effect[64], namely discouraging the use of third-party funders. This mechanism was created to ensure fair access to justice, and imposing too many entry barriers risks undermining its very purpose.

A more balanced approach, often considered an optimistic alternative, involves moderate regulation which seeks to prevent abuses while fostering private investment in litigation. From one side, it discourages harmful behaviors in litigation funding while protecting the fairness of the proceeding, from the other it encourages helpful investments and the free market. This model incorporates legislative measures or judicial oversight, granting judges the authority to review funding agreements to prevent conflicts of interest and ensure the funded party's access to justice is not unduly restricted by a strict regulation. This approach acknowledges the benefits of TPLF in enabling claimants to pursue legal action while implementing safeguards to mitigate the risks of excessive funder influence. Judicial supervision, as seen in certain self-regulated systems, allows courts to intervene when necessary to protect

Post Office, funded by a TPLF provider. Despite their desire to continue the case, the claimants were forced to accept a "full and final" settlement due to the funder's pressure. The funder's financial interest prevailed over the claimants' pursuit of justice, leading to an outcome described as coercive and unjust; In Excalibur Ventures v Texas Keystone and others the claim described by the court as "speculative and opportunistic" was funded by multiple funders. The claim lacked merit and was deemed an artificial construct maintained solely due to external financial backing. The litigation would not have been brought but for the funders' support, which allowed a weak case to proceed, wasting court resources and placing undue pressure on defendants to settle; About conflict of interests Harbour (a funder) provided £33 million in financing to law firm Slater & Gordon, specifically to fund consumer claims. These close financial ties raise concerns that lawyers may prioritize funder interests over those of clients. See Fair Civil Justice, Establishing Fairness in Litigation Funding, A British Roadmap to Protect Consumers, SMEs and Other Parties in Funded Legal Actions, June 2024.

63 Key measures include mandatory authorization, capital adequacy requirements, the imposition of a fiduciary duty on funders to act in the best interests of claimants and transparency obligations and conflict-of-interest safeguards are also central features. See EUROPEAN PARLIAMENT DRAFT REPORT with recommendations to the Commission on Responsible Private Funding of Litigation 2020/2130 (INL), Committee on Legal Affairs, Rapporteur: Axel Voss, Initiative – Rule 47 of the Rules of Procedure, Voss-Report, pp. 5 and following.

64 For instance, overly strict rules on disclosure, funding arrangements, or liability may raise compliance costs and administrative burdens for third-party funders.

the fairness and integrity of legal proceedings.[65] In contrast to an interventionist approach by the State, a more liberal regulatory framework may encourage investment. In other words, regulation should intervene where it is necessary to prevent abusive practices – excessive control over the proceeding, lack of transparency, economic interests over legality – to safeguard the legality of the proceedings, while at the same time allowing room for private initiative. For example, transparency clauses in funding agreements to impose a fiduciary duty on TPLF entities[66], the introduction of a maximum cap on the rate of return – while still allowing the parties contractual freedom to negotiate within the established limits – and the obligation to disclose the identities of the parties involved in the proceedings, limited exclusively to the judicial authority, represent measures capable of balancing the need to safeguard the integrity of the legal process with the promotion of private investment.

In contrast, some jurisdictions favor a self-regulation model, where litigation funders govern their own industry through established associations which set ethical standards and best practices.[67] By allowing private actors to take the lead in shaping financial services, this approach promotes efficiency and flexibility while encouraging responsible funding practices.[68] Self-regulation is often seen as a way to balance investor interests with fairness and transparency in legal proceedings.[69] However, concerns remain regarding its effectiveness, as self-regulatory bodies may lack neutrality and could prioritize industry interests over broader legal protections. Additionally, without mandatory participation, enforcement mechanisms may be weaker compared to formal legal regulation.[70] While self-regulation can enhance access to funding and streamline processes, its success ultimately depends on the credibility and oversight of the governing associations.[71]

---

65 See MULHERON R., England's Unique Approach to the Self-regulation of Third-Party Funding: A Critical Analysis of Recent Developments, 73(3) The Cambridge Law Journal, 2014, pp. 570-97.

66 Usually TPLF are not subject to fiduciary duties like lawyers and my not act in the best interest of the client. US CHAMBER OF COMMERCE, Institute for Legal Reform, What You Need To Know About Third Party Litigation Funding, June 7, 2024, available at https://instituteforlegalreform.com/what-you-need-to-know-about-third-party-litigation-funding/, last visited on August 28, 2025.

67 UCÍN M. C., How Can Business Best Approach Human Rights in Third-Party Litigation Funding?, Guidelines for Future Regulations, Erasmus Law Review, ELR 2023, Nr. 2, p. 108.

68 Ibidem.

69 Ibidem.

70 Ibidem.

71 Ibidem.

At the other end of the spectrum, a completely free-market approach relies on the principles of contractual freedom, allowing parties to enter into TPLF agreements with minimal or no state intervention. This model operates on the assumption market forces, rather than government oversight, should regulate litigation funding. Drawing on Adam Smith's theory of the self-regulating market, this approach assumes competition and demand will naturally establish fair conditions for funding agreements.[72] However, this lack of regulation creates the potential for significant abuses, such as excessive financial control by funders over legal representatives or the prioritization of financial gain over the protection of legal rights. Without external oversight, there is a risk weaker parties in litigation may be exploited, and the fairness of legal proceedings could be compromised.[73]

Ultimately, the regulation of TPLF reflects a broader debate over the role of financial interests in the judicial system. While some jurisdictions prohibit litigation funding to preserve the integrity of the legal process, others seek to regulate or moderate it to balance access to justice with the risks of third-party involvement. Self-regulation and free-market approaches offer more flexibility but also raise concerns about the lack of enforcement and oversight. As litigation funding continues to expand globally, the challenge for policymakers remains how to structure regulatory frameworks that protect litigants while enabling fair and responsible investment in legal proceedings. TPLF is certainly an interesting means of investment, but it is even more important when we remember it was originally created to help people access justice, especially those who cannot afford it, like in class actions brought by economically weaker groups. For this reason, a total ban on TPLF would not be a wise solution. On the other hand, fully liberalizing the market could lead to abuse and unfair practices. I also believe self-regulation is not enough, since it depends only on funders choosing to follow rules, without any real way to enforce them. In my view, the most practical solution is for the State to step in and regulate key aspects, such as creating financial authorities to oversee funders, requiring licenses with liquidity and anti-money laundering safeguards, ensuring transparency when TPLF is involved, protecting confidentiality in legal proceedings, and requiring funders to follow codes of con-

72 HEINZ D. KURZ, Adam Smith on markets, competition and violations of natural liberty, Cambridge Journal of Economics, Volume 40, Issue 2, March 2016, Pages 615–638.

73 European Law Institute, Principles Governing the Third Parties Funding on Litigation, Eli Council December 10, 2024, available at https://www.europeanlawinstitute.eu/fileadmin/user_upload/p_eli/Publications/ELI_Principles_Governing_the_Third_Party_Funding_of_Litigation.pdf?utm_source=chatgpt.com, last visited on February 25, 2025, last visited on August 28, 2025.

duct that make them act in the client's best interest, similar to lawyers' fiduciary duties. The different regulatory approaches discussed in this chapter largely depend on the perspective adopted. A framework focused on consumer protection, where the funded party is seen as vulnerable, tends to be more restrictive.

By contrast, if the funded party is viewed as a knowledgeable market participant, the approach is generally more liberal. Before providing funds, TPLFs typically assess the legal merits of the case. By assuming the financial risks and covering litigation or arbitration costs on a non-recourse basis, they enable claimants to pursue proceedings they might otherwise be unable to afford, thereby facilitating access to justice. This raises the question: is the agreement primarily commercial, and, therefore, subject to contractual freedom, or is it legal in nature, and thus subject to ethical rules and market oversight? For the time being, there is not a conclusive answer. The current practice seems to lean toward considering the relationship as a mere commercial transaction.[74] Moreover, there is no real equality of arms: where one party is classified as a legal finance service provider, it operates with greater bargaining power, expertise, and resources, while the funded party lacks comparable means to influence the process. The relationship therefore cannot be equated to two companies negotiating on equal commercial terms.

3. *Swiss Regulation*

a) Regulatory Framework

Although there is not yet a specific legislative framework regulating TPLF, this mechanism is not entirely foreign to the Swiss legal landscape. After initial skepticism, the Swiss system has shown sufficient openness to integrating this financial instrument within its legal framework. In fact, TPLF originated in Australia in the early 1990s and quickly expanded across common law jurisdictions, albeit within the constraints imposed by the prohibition of champerty.[75] Conversely, its presence remains more limited in civil law sys-

---

[74] See also notes 86, 87 and 88.

[75] For the difference between "maintenance" and "champerty": *"Roughly speaking, "maintenance" indicates the action of one who assists a litigant in prosecuting or defending a claim. "Champerty" is a particular form of maintenance, namely one made for the purpose of gain"*. See note 57 on DE MORPURGO M., A Comparative Legal and Economic Approach to Third-Party Litigation Funding, "Cardozo Journal of International & Comparative Law"(eds.), 2011, Vol. 19, p. 360, available at

tems, with notable exceptions such as Austria, Germany and Switzerland.[76] The initial skepticism surrounding TPLF led the Grand Council of the Canton of Zurich to approve the Attorney Cantonal Act in 2003, which declared the financing of litigation with a commercial nature illegal and prohibited participation in the proceeds of a successful claim.[77] The Act was set to enter into force in 2005. However, in the meantime, a leading case was decided by the Swiss Federal Court, which, in ruling BGE 131 I 223 of December 10, 2004, upheld the legitimacy of TPLF. The Court based its decision on the argument such a prohibition would constitute an excessive restriction on economic freedom under Article 27 of the Swiss Federal Constitution, as well as on the principle of contractual freedom between the parties (see consid. 4.1 and following).[78] Following this landmark ruling, the Swiss Federal Court reinforced its position in another leading decision, the BGer 2C_814/2014 of January 22, 2015, recognizing TPLF has become an established practice in Switzerland and, thereby, reaffirming its previous judgment. In the same case,[79] the Swiss Federal Court also held that, where circumstances necessitate it, the possibility of securing litigation funding falls within the professional duties of attorneys under the Federal Act on the Freedom of Movement of Lawyers.[80]

A key issue emerged from decision BGer 2C_814/2014 of January 22, 2015, with reference to BGE 131 I 223, of December 10, 2024, concerned the potential conflict of interest between the client and the funder, particularly, regarding the allocation of the proceeds from the litigation. While both parties share a common interest in winning the case[81] the real critical point lies in determining their respective shares of the proceeds and in the management of the litigation strategy. From this perspective, the relationship between the

http://biblioteca.cejamericas.org/bitstream/handle/2015/260/Morpurgo.pdf?sequence=1&isAllowed=y, last visited on August 26, 2025.

76 DE MORPURGO M., A Comparative Legal and Economic Approach to Third-Party Litigation Funding, in Cardozo Journal of International & Comparative Law, 2011, Vol. 19, p. 350, available at http://biblioteca.cejamericas.org/bitstream/handle/2015/260/Morpurgo.pdf?sequence=1&isAllowed=y, last visited on August 26, 2025.

77 Attorney Cantonal Act of the Canton of Zurich (Anwaltsgesetz des Kantons Zürich), 2003, § 41: *"Wer vor Beendigung eines Rechtsstreites gewerbsmässig und gegen die Einräumung eines Anteils am Prozesserfolg ...b) die Finanzierung eines Prozesses vereinbart oder eine solche Vereinbarung vermittelt, wird durch das Statthalteramt mit Busse bis 20'000 Franken bestraft".*

78 Decision of the Swiss Federal Court BGE 131 I 223 of December 10, 2004, consid. 4.1, p. 230.

79 At consid. 4.3.1, Decision of the Swiss Federal Court Bger 2C_814/2014 of January 22, 2015, consid. 4.3.2.

80 *Bundesgesetz über die Freizügigkeit der Anwältinnen und Anwälte,* BGFA.

81 Decision of the Swiss Federal Court BGE 131 I 223 of December 10, 2004, consid. 4.6.2, p. 236.

client and the funder differs significantly from the relationship between an insured party and an insurer: while the latter aims primarily to minimize overall costs, a litigation funder may instead pursue more aggressive strategies or prolong the proceedings to maximize its own financial return, potentially at the expense of the client's best interest.[82] This divergence of interests may create pressure on the funded party, especially in cases where the funder exerts significant influence over procedural decisions. Another critical risk factor is the potential compromise of the lawyer's independence, particularly when the lawyer has direct or indirect financial ties to the funder.[83] Current regulations, particularly Art. 8 Abs. 1 lit. d BGFA, prohibit lawyers from being directly employed by a litigation funder, yet the issue of independence becomes more complex in cases where a lawyer receives indirect benefits from a funding agreement.[84] At present, case law does not explicitly prohibit all forms of involvement between lawyers and funders, but it leaves open the possibility that certain situations could generate latent conflicts of interest, particularly if the lawyer holds stakes in litigation funding companies or has financial incentives tied to the outcome of the case. The lack of a well - defined regulatory framework in this regard may therefore create uncertainty and potential risks in legal practice.[85]

b) Rules, Restrictions and Limits

As observed above, there is no specific regulation governing TPLF in a strict sense, meaning the current legal framework is effectively shaped by the leading case law of the Swiss Federal Court. Since the issuance of these decisions, the market has evolved and experienced significant growth, raising questions regarding the sector's expansion limits, the potential oversight authorities for

---

82 It is the case where the funder decides to terminate the litigation to reach a settlement with the opposing party against the will of the funded party or opt to interrupt the financing. Decision of the Swiss Federal Court BGE 134 II 108 of April 30, 2008, consid. 4.2, p. 111 et seq. .

83 Decision of the Swiss Federal Court BGE 131 I 223 od December 10, 2004, consid. 4.6.4, p. 238; WEY R., Kommerzielle Prozessfinanzierung - ein Überblick über Angebot und Rechtsfragen, in: Fellmann/Weber (eds.), Haftpflichtprozess 2008, p. 76.

84 WEGMÜLLER M., Prozessfinanzierung in der Schweiz: Bestandesaufnahme und Ausblick, HAVE 2013, p. 243.

85 For clarification, Article 12, letters a, b, and c of the BGFA establish fundamental rules of professional ethics aimed at ensuring, on the one hand, the proper exercise of the legal profession and, on the other, the full independence of the lawyer. Additionally, these provisions impose the duty to *"avoid any conflict between the interests of the client and those of individuals with whom the lawyer has professional or personal relationships"*.

industry operators, and whether – and to what extent – the underlying contract may be classified as a pre-existing, regulated agreement. The objective of this chapter is not to provide an exhaustive overview of all potential implications but rather to highlight the sectors explicitly excluded and to equip the reader with the necessary tools to understand the risks associated with this phenomenon in the context of the present research.

The Swiss Federal Court has ruled litigation funding does not fall under the Insurance Supervision Act (*Versicherungsaufsichtsgesetz*, VAG), as it lacks a key characteristic: the insurance *premium* paid in advance to cover a future risk.[86] In TPLF, if the client loses the case, they owe nothing to the funder, who operates solely on a success-based remuneration model, therefore a performance (a *premium*) of the insured is not required. Additionally, there is no risk compensation based on statistical principles, as each case is assessed individually. While some scholars have suggested an actuarial approach, this theory finds no support in practice. Consequently, litigation funding cannot be classified as insurance, and funders are not subject to the VAG.[87]

The regulatory classification of litigation funding raises the question of whether it falls under financial market laws. However, upon closer examination, it becomes evident litigation funders in Switzerland do not fall under the Swiss Financial Market law,[88] as they do not collect public deposits, manage third-party assets, or operate collective investment schemes.[89] Consequently, their core activity is not subject to state supervision under the current legal framework.[90] This position is open to criticism, as TPLF entities can in fact operate as institutional investors and, as such, are subject to approval by FINMA.[91]

---

86 BGE 131 I 223 of December 10, 2004, consid. 4.7.

87 WEGMÜLLER M., Prozessfinanzierung in der Schweiz: Bestandesaaufnahme und Ausblick, in: HAVE 2013, p. 235 et seqq.

88 For instance, Banking and Insurance Acts, the Anti-Money Laundering Act and the Collective Investment Scheme Act.

89 About this point there is not unanimity, therefore depending on the structure of the funders, they can qualify as asset managers of collective investment. As that, they are subject to the Swiss Financial Market Supervisory Authority (FINMA) supervision in order to be granted a license for their financial services.

90 Ibidem.

91 Eg. According to Nivalion AG and after further research, it is the only TPLF in Switzerland granted a FINMA license to manage collective investments / assets. See FINMA, List of authorised fund management companies, managers of collective assets and representatives of foreign collective investment schemes, April 19, 2025, p. 8.

For their part, the aforementioned landmark decisions have not sought to provide explicit regulation from this perspective. However, through a *contrario* interpretation, certain rules can be inferred to ensure the practice of law in accordance with Article 12 lit.a–c BGFA, namely, to guarantee the independent exercise of the legal profession free from any potential conflicts of interest. In this regard, success-based fee agreements are not foreign to the Swiss legal landscape, but their practical application remains limited due to existing regulations.[92] This type of consideration, however, does not apply in a typical TPLF case, since the funder is by definition a third party in relation to both the claimant and the legal representative.

c) *Swiss Model Agreement*[93]

The question of whether a common model of funding agreement or best practices exist in Switzerland can be answered immediately with a no. Given the absence of sector-specific regulation, it is also easy to understand that the practice is left to the contractual freedom of the parties, provided it complies with the directly applicable national law. The framework is simple and operates in civil, administrative, or arbitral proceedings, allowing the creditor to enforce a claim against the debtor without bearing the legal costs. This structure is based on an agreement between the funder and the claimant, in which the claimant commits to pursuing legal action while the funder covers the litigation expenses.[94] In other words, an agreement in which the funder and the claimant set out the dispute, their respective rights and obligations until the conclusion of the proceedings, and also specify the legal representative

---

92 This is the case with the *pactum de quota litis* and the *pactum de palmario*. In the first case, banned according to art. 12 lit. e BGFA, the parties agree the lawyer's compensation will only be paid in the event of success. In the second, allowed, the parties agree on a reduced fee, with the possibility of the lawyer receiving a limited share of the proceeds from the case in the event of a favorable outcome. See Decision of the Swiss Federal Court BGer 2C_814/2014 of January 22, 2015, consid. 4.3.2 and 4.3.3; for the ratio between the success fee and the basic fee see Decision of the Swiss Federal Court 4A 240/2016 of Juni 13, 2017, consid. 2.7.5; additionally, the Swiss Federal Court has indirectly approved a success fee between 20 % and 40 % of the net income of the proceed (see Decision of the Swiss Federal Court BGE 131 I 223 of December 10, 2004, consid. 4.6.6).

93 Since in Switzerland it is not possible to transfer a legal claim in civil proceedings, the agreement between the claimant and the funder is structured as a funding contract to secure the funder's rights. See SCHUMACHER, Prozessfinanzierung, Erfolgshonorierte Fremdfinanzierung von Zivilverfahren, Thesis Zurich 2015, p. 104.

94 For definition and scope see: WEGMÜLLER M., Prozessfinanzierung in der Schweiz: Bestandesaufnahme und Ausblick, HAVE 2013, S. 235 ff., N. II.

chosen by the claimant. Regarding the classification of the investment contract, it should be clarified that depending on the service provided, there may be several interpretations. However, if we take the definition of TPLF literally, it is generally agreed it falls within the scope of a partnership agreement and, as such, follows the rules of a simple partnership according to Articles 530 and following of the Swiss Code of Obligations (*Obligationenrecht*, OR).[95]

The process of entering into a funding agreement typically has two main steps. First, after the funding request and a preliminary review of the case, the funder asks the plaintiff to sign an exclusivity agreement for a set period, usually around three weeks. During this time, the funder carries out a due diligence to decide whether to finance the case. If the decision is positive, the funder agrees to cover the costs needed for the case, such as court fees and the plaintiff's lawyer's fees.[96]

Although there is currently no sector-specific regulation, the system seems to be unaffected by this, and the current legislative framework appears to be sufficiently supported by the contractual freedom of the contracting parties. That said, this wide scope for maneuvering leaves room for uncertainty, particularly regarding the definition of the funding party, which appears not only to be free from any financial oversight but also potentially risky in light of the interests it intends to pursue. In fact, while it is true at least in the initial phase, the interests of the claimant and the funder align (simply put, winning the case and getting the money), these interests may diverge during the course of the litigation. Since one of the two parties holds the economic power, they may potentially have more influence in dictating the course of action.[97] An-

---

95 In the context of TPLF, this could imply the funder and the beneficiary of the legal action (for example, the client pursuing a lawsuit) form a partnership to achieve the goal of obtaining a favorable outcome, sharing the gains or losses based on the result of the case. See WEY R., Kommerzielle Prozessfinanzierung – ein Überblick über Angebot und Rechtsfragen, in: Fellmann/ Weber (eds.), Haftpflichtprozess, 2008, Zurich/Basel/Geneva 2008, p. 72. To avoid the automatic application of Articles 530 et seq. of the Swiss Code of Obligations, the TPLF agreement should include an exlusion clause.

96 SCHUMACHER, Prozessfinanzierung, Erfolgshonorierte Fremdfinanzierung von Zivilverfahren, Thesis Zürich 2015, p. 99 and following.

97 This situation can lead to two very different outcomes. In the first, the TPLF may push the funded claimant to accept a settlement or decide to stop the case if doing so benefits its investment—even if it goes against the claimant's interests. On the other hand, if the claimant doesn't agree with the funder's strategy, they might choose to end the funding contract early. That's why it's important for the contract to include precise rules about early termination—such as how much notice must be given, how to split the costs, whether any penalties apply, and how to handle any money already paid by the funder. If the contract doesn't cover this, Swiss law treats the relationship

other issue of no secondary importance must also be considered. In this relationship, the lawyer acts as legal representative and guardian of the claimant's interests. At the same time, the lawyer is required to account for their actions to the TPLF. This dual obligation raises significant concerns regarding professional ethics. Matters such as confidentiality, legal privilege, and diligence in fulfilling the mandate are compromised by the potential risk of a third party dictating the direction of the proceedings and seeking access to detailed information.

For this reason, the funding agreement must safeguard the confidentiality of information and restrict its disclosure to essential parties only. At the same time, however, the confidential relationship between lawyer and client is stripped of its meaning, as the information leaves the protective sphere of the law firm and enters that of a legal finance entity.

IV. Conflict of interests

Potential conflicts of interest among the various actors involved in arbitration or state court proceedings are a real and significant concern. It is no coincidence both public and private institutions have intervened to mitigate these risks. However, since litigation funding operates within a financial framework, economic interests often prioritize investment profitability over ensuring access to justice. Switzerland has been relatively flexible in its legislation, giving industry operators considerable freedom. In contrast, the European Union, known for its stricter regulations, has tried to impose more restrictions. Currently, there is no EU-wide rule requiring mandatory disclosure of interests or involved parties beyond national laws. When such a rule is introduced, Switzerland will have to decide how to adapt. Switzerland has traditionally kept its financial regulations liberal to stay competitive internationally. However, it has also had to adopt some European and international rules to access foreign markets. For now, regulation mainly depends on national laws and financial market authorities. As mentioned earlier, litigation funders in Switzerland are not subject to standard financial oversight. The only possible regulation would be if they were classified as investment funds,

like a simple partnership. In such case, if one side leaves, the partnership must be closed and the funder gets their money back. It may also be important to check whether the claimant is to blame for the project failing. In any case, if the claimant leaves the contract without a valid reason under Swiss law, they could be held legally responsible. A useful example can be found in the draft agreement used by Profina Prozessfinanzierung GmbH., available at http://www.profina.ch/fileadmin/profina_finanzierungsvertrag.pdf, last visited on August 28, 2025.

requiring FINMA supervision and disclosure. Otherwise, oversight remains up to individual entities. Without state supervision, there are no effective coercive tools to ensure compliance with ethical or procedural standards. This creates a regulatory gap in which potential abuses may occur without consequences. While self-regulation might work in theory, in practice it lacks the enforceability needed to truly protect claimants and uphold the integrity of the legal process. Therefore, some level of public oversight is not only advisable, but necessary.

A. What is a Conflict of interests?

From an etymological perspective, the term "interest" derives from the Latin word *"interesse"*, composed of *"inter"* (to be between, take part) and *"esse"* (to be). In other words, it refers to a connection binding a subject to someone or something, creating a relationship between the two. Defining what constitutes a conflict of interest in a precise and comprehensive manner is challenging, as it often emerges from the specific circumstances of a case rather than from a fixed definition. At a purely abstract level, one could argue a conflict of interest arises when an individual derives some form of benefit from a particular relationship. However, reaching a universally accepted definition is difficult, and conflicts of interest are often identified through a negative approach, by determining when impartiality or independence is compromised. In this regard, the United Nations Commission on International Trade Law (also UNCITRAL) attempts to define the concept of an arbitrator's "independence" in an objective sense, considering both factual circumstances and external perception. Impartiality, on the other hand, is understood as a subjective and internal state of mind, which must be inferred from the arbitrator's outward conduct toward the parties. Both principles are essential for the proper functioning of arbitration proceedings and must not give rise to any reasonable doubts regarding their integrity. To this end, an objective standard – the perspective of a reasonable person – is often applied as an additional safeguard in assessing potential conflicts of interest.[98]

While not legally binding, the IBA Guidelines on Conflicts of Interest in International Arbitration are widely recognized as a persuasive soft law instrument in both institutional and ad hoc arbitrations seated in Switzerland. Based on Article 12 of the UNCITRAL Model Law, which corresponds to

98 HIARLOUSKE V., Arbitrator's Impartiality and Independence, available at https://jusmundi.com/en/document/publication/en-arbitrators-impartiality-and-independence, last visited on March 12, 2025; See also BGer 4A_54/2012 of June 27, 2012, consid. 2.2.1.

Article 180(1)(c) of the Swiss Private International Law Act (PILA), the Guidelines provide a structured framework for assessing whether justifiable doubts exist as to an arbitrator's impartiality or independence.[99] Similarly, the International Chamber of Commerce (also ICC) has published its own guidelines aimed at preventing conflicts of interest. Although there is no direct reference to TPLF, it cannot be excluded such agreements could fall under one of the macro-categories exemplified by these institutions. Since these are ultimately funding agreements based on business relationships related to legal finance, any business-oriented connection referred to in the current guidelines could be included. Therefore, even in the absence of an explicit reference, these guidelines should be considered in the analysis of the potential degree of bias.

B. Involved Interests

Regardless of how it is defined, both potential and actual conflicts of interest are well recognized in both common law and civil law systems. Chief Justice Sundaresh Menon's concerns on this issue were based on the premise of a small, specialized community of professionals who may act as arbitrators in some cases and serve as counsel or experts for one of the parties in others[100]. In other words, a closed ecosystem of professionals where interests and roles can easily overlap and come into conflict.

As it stands, the procedural elements directly or indirectly affected by the interests of a TPLF are numerous, inevitably leading to the need for disclosure regarding the nature and terms of the funding arrangement. Key issues include the independence and impartiality of arbitrators in relation to the TPLF, security for costs, the allocation of costs in the presence of a third-party funder, and the confidentiality of the proceedings. While other potential concerns may arise, this paper will focus solely on the influence TPLF may exert on the proceedings and the parties involved. Issues related to confiden-

---

99 "Doubt are justifiable …" General Standard 2(c) in International Bar Association, IBA Guidelines on Conflicts of Interest in International Arbitration, May 24, 2024; "…legitimate doubt…" Artt. 179 (6) and 180 (1)(c) Swiss Private International Law Act (PILA); "…justifiable doubts …" Art. 12 United Nations Commission on International Trade Law (UNCITRAL); "reasonable doubts" Art. 11 (2) International Chamber of Commerce (ICC), Arbitration Rules, September 2022.

100 See SUNDARESH M., Some cautionary notes for an age of opportunity, Keynote Address by, Chartered Institute of Arbitrators International Arbitration Conference Penang, 22 August 2013, p. 7.

tiality will be addressed alongside disclosure obligations in the following Section C.

1. Arbitrators

As a participant in the proceedings and a holder of external interests beyond the arbitration process, the arbitrator – or one of the arbitrators in the case of an arbitral tribunal – may find themselves in a conflict situation due to direct or indirect personal relationships with a TPLF. This can occur in various ways and stems from the premise already outlined above[101]: the world of international arbitration professionals is an ecosystem where individuals, law firms, and third-party funders operate and interact within the same network of exchanges and mutual relationships.

For instance, an individual may, at one time, act as counsel for a party funded by a TPLF and, at another, serve as an arbitrator in a different case where one party is supported by a TPLF. Likewise, a law firm may have an ongoing collaboration with a TPLF currently funding the opposing party's client in the proceeding. Additionally, a funder may be repeatedly chosen by financed parties to support their cases, or an arbitrator may hold shares in a litigation funding entity.[102] All these scenarios can create a situation in which the funder gains significant influence over arbitral (or judicial) proceedings, potentially jeopardizing the impartiality of the process. The principles of independence and impartiality of arbitrators are not merely semantic concepts or requirements of honorability; they are fundamental pillars of the integrity of the proceedings and, more broadly, relate to the principle of equal treatment

---

[101] See note n. 9.

[102] See LANDI N., The Arbitrator and the Arbitration Procedure: Third Party Funding in International Commercial Arbitration – An Overview, in Christian Klausegger and Peter Klein (eds), Austrian Yearbook on International Arbitration 2012, Manz'sche Verlags- und Universitätsbuchhandlung, p. 102; VON GOELER J., Third-Party Funding in International Arbitration and Its Impact on Procedure, Kluwer Law International, 2016, p. 267; GOLDSMITH A. / MELCHIONDA L., Third Party Funding in International Arbitration: Everything You Ever Wanted to Know (but Were Afraid to Ask), 2012, 1 International Business Law Journal 53, p. 225; SHANNON SAHANI V., Blurred Lines between Third-Party Funders and Law Firms, Kluwer Arbitration Blog, 2016, available at http://arbitrationblog.kluwerarbitration.com.eur.idm.oclc.org/2016/11/03/blurred-lines-between-third- party- funders-and-law-firms, last visited on August 26, 2021.

of the parties, procedural fairness, and ultimately, the enforceability of the arbitral award.[103]

If elements emerge undermining this principle of independence and impartiality, the parties may at any time challenge the legitimacy of the arbitrators,[104] leading to two possible consequences: on the one hand, the parties may request the appointment of a new arbitrator, at the expense of the efficiency and speed of the proceedings; on the other hand, if an arbitral award has already been issued, its validity may be contested, potentially resulting in its annulment or refusal of recognition and enforcement.[105] The presence of a third party, separate from the parties directly involved in the proceedings, legitimately raises questions about the arbitrators' compliance with the requirements of independence and impartiality.[106] Conversely, the identity of the funders should not remain undisclosed to address this procedural concern. The need to ensure the highest standards of independence and impartiality of arbitrators concerning the parties and TPLF is closely linked to the principle of transparency, which aims to provide guarantees to the parties and the public regarding the reliability and predictability of arbitral proceedings. In this regard, arbitrators have a duty to investigate their personal involvement and disclose any potential conflicts of interest. Likewise, it is essential to make the identity of the TPLF involved known, a point that will be analyzed separately in the next Section C.

---

103 PARK W. W., 'Rectitude in International Arbitration' (2011) 27 Arbitration International 473, pag. 526.

104 E.g. the following provisions in which the possibility of challenging an arbitrator is stipulated: Art. 14 par. 2 ICC Arbitration Rules, Art. 14 par. 3 ICDR Arbitration Rules, Art. 10.3 LCIA Arbitration Rules; Art. 13 par. 1 UNCITRAL Arbitration Rules, Art. 180a par. 1 Swiss PILA.

105 The lack of impartiality and independence of arbitrators may prevent the recognition and enforcement of an arbitral award under the 1958 New York Convention, particularly when it violates the right to a fair hearing (Art. V par. 1 lit. b), the agreed-upon composition of the arbitral tribunal (Art. V par. 1 lit. d), or public policy (Art. V par. 2 lit. b). Conflicts of interest, improper appointments, or biased decisions may lead national courts to refuse enforcement of the award. See also BRAVIN M., An Arbitrator's Failure To Disclose Conflicts: Practical Advice Before Starting & After Completing An Arbitration, Corporate Livewire, 7 August 2012, available at. https://www.corporatelivewire.com/top-story.html?id=an-arbitrators-failure-to-disclose-conflicts-practical-advice-before-starting-after-completing-an-arbitration, last visited on August 29, 2025.

106 This raises further questions falling outside the scope of this submission, such as whether it makes a difference if the connection involves a co-arbitrator as opposed to the presiding arbitrator, or whether the degree of concern varies depending on the nature and extent of the relationship with the third-party funder.

Not least, according to well-established Swiss Federal Court jurisprudence, arbitrator independence is presumed and can only be rebutted by concrete and substantiated circumstances capable of objectively raising doubts about impartiality.[107]

2. *Parties*

Third-party funding presents a valuable opportunity from multiple perspectives, as it enables litigants to pursue their claims in legal proceedings, thereby expanding access to justice. This strategy is applicable both to financially disadvantaged individuals and to those who, despite having the means to cover litigation costs, prefer to shift the risk onto a third party who is external to the proceedings but willing to invest in anticipation of a potential economic benefit resulting from a successful outcome. From this perspective, the potential influence of a TPLF is foreseeable, given its vested interest in maximizing the return on investment.

At this point, a prudent lawyer may question how to navigate the relationship with their client and what kind of service they can provide when the *"sponsor"* of the case, the one financing it, is also involved in shaping the litigation strategy. National laws across different jurisdictions safeguard the principles of lawyer independence and professional autonomy to varying degrees, as these are fundamental to the practice of law. However, the lawyer's economic dependence on the funder, combined with the funder's interest in monitoring and controlling its investment, creates a potential conflict of interest with the lawyer's duty to the client.[108] In Switzerland, the landmark rulings BGE 131 I 223 of December 10, 2004 and BGer 2C_814/2014 of January 22, 2015, consid. 4.3.1 have clarified the role of lawyers with regard both to their duties towards the client and to a possible third-party funder. Article 12 BGFA identifies the duty to avoid any conflict of interest as a core element of the legal profession (lit. a), closely linked to the guarantee of independence (lit. b) and to the obligation of professional secrecy (Art. 13 BGFA). In addition, the Swiss Code of Professional Conduct (SSR), Article 5 on conflicts of interest, establishes the priority for the lawyer to protect the client's interests in carrying out their mandate, taking care to avoid any possible direct or indirect involvement by themselves or third parties that could potentially harm their principal. These are fundamental principles aimed not only at protecting the

[107] Decision of the Swiss Federal Court BGE 129 III 445 of May 27, 2003, consid. 4.2.2.2. p. 467 with references.

[108] WAYE V., Conflicts of Interests Between Claimholders, Lawyers and Litigation Entrepreneurs, 19 BOND L. REV. 225, Austl., 2007, p. 237 n.56.

client and their defense but also at ensuring the proper conduct of proceedings and the lawyer's full capacity to represent the client. For this reason, a lawyer may inform the client of the possibility of obtaining third-party funding and assist them in entering into the relevant agreement, but may not act as the funder themselves or otherwise be involved in the funding institution.[109] It is, therefore, the lawyer's responsibility to take all necessary precautions to protect both the client and their own position, avoiding situations that could undermine their independence or the integrity of their mandate. Otherwise, they risk incurring the disciplinary measures provided for in Art. 17 BGFA.[110]

Complicating the issue further is the existence of two distinct contractual relationships: one between the legal representative and the client, and the other between the funding entity and the claimant. As a result, the lawyer assumes a dual role, simultaneously providing legal counsel while also receiving instructions regarding the management of the proceedings. In some cases, the funder's involvement is even more pronounced, extending to the direct selection of the legal representative or requiring, within the funding agreement, the acknowledgment of both a duty of care and a fiduciary duty toward the funder as well as the client.[111] In any case, the lawyer's role is undermined in terms of professional autonomy, often having to prioritize the funder's interests over those of the client, resulting in an explicit conflict of interest.[112]

In principle, therefore, a lawyer who limits their role to providing legal advice and counselling the client exclusively in the client's best interest does not

---

109 BGE 131 I 223 of December 10, 2004, consid. 4.6.4.

110 Art. 17 BGFA – Disciplinary Measures: In the event of a violation of this Act, the supervisory authority may impose the following disciplinary measures: a. a warning; b. a reprimand; c. a fine of up to 20,000 Swiss francs; d. suspension from the practice of law for a maximum of two years; e. a permanent ban from practicing. The fine may be combined with suspension from the practice of law or with a permanent ban from practicing. Where necessary, the supervisory authority may also order suspension as a precautionary measure.

111 Ibidem. As an example, we can imagine the situation where funding agreement requires the claimant to appoint one of three law firms pre-approved by the funder and grants the funder veto power over any settlement offers. During proceedings, the respondent offers a settlement that would preserve a key future supply contract, highly valuable for the claimant's commercial viability, though the financial payout is lower than the funder's expectations. The funder instructs the legal team to reject the offer, seeking a larger award. The lawyers, now caught between their duty to act in the claimant's best interest and their contractual obligations to the funder, advise rejecting the offer, against the claimant's preference. The dispute continues, and the claimant later accuses the law firm of negligence and breach of fiduciary duty.

112 ATTRILL W., Ethical Issues in Litigation Funding, IMF 16 February 2009, p. 16.

incur any disciplinary risk. In this sense, the lawyer must act as an intermediary between the client's wishes and the third-party funder's requirements, ensuring transparency of information and upholding the highest standards of professional ethics.

However, regardless of the applicable jurisdiction, a lawyer has both a legal and moral duty to always act in the best interest of their client. The greatest risk, on the other hand, is if the lawyer does not adhere to the third-party funder's directives, the funder may choose to withdraw, effectively halting the proceedings due to a lack of resources. Another significant drawback to consider is the client may be forced to accept a settlement not in their best interest but financially advantageous for the funder.[113] The client loses part of their decision-making autonomy, while the lawyer, in their role as advisor and advocate, is weakened by the constant tension between the interests of the funder and those of the client. Naturally, funders are aware of these risks and make a point of stating they adopt a purely passive role in the dispute, acting solely as external financial backers with no direct involvement in the case.[114] It is somewhat implausible overall, as rationally, a fund will be more inclined to finance cases from law firms aligning with their investment policy.

Similarly to what is required of arbitrators, the most appropriate solution once again seems to be requiring the lawyer to disclose their interests or the degree of their involvement with the TPLF they present within the scope of their legal counsel and assistance to the client.

C. Disclosure

The existence of a TPLF rightly raises concerns about potential conflicts of interest among the various actors involved in the proceedings, given the funder's personal and direct interest in the case due to its investment, which is made with the aim of securing a profit margin. This issue becomes even more critical when control over the litigation strategy shifts from the traditional lawyer-client relationship to a tripartite dynamic, where the funder – as the sponsor of the proceedings – holds the true contractual power.

---

113 WAYE V., Conflicts of Interests Between Claimholders, Lawyers and Litigation Entrepreneurs, 19 BOND L. REV. 225, Austl., 2007, p. 237 n.56.

114 See e. g. ALF of England and Wales, Code of conduct for litigation funders, January 2018, art. 9; ELFA, Code of Conduct, June 2022, art. 5; also WEGMÜLLER M. / BERGER I. / STUDER F., PANORAMIC LITIGATION FUNDING 2024 Switzerland, Nivalion AG, points 4, 6 and 8.

1. Pro – Disclosure Arguments

The debate on the necessity of a disclosure obligation has not reached unanimity within the international arbitration community. Those in favor argue the disclosure of the existence of a TPLF agreement serves not only to protect the arbitral tribunal from potential conflicts of interest but also to assess the extent of the funder's control over the funded party, ensure cost predictability, allocate procedural expenses fairly between the parties, and uphold the principle of confidentiality in the proceedings.

As previously stated in this research, parties have the right to challenge the impartiality of arbitrators at any time.[115] Therefore, it is advisable for disclosure to take place at an early stage of the proceedings to prevent unnecessary delays or, in the worst case, the non-enforcement or annulment of the arbitral award.[116] Currently, there is no state regulation on duty to disclose. While some arbitral courts have ruled in favor of such an obligation, the principle of *stare decisis* does not apply in the field of international arbitration law.[117]

Article 11 (2) and (3) of the ICC Rules imposes a duty of disclosure on arbitrators. Similar provisions can be found in various arbitration institutions, though their scope and meaning may differ. For instance, the UNCITRAL Rules require disclosure when circumstances are "likely to give rise to any justified doubts". [118] The IBA Guidelines, although non-binding, go further by requiring arbitrators to disclose any circumstance "may in the eyes of the parties, give rise to doubts". [119] The IBA Guidelines also categorize potential conflicts of interest into three lists (Red, Orange, and Green) based on their severity. Moreover, under Standard 7 lit. a, the Guidelines mandate parties disclose any potential conflict of interest between the funder and the arbitrator

---

[115] See supra note 82.

[116] BLACKABY N. / PARTASIDES C. / REDFERN A. / HUNTER M., Redfern & Hunter on International Arbitration, 5th edition, Oxford: Oxford University Press, 2009, par. 4.72; see also TRUSZ J. A., Full Disclosure? Conflicts of Interest Arising from Third-Party Funding in International Commercial Arbitration, 101 GEO. L.J. 1649, 2013, p. 1652.

[117] UGUALE A., RIDI N., Precedent, Jus Mundi, February 11, 2025, available at https://jusmundi.com/en/document/publication/en-precedent, last visited on August 29, 2025.

[118] Art. 17F cpv. 2 UNCITRAL Model Law.

[119] Art. 3 lit. a IBA Guidelines on Conflicts of Interest in International Arbitration. The Swiss Federal Court itself recognizes their practical value. They are used as a helpful reference tool to promote consistency in assessing arbitrator independence, especially in international sports arbitration. However, the Court ultimately bases its decisions on the specific circumstances of each case. See Decision of the Swiss Federal Court BGer 4A_506/2007 of March 20, 2008, consid. 3.3.2.2.

if the arbitrator has a conflict with any person or entity holding a direct economic interest in the outcome of the case.

Since TPLF is a relatively recent phenomenon, it is not explicitly mentioned in the various applicable rules. However, arbitrators are required to disclose any potential connection that could compromise their impartiality and independence in the arbitral proceedings. In doing so, they must also ensure they are released from any confidentiality obligations stemming from their prior professional engagements.

If, as seen above, a disclosure obligation is required when the relevant regulations apply, no explicit provision addresses whether the parties to the proceedings themselves have such a duty. Most existing regulations tend to impose this obligation on the funded party, regardless of the specific terms of the funding agreement between the parties.[120] Moreover, these agreements typically include confidentiality clauses, which further discourage the funded party from voluntarily disclosing their existence.

Given that arbitral proceedings are generally subject to strict confidentiality, even if a general obligation to disclose third-party funding agreements were established, such disclosures would primarily be known only to the parties involved in the arbitration. However, one counterargument to this reasoning is once a third-party funder becomes involved in the proceedings and gains access to certain statements or evidence, the private and confidential nature of arbitration is already compromised. Therefore, both the arbitrators and the opposing party have a legitimate interest in knowing who is influencing the case.[121]

As for whom the disclosure should be made to, the most efficient approach for procedural integrity and the future enforcement of the arbitral award would be to notify both the arbitrators and the opposing party of the existence of a TPLF arrangement, allowing them to conduct appropriate due diligence. Regarding the content of the disclosure, the most effective method would be to provide access to the funding agreement itself. This would safeguard the non-funded party from a disproportionate allocation of costs and clarify the extent to which the funder assumes responsibility for covering procedural expenses.[122]

---

[120] OVERGAARD / CAROLINE & JOHAN TUFTE-KRISTENSEN, Disclosure of Third-Party Funding in Commercial Arbitration, 2020, 2, NORDIC JOURNAL OF COMMERCIAL LAW, 2020, pp. 10 -11, 16.

[121] ATTRILL / WAYNE, ETHICAL ISSUES IN LITIGATION FUNDING, IMF, 2009, p. 7.

[122] Of great relevance to the security of costs in the event the financed party loses and is required to compensate the other party. It goes without saying that based on the level of control, the arbitrator should be able to grant a request for security of costs filed by

2. *Anti – Disclosure Arguments*

It should be noted the agreement between the funded party and the third-party funder is a private contract, external to the investigative powers of the arbitral tribunal and, therefore, beyond its jurisdiction.[123] This perspective aligns with the fundamental purpose for which the arbitral tribunal is established – resolving disputes between the contracting parties. Consequently, the funding agreement is not a subject for discussion before the tribunal and cannot be examined as part of the proceedings. Otherwise, a valid objection regarding a lack of jurisdiction could be raised against the tribunal. The tribunal's authority stems from an arbitration clause agreed upon by two parties who have mutually consented to submit their disputes to arbitration. Since the third-party funder is not a signatory to the arbitration agreement, it remains, in principle, a non-party to the proceedings.[124]

Additional arguments against a mandatory disclosure obligation are of a practical nature. One key concern relates to time and cost implications. If disclosure were required and the opposing party became aware of the existence of a funder, it might exploit this information to engage in procedural maneuvers in bad faith, with the aim of prolonging the proceedings and inflating expenses. Such a strategy would aim to burden the funded party financially, potentially forcing the funder to withdraw its financial support.[125] This leads to further concerns regarding cost allocation and security for costs. Without a third-party funder, the funded party may lack the financial means to cover procedural expenses. Consequently, some argue financial guarantees should be required when a third-party funder is involved to ensure the opposing party is not unfairly disadvantaged.[126]

---

the funded party. See Goeler, Jonas Von (2016), Third-Party Funding in International Arbitration and Its Impact on Procedure, 35 INTERNATIONAL ARBITRATION, pp. 144 – 145.

123 FRIGNATI V., Ethical Implications of Third-Party Funding in International Arbitration, 32 ARB. INT'L 516, 2016.

124 GOELER, V., Third-Party Funding in International Arbitration and Its Impact on Procedure, 2016, pp. 85-86, at 143.

125 GOLDSMITH A / MELCHIONDA L., Third Party Funding in International Arbitration: Everything You Ever Wanted to Know (But Were Afraid to Ask) – Part Two, 2012 INT'L BUS. L.J., 2012, at 223; also HONLET J., Recent Decisions in Third-Part Funding in Investment Arbitration, 30 ICSID REV. 699, 2015, p. 711.

126 The rationale behind the request for financial guarantees when an external funder is involved relates to the concern the funded party may not have the means to cover procedural expenses or any adverse costs if the proceedings do not go in their favor. Requiring such guarantees is particularly relevant when an external funder is involved, as the funded party may not have the means to cover potential costs directly, and the

Given the opinions of supporters on both sides, I feel obliged to note, likewise, the matter is not without risks. Indeed, a third funder is represented by a professional investor whose clients are served under strict confidentiality clauses in compliance with the financing agreement. Such a funder may have no interest in being exposed in legal proceedings, in order to protect both themselves and the clients who invest in their fund. For this reason, any potential obligation of disclosure could prove counterproductive, pushing the TPLF towards relying on a Special Purpose Vehicle (SPV). The SPV is a limited liability company, an empty shell outwardly presentable in any potential proceedings, but poses a risk in terms of its potential solvency[127]. Conversely, the opposing argument, namely, not to require disclosure, also fails because in a growing market, with numerous investor players and few rules, the risk investment market would be favoured to the potential detriment of consumers. Therefore, in my view, a disclosure clause alone is not sufficient; an ethical code applicable to legal finance service providers is also necessary.

3. *Swiss Practice*

Under the Swiss Civil Procedure Code (Zivilprozessordnung, ZPO), a party may request the production of documents from the opposing party, provided the request is precise and specific, in compliance with the prohibition against fishing expeditions.[128] While the Swiss Procedure Code does not directly

---

funder could theoretically withdraw its support during the proceedings, leaving the claimant without the ability to meet their financial obligations. Although there is no obligation to actively disclose one's financial status, there is a need to question the fairness of the process, i. e., to ensure all parties have equal access to the proceedings, preventing the more financially supported party from hindering the opposing party's ability not only during the proceedings but also in recovering costs in case of a victory. Harwood M. K. / BATIFORT S.N. / TRAHANAS C., Third-Party Funding: Security for Costs and Other Key Issues, THE INVESTMENT TREATY ARBITRATION REVIEW 108, Barton Legum ed., 2d ed., 2017.

127 In such circumstances, the doctrine of piercing the corporate veil may apply, allowing action to be taken directly against the ultimate economic actor. A similar approach comes into consideration by drawing an analogy with two cases decided by the Supreme Court of the Canton of Zurich, which, in two 2018 decisions (RT180059-O/U, 24 May 2018; RT180057-O/U, 17 May 2018), recognised, respectively, the liability of a third-party funder for adverse costs and the possible qualification of a litigation funding agreement as a contract for the benefit of a third party, thereby granting the funded party's lawyer a direct claim against the funder for the payment of their fees.

128 Art. 160 (1) lit. b ZPO ; SCHUMACHER, Prozessfinanzierung, Erfolgshonorierte Fremdfinanzierung von Zivilverfahren, Thesis Zurich 2015, cited Schumacher, *Prozessfinanzierung*, p. 100.

govern international arbitration proceedings seated in Switzerland, it may still become relevant in certain cases. The applicable legal framework for such arbitrations is Chapter 12 of the Swiss PILA, which serves as the *lex arbitri*. However, pursuant to Art. 184 (2) Swiss PILA, if the arbitral tribunal or a party – with the tribunal's consent – requires judicial assistance for evidentiary matters (such as compelling third-party document production), the Swiss State Courts at the seat of the arbitration may intervene. In doing so, these courts apply their own procedural law, namely the ZPO. Accordingly, provisions such as Art. 150 ZPO, which governs document production in civil litigation, can be applied by analogy when State Court assistance is sought in international arbitration.

An exception applies to documents related to communications between a party or a third party and their legal counsel[129], which are protected regardless of whether they are held by the lawyer, the client, or a third party.[130] This protection extends to legal assessments conducted by third-party litigation funders (TPLF). Swiss civil procedure law does not impose any obligation to disclose third-party litigation funding.[131] Specifically, any request for the production of documents must be justified and relevant to the court's decision, which litigation funding agreements typically are not.[132] As a result, in most cases, the existence of such agreements remains entirely confidential.

Conversely, in the field of international arbitration, the debate on disclosure obligations aligns with the previously discussed arguments for and against mandatory disclosure.

In Switzerland, litigation funding agreements are generally subject to strict confidentiality clauses, and their disclosure requires the consent of the opposing party.[133] However, this does not prevent disclosure from being used as a strategic tool to facilitate settlement before a final ruling.[134] The idea is re-

---

129 Article 160 (1) lit. b ZPO.

130 SCHMID, in: SPÜHLER/TENCHIO/INFANGER (eds.), Basler Kommentar Schweizerische Zivilprozessordnung, 3rd ed., Basel 2017, para. 24 ad Article 160; SCHMID, in: OBERHAMMER/DOMEJ/HAAS, Kurzkommentar ZPO, 2nd ed., Basel 2014, para. 6a ad Article 160; Hasenböhler, in: Sutter-Somm/Hasenböhler/Leuenberger (eds.), Kommentar zur Schweizerischen Zivilprozessordnung, 3rd ed., Zürich 2016, para. 18 ad Article 160.

131 For exception see, e. g., Swiss Federal Court 2C_814/2014 of 22 January 2015 c. 5.2.

132 Art. 150 ZPO.

133 See SCHUMACHER, Prozessfinanzierung, Erfolgshonorierte Fremdfinanzierung von Zivilverfahren, Thesis Zürich 2015, cited Schumacher, *Prozessfinanzierung*, p. 100.

134 WEY R., Kommerzielle Prozessfinanzierung – ein Überblick über Angebot und Rechtsfragen, in: Fellmann/ Weber (eds.), Haftpflichtprozess,2008, Zürich/Basel/Geneva 2008, pp. 54 et seqq. .

vealing the financial strength and legal soundness of a claim early on – by demonstrating it has passed the due diligence of a third-party funder – could encourage the opposing party to consider an early resolution.[135]

V. How to trust the System

There are numerous interconnected aspects to consider. While regulations exist, much of the current framework relies on the responsibility of arbitration participants to ensure the proper functioning of the proceedings;[136] failure to do so may compromise the enforceability of the arbitral award. Below, several key elements are succinctly outlined, all of which play a role in this dynamic and have been addressed at various points in this research.[137] Above all, the principle of transparency must prevail. Not as a mere procedural formality, but as the cornerstone of legitimacy and enforceability in arbitration. Only by embracing openness regarding third-party involvement and potential conflicts of interest can the process preserve its credibility and ensure justice is not only done, but seen to be done.

A. Follow a transparency principle

The principle of transparency is foundational and intrinsic to the entire arbitral process. On one hand, it is a requirement in relation to TPLF disclosure; on the other, it is inherent to the arbitration proceedings as a parameter for assessing the legitimacy of the decision.[138] Arbitrators alone are not always

---

135 Ibidem.

136 Art. 179 (6) Swiss PILA refers to the individual responsibility of the person appointed as arbitrator to make a disclosure. By contrast, Article 180(2) of the Swiss PILA leaves it to the parties in the proceedings to raise objections under paragraph (1)(c). The same principle can be found in the UNCITRAL Arbitration Rules ex art. 11 and following and in the ICC Arbitration Rules under art. 11 (2) and 14 (1). The difference lies in the time limit within which a challenge must be raised: 30 days from the date on which the grounds compromising the principles of impartiality and independence became known (Article 180a (1) Swiss PILA, Article 14 of the ICC Arbitration Rules), and 15 days under Article 13(1) of the UNCITRAL Arbitration Rules.

137 See also Section III B.2.b at page 13, 14; Section IV B.1 at page 22 ; Section IV B.1 at page 21.

138 SCHIMMEL D. and others, Transparency in Arbitration, *Practical Law*, 2018, available at https://uk.practicallaw.thomsonreuters.com/w-013-1478, last visited on August 29, 2025.

able to effectively carry out due diligence on potential conflicts of interest.[139] This is why it is essential to adhere to a principle of transparency between the parties, both in the relationship between the legal representative and the funder, as well as between the client and the lawyer, in order to minimize the potential risk of a conflict of interest. In some cases, it also strengthens the position of the funded party by exposing the strength of the case, while at the same time allowing them to maintain control over the proceedings.[140] Therefore, the principle of transparency serves not only as a tool to mitigate possible conflicts of interest but also as a procedural mechanism to return control of the proceedings[141] to its rightful owner,[142] despite the potential influence of the third-party investor, who, once known to the parties, will have to act with great discretion or adhere to the choices of the party holder or the opinion of their legal representative.

B. Enforceability

As outlined in the preceding paragraphs,[143] the enforcement of an arbitral award, beyond representing the culmination of the entire extrajudicial proceeding, is an essential element, as without it, the decision cannot be implemented, and the prevailing party is unable to satisfy its claim. To this end, the principle of transparency, along with the duty of arbitrators and parties to disclose any potential conflicts of interest, serves the purpose of ensuring the enforceability of the decision in accordance with the Convention on the

139 STONE W., Third Party Funding in International Arbitration: A Case for Mandatory Disclosure?, 2015, 17 Asian Dispute Review 62, 68.

140 STEINITZ M., Whose Claim Is This Anyway? Third-Party Litigation Funding, 95 Minnesota Law Review 1328, 2011.

141 Even in the absence of an actual conflict of interest, lies in the potential erosion of party autonomy. When control over key decisions (e. g., settlement strategy, appointment of counsel, or even the continuation of the claim) is shifted to a third-party funder, the funded party may no longer be acting on its own will. Even without a direct conflict of interest, this undermines the legitimacy and integrity of the proceeding, blurring the line between legal representation and commercial investment, and potentially weakening trust in the fairness of the process.

142 The claim belongs to the party with the legal interest in the underlying dispute. Even if a funder finances the entire proceeding, it remains a commercial contract between the funder and the claimant, not a transfer of substantive legal rights. Allowing funders to assume ownership just because they pay would fundamentally alter the legal architecture of arbitration. It could also trigger concerns under doctrines like champerty or maintenance in some jurisdictions (eg. Ireland) and might affect enforceability, confidentiality, and party autonomy.

143 Section IV B.1 at p. 21 and C.1 at p. 24.

Recognition and Enforcement of Foreign Arbitral Awards (commonly known as the New York Convention). Any objections based on an alleged violation of the duty of impartiality and independence of arbitrators, such as a personal connection with the parties or their third-party funder, may jeopardize the enforceability of the award under the New York Convention.

Another issue worth mentioning concerns the enforcement of awards issued in proceedings involving TPLF in jurisdictions where such practice is prohibited. It is important to emphasize signatory states to the New York Convention generally cannot hinder enforcement solely on the basis of third-party funding. The only permissible limitation relates to a potential violation of public policy.[144] However, the public interest in ensuring the stability of the international arbitration system outweighs the interest in refusing enforcement, even if it entails upholding contractual provisions might otherwise be deemed unacceptable.[145] In other words, the public interest in enforcing the arbitral award prevails over the interest in upholding domestic legal norms.[146]

C. Trust and Involvement

It can be said the system is here to stay, and TPLF will consolidate its role in the landscape of international arbitration law. The challenge now is to push the current framework in a direction fostering genuine trust, not only in the individual arbitrators but in the integrity of the arbitral institution as a whole. This can best be achieved by codifying an unambiguous and consistent obligation of disclosure – particularly regarding third-party funding arrangements – which would apply uniformly across arbitral institutions and jurisdictions. The goal is not to discourage funding, but to ensure any involvement by funders does not undermine the transparency or perceived neutrality of the process. This approach would enhance predictability, reduce the risk of post-

---

144 Eg. In Ireland where third - party litigation funding is prohibited based on the champerty and maintenance rules, can raise public policy concerns, particularly when it comes to enforceability of arbitral awards or admissibility of funding arrangements. According to the NY Convention Art. V (2)(b) recognition and enforcement of the award can be refused. In 2023, the Supreme Court decision R v Competition Appeal Tribunal, 2023, UKSC 28, held certain litigation funding agreements were unenforceable as damages - based agreements, creating uncertainty in one of the world's largest funding markets.

145 KNOWLES B / BAKER P., Enforcing a funded award in an anti-funding environment, in Global Arbitration Review, 19 August 2017, available at https://globalarbitrationreview.com/article/enforcing-funded-award-in-anti-funding-environment, last visited on August 29, 2025.

146 Ibidem.

award challenges, and reinforce the legitimacy of arbitration as a fair and impartial forum for dispute resolution. However, it is essential to lay the groundwork to ensure those parties, or external parties involved, trust in a fair judgment. Here, an obligation of disclosure does not appear to be an extraneous burden or an excessive intrusion into the parties' confidential relationships, but rather a tool enhancing the reliability of the arbitration process and the validity of the future arbitral award. Thus, transparency, coupled with the duty of arbitrators and parties to declare any potential conflicts of interest, serves to strengthen the system's credibility, ensuring all parties involved can trust the outcome. While the two concepts are linked in a cause – effect relationship, disclosure is the means by which transparency is achieved making it essential for maintaining trust in the arbitral process.[147]

VI. Conclusion

TPLF is a complex phenomenon developed both as a means to ensure more equitable access to justice and as a financial investment tool. As such, it must be approached from a financial perspective, based on investment assessments and strategic decisions aimed at maximizing profit. This very aspect, however, raises concerns when TPLF becomes involved in arbitration proceedings, traditionally structured around other actors, as it can disrupt the balance between claimant, respondent, and arbitrators.

By choosing to support one party's claim, a third-party funder introduces personal interests into the proceedings, which may compromise the validity of the arbitral award. Existing or past business relationships, as well as the funder's interest in securing a favorable return on investment, increase the likelihood of conflicts of interest: both between the funded party and the funder, and in terms of the neutrality and impartiality of the arbitrators in rendering their decision.

TPLF has undoubtedly become permanent in the international arbitration landscape. What began as a tool to enhance access to justice has evolved into a sophisticated financial instrument with its own dynamics, incentives, and risks. The complexity of the system now requires a shift from reactive scrutiny to proactive regulation. While TPLF offers valuable benefits, including financial accessibility and risk mitigation, it simultaneously introduces the potential for conflicts of interest, imbalances in procedural control, and threats to the enforceability of arbitral awards.

---

[147] To summarise the concept in a motto: disclosure is the tool, transparency is the goal.

To preserve trust in the system, a robust disclosure regime is no longer optional, it is essential. Disclosure should be seen not as a burden or intrusion, but as a safeguard reinforcing transparency, ensures the integrity of the tribunal, and strengthens the enforceability of awards. While the current framework focuses primarily on arbitrators, future regulation must extend to lawyers and parties themselves, especially where the funder exerts control or influence over case strategy. In practical terms, a tiered approach to disclosure could be adopted, one that distinguishes between the mere existence of funding - always disclosable - and the specific contractual terms - protected unless they affect neutrality or cost allocation.

From a regulatory perspective, the future lies in a balanced, harmonized approach: neither a blanket prohibition nor unchecked liberalization. A minimum international standard should be encouraged; for example, through a revised IBA or UNCITRAL model provision, to ensure uniformity, predictability, and procedural fairness. By embracing precise but flexible rules, including disclosure obligations, conflict of interest guidelines, and optional codes of conduct for funders, it can enhance its competitiveness while maintaining the integrity of its legal framework. Ultimately, the way forward is not to reject TPLF, but to regulate it smartly aligning commercial innovation with procedural justice, and investor confidence with party autonomy. Only by doing so can the arbitral system continue to inspire the trust it depends upon.

As an example, a possible model clause for such a disclosure framework could be:

1. Disclosure of third – party funding: Each party shall, at the earliest possible stage of the proceedings, disclose the existence of any third-party funding arrangement related to the arbitration. This includes any agreement under which a non-party has an economic interest in the outcome of the dispute or is providing financial support to a party.
2. Scope of disclosure: The disclosure shall, at a minimum, identify the identity of the funder and the nature of the funding arrangement (e. g., non-recourse loan, contingency-based support). Specific terms of the funding agreement, including financial details, shall remain confidential unless they may reasonably affect the impartiality or independence of an arbitrator, the cost allocation, or the enforceability of the award.
3. Duty to disclose: Parties shall have a continuing obligation to update their disclosure if the funding arrangement is modified or terminated, or if additional funders become involved.
4. The arbitral tribunal shall have the authority to request further information to assess potential conflict of interest ant take appropriate procedural orders.

A uniform international regulatory approach could help strike a balance between protecting the confidentiality of funding agreements and preserving the integrity of arbitration proceedings. In this context, Switzerland, historically known for its liberal approach, may find itself needing to reconcile its competitive position with growing international pressure for increased regulation of third-party funding in arbitration. By preserving party autonomy and offering a funder-friendly environment with minimal regulatory interference, Switzerland could enhance its appeal as a flexible and confidential seat of arbitration. Yet this same reluctance carries risks: without baseline disclosure requirements, Swiss-seated awards may face legitimacy challenges, particularly in cases involving undisclosed funders or potential conflicts of interest. In a legal landscape increasingly shaped by transparency norms, Switzerland's regulatory hesitance may be perceived as out of step with evolving international standards. The challenge, therefore, lies not in choosing between regulation and deregulation, but in crafting a balanced framework: one maintaining Switzerland's traditional strengths while reinforcing the procedural integrity global users now demand.

VII. Description of the author

Alex Alvise Corti is a Swiss-admitted lawyer at Berra, Vigilante & Partners in Lugano. He holds a Master of Laws (MLaw) from the University of Insubria, Como, and has over three years of legal experience across multiple jurisdictions and practice areas, including arbitration, corporate, contract, and administrative law. His academic and professional background includes international scholarship programs, Model United Nations participation, and exchanges at institutions such as Harvard University and the University of Regensburg. Currently pursuing a Certificate of Advanced Studies in arbitration, he is an active member of the International Association of Young Lawyers (AIJA) and brings multilingual and cross-cultural expertise to international legal research and practice. Beyond his professional work, he contributes to community service through leadership roles in Leo Club organizations.

Investment Treaty Arbitration and Access to Medicines: Post-Pandemic Developments[1]

SAMANTHA REGENTHAL

1 This paper is an augmented version of an article previously published in the ASA Bulletin, Volume 43, No. 1/2025. The author wishes to thank Joachim Knoll, Partner at LALIVE, Geneva, for his invaluable guidance and insights throughout its development.

Table of Contents

I. Summary

Investment treaties are entered into by and between States in order to promote investments and greater economic cooperation by providing an international legal framework establishing standards of protection and a mechanism for dispute resolution for foreign investors. Restrictions in States' right to regulate are integral parts of these agreements.

Despite many modern investment treaties being entered into between developed economies that are both capital importing and exporting and where the risk of exposure to investment treaty arbitration could be said to be a calculated risk, a part of the 'cost' of attracting foreign investment, criticism towards the investment treaty arbitration system has been growing in the past decades. Concerns surrounding an anticipated increase in investment treaty arbitration cases as a result of States' measures during the COVID-19 pandemic further highlighted the perceived need to safeguard States' regulatory space in investment treaties to protect public health. A number of reforms of relevance to investment treaty arbitration are currently ongoing and recently signed treaties show a clear trend towards including provisions intended to safeguard States' regulatory autonomy.

International investment treaties protect foreign investors against a wide range of State measures relevant to pharmaceutical investments, but investment treaty arbitration involving pharmaceutical investors is still relatively uncommon. The relationship between States and pharmaceutical investors is characterised by complex interdependencies, which may at least in part explain this reluctance to engage in investment treaty arbitration. With increased pressure on health systems and in light of global challenges relating to access to medicines, including serious drug supply shortages, the path of investment treaty arbitration may be of increased relevance to pharmaceutical investors in the future.

II. Introduction

As the COVID-19 pandemic unfolded, States took to a broad variety of measures in attempts to mitigate the spread of the virus, support investment or protect critical industries. Of great visibility to the public at large were quarantine measures, border closures, restrictions on the movement of people and goods, city lockdowns or the expropriation of private property for quarantine sites or medical treatment. But there were also more sophisticated measures States resorted to, such as the speeding up of investment approval procedures and incentive schemes for health-related research and development (R&D).

Some States intervened specifically to protect their domestic health sector, for example by tightening foreign investment screening mechanisms, issuing State loans and guarantees, or acquiring equity in struggling domestic key companies, introducing new regulations, mandatory production requirements and export bans for medical equipment or by reducing import duties for medical devices.[2]

At the time, an increase in investor-State dispute settlement through investment treaty arbitration under existing investment treaties, such as bilateral investment treaties (BITs) or other treaties with investment provisions (TIPs) was considered a probable consequence of such State measures, given their potential to trigger claims for breaches of substantive protection standards of investment treaties, such as fair and equitable treatment (FET) or the protection from unlawful indirect expropriation.[3] Already in the initial phase of the pandemic, the Columbia Center on Sustainable Investment called for an:

"[...] immediate moratorium on all arbitration claims by private corporations against governments using international investment treaties', and a *'permanent restriction on all arbitration claims related to government measures targeting health, economic, and social dimensions of the pandemic and its effects."*[4]

The concerns surrounding the anticipated investment treaty arbitration upswing gave new wind in the sails to the longstanding policy debate around the need to safeguard States' regulatory space in investment treaties to protect public health as well as corresponding investment treaty reform initiatives.[5]

Access to medicines is a field of complex interdependencies. The medicines market is one of the most regulated markets and national and regional policy and regulation largely determine not only market access by establishing the safety and efficacy standards and procedure for product development and

---

2 UNCTAD, Investment Policy Responses to the COVID-19 Pandemic, Investment Policy Monitor, Special Issue No. 4, May 2020.

3 See for example: PADDEU, FEDERICA I. / KATE PARLETT, COVID-19 and Investment Treaty Claims, Kluwer Arbitration Blog, 30 March 2020, available at https://arbitrationblog.kluwerarbitration.com/2020/03/30/covid-19-and-investment-treaty-claims/, last accessed 30. September 2024; QU, GUANGYI / WEI, SHEN, Public Health and Investment Protection in the Context of the COVID-19 Pandemic - From the Sustainable Perspective of Exception Clauses, Sustainability, 2022, 14, 6523.

4 Columbia Center on Sustainable Investment, Call for ITA Moratorium During COVID-19 Crisis and Response, 6 May 2020.

5 UNCTAD Investment Policy Responses to the COVID-19 Pandemic, (see footnote 2), p. 11 f.

marketing approval but also the pricing, as reimbursement is highly dependent on States' reimbursement policy, negotiation and tenders.[6]

Securing 'access to medicines' is part of State activities, but also of activities and investments by the pharmaceutical[7] sector. Pharmaceutical companies engaged in R&D bring new innovative medicines to market and provide access to clinical trials, engage in capacity building for manufacturing and supply chains incl. education and training of health care staff and maintain product registrations through compliance with sometimes rigorous local market requirements over time[8]. Clinical trials and early access schemes offer patients an opportunity to receive new, potentially life-saving medicines before final regulatory and/or reimbursement approval, which can be very lengthy procedures. For the purpose of this paper, investment treaty arbitration on 'access to medicines' refers to cases involving State measures that may impact the full spectrum of investments by pharmaceutical companies, as such investments are defined in the relevant investment treaties.

This paper examines the dynamics between States' right to regulate and investor protection standards in investment treaties in cases relevant to access to medicines. To identify future trends this paper includes an analysis of 19 investment treaties, signed between 1. January 2022 and 31. December 2023 as well as three new model investment treaties released by States during the same time frame, with regard to inclusion of provisions specifically safeguarding States' right to regulate in the field of public health and clarifications or limitations of the protection standards most relevant to access to medicines investment treaty arbitration cases.

III. Investment treaties

A. Introduction

Investment treaties are entered into by and between States in order to promote investments and greater economic cooperation by providing an international legal framework establishing standards of protection and a mechanism for

[6] For a compact summary of the sector, see for example OECD, Pharmaceutical Innovation and Access to Medicines, OECD Health Policy Studies, OECD Publishing, 2018.

[7] When referring to the 'pharmaceutical sector' herein, also the biotech and other related sectors developing medicines for human consumption are meant to be included.

[8] Such as for example pharmacovigilance i. e. safety reporting.

dispute resolution for foreign investors.[9] The investment treaty protection standards commonly guarantee predictability and security to the foreign investor through stipulating restrictions on the regulatory autonomy of the host State. Therefore, as such, restrictions in States' right to regulate are indispensable parts of the purpose of investment treaties.[10] It could be held that disciplining domestic policymaking is one of the key reasons why countries commit to enforceable international rules.[11]

Notably, investment treaties only provide a legal framework for foreign investors to bring a claim against a host State in which such investor has made an investment when the host States acted as a sovereign authority. In cases of disputes relating to commercial contracts to which a State might be a party, the State would commonly act in another capacity and the dispute would not be subject to investment treaty arbitration under the investment treaty.[12] For the purpose of this research paper, whenever referring to 'State regulation' or 'State regulatory measures' such cover any measure taken by a State exercising its authority as a sovereign, such as decisions, enactment of regulations or policy enforcement.

B. Investment treaty protection standards

Investment protection standards commonly included in investment treaties and relied on by foreign investors in investment treaty arbitration cases are:

- Fair and equitable treatment (FET): requiring the host State to provide a stable and predictable investment environment in line with the investor's reasonable and legitimate expectations;
- Full protection and security (FPS): obliging the host State to take active and reasonable measures to protect a foreign investment from adverse effects or actions of physical or legal nature;
- Free transfer of funds related to the investment;

---

9 GIRSBERGER, DANIEL / VOSER, NATALIE, International Arbitration Comparative and Swiss Perspectives, Fourth Extended Edition, Zürich, 2021, para 1786.

10 NOWROT, KARSTEN, How to Include Environmental Protection, Human Rights and Sustainability in International Investment Law, The Journal of World Investment & Trade, 2014, p. 622.

11 See for example BERGE LAUDAL, TARALD / BERGER, AXEL, Do Investor-State Dispute Settlement Cases Influence Domestic Environmental Regulation? The Role of Respondent State Bureaucratic Capacity, Journal of International Dispute Settlement, March 2021

12 GIRSBERGER / VOSER, (see footnote 9), para 1814.

- Protection against direct or indirect expropriation which does not fulfil defined requirements; and
- National treatment and most favoured nation (MFN) principles, requiring host States to treat foreign investors no less favourable than their domestic entities in similar circumstances or no less favourable than investors from another State that has an investment agreement with the host State.[13]

Investment treaties may also contain other substantive standards and protections impacting States' right to regulate, such as specific intellectual property (IP) rights protection or protection against performance requirements for the investor. FET and the protection against unlawful direct and indirect expropriation are most often invoked in known investment treaty arbitration claims relevant to access to medicines.[14]

1. Fair and equitable treatment

The FET clause is the most litigated provision in investment treaties. It is included in over 80 per cent of known investment treaty arbitration cases and FET breaches are the most commonly found violations in cases decided in favour of the investor.[15] Due to the vagueness of the concept and resulting lack of predictability regarding investment tribunals' interpretation, UNCTAD identified the FET standard as a major issue of the current investment law regime in terms of its impact on developing countries' ambitions to realize the UN's Sustainable Development Goals and has explicitly argued for its reform for the past decade.[16] Although each tribunal interprets a FET provision as per the investment treaty applicable in a specific case and although the system is one without binding precedent, there is consistency in that the FET standard incorporates the following terms:

- Prohibition of manifest arbitrariness in decision-making, that is, measures taken purely on the basis of prejudice or bias without a legitimate purpose or rational explanation;

---

13 GIRSBERGER / VOSER, (see footnote 9), para 1822.

14 More on this in chapter III C.

15 UNCTAD, International Investment Agreements Reform Accelerator, UNCTAD/DIAE/PCB/INF/2020/8, 2020, (hereinafter referred to as UNCTAD IIA Reform Accelerator), p. 20.

16 UNCTAD, Fair and equitable treatment, Series on Issues in International Investment Agreements II, 2012, p. 61 f., 89 ff.; UNCTAD IIA Reform Accelerator, (see footnote 15), p. 2 ff.

- Prohibition of the denial of justice and disregard of the fundamental principles of due process;
- Prohibition of targeted discrimination on manifestly wrongful grounds, such as gender, race or religious belief;
- Prohibition of abusive treatment of investors, including coercion, duress and harassment;
- Protection of the legitimate expectations of investors arising from a government's specific representations or investment inducing measures, although balanced with the host State's right to regulate in the public interest.[17]

In arbitral practice, a broad variety of governmental conduct, including legislative, administrative and judicial practices can potentially be found to breach the FET obligation.[18]

2. *Protection against unlawful expropriation*

Almost all investment treaties prohibit unlawful expropriation, as one of the most obvious threats to an investment. Commonly, to be lawful, expropriation measures must i) serve a public purpose, ii) not be arbitrary or discriminatory, iii) follow the principles of due process, and iv) be accompanied by prompt, adequate and effective compensation.[19] Expropriation may be either direct or indirect and these concepts are increasingly defined in investment treaties.[20] The EU model clauses from 2023 provide the following definitions:

- *"[...]direct expropriation occurs when an investment is nationalised or otherwise directly expropriated through formal transfer of title or outright seizure.*
- *indirect expropriation occurs where a measure or series of measures by a Party has an effect equivalent to direct expropriation, in that it substantially deprives the investor of the fundamental attributes of property in its investment, including the right to use, enjoy and dispose of its investment, without formal transfer of title or outright seizure."*[21]

---

17 UNCTAD, Fair and equitable treatment, (see footnote 16), p. 61 ff.

18 More on this in Chapter III C.

19 GIRSBERGER / VOSER, (see footnote 9), para 1822.

20 See Chapter IV B.

21 European Union (EU) Model BIT Clauses (2023), EU Annotations to the Model Clauses for negotiation or re-negotiation of Member States' Bilateral Investment Agreements with third countries from 21. September 2023, p. 32.

With regard to indirect expropriation, measures having an effect equivalent to expropriation are often not intentionally expropriatory. Therefore, it is necessary to assess if a measure has a sufficiently substantial effect to be considered equivalent to an expropriation. In addition, there are conditions which, if fulfilled, remove the expropriatory nature of the measure. If there is no expropriation there is no compensation to be paid to the investor who suffers damages.[22] If there is a case of expropriation, to be lawful under the investment treaty, such needs to fulfil the criteria stated in such investment treaty.

C. Limitations to the investment protection standards

When a foreign investor challenges State decisions or regulatory measures impacting its investment, the host State may defend itself by referring to justifiable reasons under the investment treaty. That would be the case if the substantive provisions of the investment treaty explicitly allow such measures. If the measures are inconsistent with the obligations established by the relevant substantive provisions the question will be if the State has a valid defence? Under the international investment legal framework, the host State may then build its defence based on investment treaty exception clauses covering regulatory measures or, when the investment treaty does not expressly include such exceptions, on customary international law as per article 31(3)(c) of the Vienna Convention on the Law of Treaties ('VCLT'), referring for example to reasonable, bona fide, non-discriminatory and proportionate exercise of police powers.[23]

Since older investment treaties only rarely include explicit language safeguarding the States' right to regulate and an overwhelming majority of investment treaty arbitration cases are brought under such old-generation investment treaties [24], most tribunal assessments of States' rights to regulate to date have involved elements of customary international law. The *Philip Mor-*

---

22 MANCIAUX, SÉBASTIEN, Big pharma and investment arbitration, Vietnamese Journal of Legal Sciences, Vol. 04, No. 01, 2021, p. 107 f.; see also Article 1 of Protocol No. 1 to the European Convention on Human Rights.

23 BALTAG, CRINA / JOSHI, RIDDHI / DUGGAL, KABIR, Recent Trends in Investment Arbitration on the Right to Regulate, Environment, Health and Corporate Social Responsibility: Too Much or Too Little?, ICSID Review, 2023, p. 395; The concept of 'police powers' was incorporated already in the 1961 Harvard Draft Convention on the International Responsibility of States for Injuries to Aliens and is commonly referred to in arbitral awards, as also noted by the tribunal in *Marfin Investment Group v. Republic of Cyprus*, ICSID Case No ARB/13/27, award 26. July 2018, para 828.

24 UNCTAD IIA Reform Accelerator, (see footnote 15), p. 2.; UNCTAD Investment Dispute Settlement Navigator.

ris v. Uruguay[25] award from 8. July 2016 sets a non-binding but often cited precedent for the State's right to regulate in the interest of public health and the assessment of customary international law in the absence of explicit exceptions from the investment treaty protection standards. The tobacco products manufacturer Philip Morris challenged new rules released in Uruguay requiring that 80 % of cigarette pack surfaces must be covered by graphic warnings of the dangers associated with smoking, a prohibition of the use of variants of any brand as well as increases in tobacco taxes under the Switzerland–Uruguay BIT from 1988. Uruguay had become a party to the 2003 Framework Convention on Tobacco Control (FCTC) of the World Health Organization (WHO) and enacted a series of domestic measures of tobacco control.[26] The company argued that the requirement for plain packaging and the single presentation requirement which restricted tobacco companies to selling only one variant per brand amounted to an expropriation of its intellectual property rights, including trademarks and goodwill, without compensation. In the absence of explicit exceptions from the protection standards for regulatory measures taken in the interest of public health, Uruguay's defence and the tribunal's assessment were based on principles of customary international law. The tribunal rejected Philip Morris' claim and found that the State measures were a legitimate exercise of Uruguay's police powers to protect public health and therefore no compensation was required under international law for this type of regulation.[27]

In broad terms, investment treaties may contain provisions stating a general right to regulate for the host State[28] or a more articulated right to regulate for specific purposes, such as taxation, State finances (prudential measures), anti-

25 *FTR Holding S. A. (Switzerland), Philip Morris Products S. A. (Switzerland) and Abal Hermanos S. A. (Uruguay) v. Oriental Republic of Uruguay*, ICSID Case No. ARB/10/7, registered 26 March 2010, award 8. July 2016 (hereinafter referred to as '*Philip Morris v. Uruguay*').

26 The measures challenged by Philip Morris were Ordinance 514 of August 18, 2008 (the Single Presentation Regulation [SPR]) and Presidential Decree 287/009 of June 15, 2009 (the 80/80 Regulation).

27 See *Philip Morris v. Uruguay*, (see footnote 25), para 291 ff. The tribunal noted the inclusion of states' police powers already in the inclusion in the 1961 Harvard Draft Convention on the International Responsibility of States for Injuries to Aliens.

28 Such as for example in the EU–Singapore Investment Protection Agreement from 2018, Art. 2.2: *"The Parties reaffirm their right to regulate within their territories to achieve legitimate policy objectives, such as the protection of public health, social services, public education, safety, environment or public morals, social or consumer protection privacy and data protection and the promotion and protection of cultural diversity."*

corruption etc. General recognition of the State's right to regulate might also be found in the preamble of the investment treaty.[29]

Common inclusions of the right to regulate in more recent investment treaties, as further investigated in this paper, would be[30]:

- Explicit exemptions: Commonly seen in the context of indirect expropriation and excluding State liability for breach of the investment treaty when regulating to achieve specific objectives, such as environment and health objectives. The Turkey-Venezuela BIT from 2023 contains the following example:

  "Non-discriminatory legal measures, designed and implemented to ensure legitimate objectives of public welfare, such as health, security, and the environment, do not constitute indirect expropriation." [31]
- Non-precluded measures: Are clauses that recognise exceptional situations in which it would be permitted for States to impose measures that may impair investor rights. These clauses tend to follow the language of the general exceptions of Article XX of the GATT, such as in the Turkey-Serbia BIT from 2022:

  "Nothing in this Agreement shall be construed to prevent a Contracting Party from adopting, maintaining, or enforcing any non-discriminatory legal measures: (a) designed and applied for the protection of human, animal or plant life or health, or the environment; (b) related to the conservation of living or non-living exhaustible natural resources; (c) for maintaining the safety, solvency, integrity or financial responsibility of financial institutions and ensuring the integrity and stability of a Contracting Party's financial system."[32]
- Wording referring to general consistency with investment treaty obligations: Such wording recognises States' rights to regulate by imposing measures consistent with obligations in the investment treaty, such as in the Pacific Alliance-Singapore FTA from 2022:

  "Nothing in this Chapter shall be construed to prevent a Party from adopting, maintaining or enforcing any measure, otherwise consistent

---

29 See for example China-Angola BIT signed in 2022: *"Recognizing the right to regulate, and resolving to preserve the flexibility of the Parties to protect legitimate public welfare objectives, including public morals, public health, safety, the environment, and the conservation of living or non-living exhaustible natural resources."*

30 Part of categorisation of investment treaty language on the right to regulate as defined by BALTAG / JOSHI / DUGGAL, (see footnote 23), p. 387 ff.

31 Art. 7.4., Turkey-Venezuela BIT from 2023.

32 Art. 5.1., Turkey-Serbia BIT from 2022.

> *with this Chapter, that it considers appropriate to ensure that investment activity in its territory is undertaken in a manner sensitive to environmental, health or other regulatory objectives."*[33]

Within the universe of investment treaties currently in force there are vastly different approaches to both the protection standards and the language referring to the host States' rights to regulate. Looking closer at the potential impact of investment treaty provisions on access to medicines cases in the next chapter, the importance of a thorough assessment of the wording of the treaty in question is therefore emphasised.

IV. Investment treaty arbitration and access to medicines

A. Introduction

State regulation and access to medicines is an area of interdependencies across several dimensions, including, but not limited to, regulatory approval, pricing, intellectual property, market incentives, and public health needs. Accordingly, investment treaty arbitration in cases relevant to access to medicines involve complex considerations on the intersection between international investment law and public health policy.

Medicines R&D and marketing are highly regulated, costly and risk-prone and largely rely on private capital. In the research-based pharmaceutical sector, returns on investment are highly dependent on the costs of R&D, the probability of marketing authorisation and the value of expected sales.[34] The probability that a medicine candidate entering phase one clinical trials will make it all the way to marketing authorisation is low.[35] Medical manufacturing supply chains have become more internationalised in the past decades.

---

33 Art. 8.3.2., Pacific Alliance-Singapore FTA 2022.

34 OECD, Pharmaceutical Innovation and Access to Medicines, (see footnote 6), p. 85.

35 OECD, Health at a Glance 2023: OECD Indicators, OECD Publishing, 2023, p. 206. The estimated rate of successful transition of medicine candidate compounds from pre-clinical R&D into phase one is 35 % after more than five years on average and only an average 14 % of such candidates are receiving marketing authorisation after an additional median time of eight years of clinical development. Whereas governments typically contribute to basic and early-stage research through budget allocations, research grants and public administration of research and higher education institutions, the research based pharmaceutical industry funds medical R&D across all R&D phases and dominates clinical development, marketing as well as the manufacturing and distribution of medicines.

This has played an important role in the development of capacities to produce more affordable medicines and in providing flexibility to manufacturers and governments to source medical products. As shown in the COVID-19 pandemic, however, the internationalisation of medical supply chains has also created interdependencies between producing and consuming economies.[36] Shortages of medical goods were common and increasing in frequency prior to the COVID-19 pandemic, but the pandemic significantly magnified pre-existing issues.[37] Apart from attributing supply shortages to manufacturing and quality issues, manufacturers commonly cite market dynamics, where poor profitability and a lack of economic incentives make the production of older off-patent products, in particular, unattractive. Competitive public and private procurement processes are held to often drive prices down to near the marginal cost of production, discouraging maintenance of surplus stock or investment in quality improvement.[38]

With heavy reliance on the private sector for investment, especially in the riskier and more high-cost phases of medical R&D and the subsequent manufacturing and marketing of approved products, the policy challenge for States is to strike a balance between medicine prices[39] and other measures that encourage such investment and the development of treatments that address unmet needs while at the same time ensuring the most efficient allocation of health care budgets.[40] Therefore State measures in this field frequently impact foreign investors.

As not all investment treaty arbitration awards are published, it is not possible to say exactly how many cases concern access to medicines. The number of known investment treaty arbitration cases in the pharmaceutical sector appears to still be quite low. As per UNCTAD's Investment Dispute Settlement Navigator, there are only 12 reported cases involving the 'manufacture of basic pharmaceutical products and pharmaceutical preparations', among

36 OECD, Securing Medical Supply Chains in a Post-Pandemic World, OECD Health Policy Studies, OECD Publishing, 2024, p. 8.

37 Ibid. p. 58.

38 Ibid. p. 32.

39 Governments or compulsory health insurance schemes financed around 58 % of retail pharmaceutical spending in OECD countries on average in 2021. Spending on medicines in the hospital sector, which is commonly also funded through governments and compulsory health insurance coverage, and other settings typically accounted for 20 % or more on top of such retail spending, see OECD, Health at a Glance 2023: OECD Indicators, (see footnote 35), p. 198 ; Retail pharmaceuticals are those provided outside hospital care, dispensed by a retail pharmacy or bought from a supermarket. See OECD / Eurostat / WHO, A System of Health Accounts 2011: Revised edition, OECD Publishing, 2017.

40 OECD, Pharmaceutical Innovation and Access to Medicines, (see footnote 6), p. 85 ff.

which three have been concluded in favour of investors and five cases have been concluded in favour of the States, one case has been settled, two are pending and one has been discontinued.[41]

B. Protected investments particularly relevant to access to medicines

A prerequisite for investment treaty arbitration is that the dispute relates to an investment protected under the relevant investment treaty. Apart from the classical types of investment common for any sector, such as investment in research or production facilities, the pharmaceutical sector heavily relies on investment in more abstract rights, such as various forms of market exclusivity or marketing rights through patents, trademarks, marketing authorisations or regulatory data protection for the purpose of conducting business in a given market.

1. Patents

Most States have agreed to the international minimum standards of IP protection contained in the Paris Convention[42] and the TRIPS Agreement[43], the latter also being referred to as the third pillar of the World Trade Organisation (WTO) due to its central importance for international trade.[44] Most invest-

---

41 UNCTAD Investment Dispute Settlement Navigator.

42 Convention for the Protection of Industrial Property, Paris, 20 March 1883, revised at Stockholm on 14 July 1967, and amended on 28 September 1979.

43 WTO Agreement on Trade-Related Aspects of Intellectual Property Rights (TRIPS), Annex 1C of the Marrakesh Agreement Establishing the World Trade Organization, signed in Marrakesh, Morocco on 15 April 1994

44 Such as equal levels of patent protections with respect to national and foreign patent holders, the right of priority in relation to the original filing of a patent application enabling filing of subsequent applications in other member countries, a patent application in one member country to be examined independently from applications for patents for the same or related inventions filed in other countries, compulsory licences as a means to prevent abuses (Art. 2(1), Art. 4., Art. 4bis., Art. 5A(2) and (4) Paris Convention) and harmonisation of the definition of patentable subject matters, the provision of exclusive rights for patent holders, a standard period of enjoyment of patent rights of 20 years, shift in the burden of proof to the party accused of reproduction to demonstrate the uniqueness of its creation, inclusion of the most-favoured-nation (MFN) principle with respect to all WTO members and allowing members to resort to parallel importation, provided that the principles of national treatment and

ment treaties therefore also explicitly recognise patents and other IP rights as protected investments. [45] Historical tensions between enforcement of IP rights and States' health policy autonomy, in particular relating to access to medicines, has resulted in several adjustments to TRIPS.[46] Despite such adjustments, as part of their efforts to attract foreign investment[47], many States have historically negotiated so called 'TRIPS plus protections' into their investment treaties, again increasing the level of protection given to IP rights.[48] Most investment treaties also contain investors' rights to challenge measures impacting their patents via investment treaty arbitration proceedings.[49] It should be noted that in order for there to be an investment, since patents are granted on a territorial basis, the patent must be registered or at least a license to use the patent must be used in the host State confronted with the claim under the investment treaty.[50]

---

most favoured-nation are respected (Art. 27(1), Art. 28., Art. 33., Art. 34., Art. 4., Arts. 31 and 6 TRIPS).

45 For an overview relevant to access to medicines, see RUTLEDGE, PETER B., TRIPS and BITs: An Essay on Compulsory Licenses, Expropriation, and International Arbitration, N.C. J. L. & Tech, 2012

46 Of particular importance is the Doha Declaration on the TRIPS Agreement and Public Health adopted in 2001, which recognised the right of states to interpret TRIPS provisions broadly when public health is at stake and clarified conditions for compulsory licenses and exemptions for least developed countries. The Doha Declaration on the TRIPS Agreement and Public Health, adopted on 14 November 2001, was followed by a WTO Council Decision in 2015 on an exemption until 2033 of applicability of TRIPS provisions in least developed countries (LDCs) and the introduction of TRIPS Art. 31 in 2017, which affirms states' ability to export and import pharmaceutical products, coupling it with a compulsory licence issued by the exporting member state, in exceptional circumstances. In 2022 another WTO Ministerial Decision clarified the scope available to WTO members to limit the exclusive effect of patent rights in order to support equitable access to COVID-19 vaccines. See World Trade Organisation, TRIPS and public health.

47 While IP rights may be considered an obstacle for market entry of generic competition and thereby (presumably) more affordable medicines, the same IP rights are a main tool for incentivising investment in high-risk medical research.

48 WTO members may enter into preferential trade agreements, which aim to increase freedom of trade by the development of closer ties between the economies of countries that are parties to such agreements, see Art. XXIV General Agreement on Tariffs and Trade (GATT).

49 UNCTAD, International Investment Policies and Public Health, IIA Issues Note, 2021, p. 4.

50 MANCIAUX, (see footnote 22), p. 91 ff.

2. *Marketing authorisations*

The assessment if a marketing authorisation is a protected investment is more complex. Whereas it has a substantiable value and can be transferred to a third party, like an IP right, it is an authorisation to sell the corresponding product on the market and sales are at times explicitly excluded from the investment treaty definitions of protected investments.[51] This topic was in part addressed in *Apotex v. United States.*[52] Apotex had filed Abbreviated New Drug Applications (ANDAs) with the US Food and Drug Administration (FDA), for two generic drugs. Apotex's ANDAs were ultimately rejected by the US courts, in part as a result of proceedings brought by its competitors. Apotex argued that these decisions constituted violations by the United States of its obligations under NAFTA. The United States objected to the jurisdiction of the tribunal stating that applications for authorisation could not be considered as investments. In its award of June 14, 2013, the tribunal decided that it did not have jurisdiction to hear the dispute. It noted that the ANDA was only "an exercise in securing regulatory clearance" and did not fall within any of the categories of the exhaustive list of Article 1139 of the NAFTA Treaty, which expressly excludes claims arising solely from commercial contracts for the sale of goods or services. [53] With reference to findings by other tribunals, the tribunal in Apotex v. United States further stated that where a company must meet "regulatory requirements" to sell its products, the costs of such compliance themselves are not investments.[54] While it may be considered justified to distinguish an application for authorisation to sell from a granted license to sell, which may more clearly constitute an 'investment', in particular where the investment treaty explicitly does not recognise sales as investments, it is not necessarily a logical consequence to refuse to classify the authorisation to sell in itself as an intangible asset and thereby, potentially, as an investment. Especially not when such authorisation generates transferable rights as well as considerable maintenance costs for its holder, such as in the case of marketing authorisations for medicines.[55]

In any event, the determination if a pharmaceutical investment can be considered to be a protected investment can only be done on a case-by-case basis as it depends on the definition of investments in the applicable investment treaty.

---

51 Ibid., p. 93 ff.

52 *Apotex Inc. v. United States of America*, ICSID Case No. UNCT/10/2, award 14. June 2013 (hereinafter referred to as *'Apotex v. United States'*)

53 Ibid., para 193.

54 Ibid., para 194. For a summary of the case, see also MANCIAUX, (see footnote 22), p. 93 f.

55 Compare MANCIAUX, (see footnote 22), p. 98.

C. Application of the protection standards to pharmaceutical investments

1. State sovereign measures impacting access to medicines

Some categories of State measures may be particularly prone to play a role in investment treaty arbitration because they have a profound impact on the conditions under which foreign investors operate in the host State.

- Regulation, regulatory assessments and decisions: National and regional regulatory agencies are responsible for ensuring that medicines are safe, effective and of high quality before they enter the market. Regulatory frameworks establish the processes and criteria for clinical trials, manufacturing practices, and post-market surveillance and thereby directly impact access to medicines and related investments. A decision of State authorities to grant, refuse or withdraw a marketing authorisation is central to the business of pharmaceutical investors in any given market.
- Pricing and tenders: In particular in countries with national healthcare systems, the State often plays a direct role in drug pricing and reimbursement decisions. As part of such centralised medicines procurement systems, States may for example grant companies who have been successful in pricing negotiations rights to market the drug on an exclusive basis in their territory. Such systems bear inherent integrity risks. Should the granted exclusivity be violated through distribution of similar marketing rights to competitors, this may conceivably lead to at least perceived violations of any investment treaty protecting the related investments.
- Incentives for R&D: States may create policies and incentives, such as tax credits, grants, or public-private partnerships to encourage investment in the development of new medicines, including for rare diseases or neglected tropical diseases. This area may be sensitive for example to discriminatory practices.
- Intellectual property: The protection of IP rights highlights the tension between investment treaty investment protection standards and States' regulatory autonomy in the pursuit of achieving public health related goals. Investment treaties usually cover IP rights in line with TRIPS as protected investments. By their nature, IP rights restrict competition and, arguably, enable the rights holder to exercise greater control over market access and/or prices. States can intervene through mechanisms like compulsory licensing, which allows other manufacturers to produce generic versions of patented medicines in certain situations (e. g. during a public

health crisis).[56] Examples of exclusivity relating to IP rights are patents or the protection of the regulatory dossier used for the marketing authorisation application for a medicine (trial data exclusivity), which prohibits a generic competitor from copying and re-using the clinical data of the originator who has performed the R&D for its own marketing authorisation application.

2. *Violation of the fair and equitable treatment standards*

In light of the established investment treaty arbitration practice, sovereign acts of States may be held to breach FET if they are arbitrary, taken purely on the basis of prejudice or bias without a legitimate purpose or rational explanation, involve a denial of justice or disregard of the fundamental principles of due process, discriminatory, abusive or go against the legitimate expectations of investors to the extent such arise from a government's specific representations or investment inducing measures.[57]

When faced with an application for a patent or marketing authorisation, for example, authorities retain the right to refuse the application, but the refusal must be based on an analysis of the application that is neither arbitrary nor discriminatory and carried out in accordance with the legal procedures in force.[58] In *Servier v. Poland*[59], the applicable BIT between France and Poland only enabled arbitration in the event of expropriation and therefore, the Polish authorities' refusal to renew marketing authorisations could not be assessed in the light of the FET standard. Nevertheless, the tribunal in its award of 14 February 2012 did refer to the discriminatory and disproportionate nature of the measure as contributing factors for the unlawfulness of the expropriation. These characteristics would also apply to a violation of the obligation of fair and equitable treatment.[60] The case concerned the refusal of Polish authorities

56 For a detailed review of the tension between IP rights and access to medicines see for example PIERGIUSEPPE PUSCEDDU, Assessing Access to Medicines in Preferential Trade Agreements: From the Trans-Pacific Partnership to the Comprehensive and Progressive Agreement for Trans-Pacific Partnership, IIC - International Review of Intellectual Property and Competition Law, 2018, pp.1048-1079; RUTLEDGE, (see footnote 45); URIAS, EDUARDO / RAMANI, SHYAMA V., Access to medicines after TRIPS: Is compulsory licensing an effective mechanism to lower drug prices? A review of the existing evidence. J Int Bus Policy, 2020.

57 See above Chapter II B.

58 MANCIAUX, (see footnote 22), p. 102 f.

59 *Les Laboratoires Servier, S.A.A., Biofarma, S.A.S., Arts et Techniques du Progres S.A.S. v. Republic of Poland,* UNCITRAL, award 14. February 2012

60 Ibid. para 576.

to renew marketing authorisations for certain Servier pharmaceutical products in Poland following a harmonisation of Poland's pharmaceutical regulatory framework with the standards applicable under EU rules. The case is partly redacted, which limits the possibilities for analysis.

Pharmaceutical investors may also argue that abrupt regulatory changes, including changes in regulation or enforcement approaches, without proper notice or consultation when used excessively or without due process amount to unfair treatment and go against their legitimate expectations.[61] This was assessed in *Eli Lilly vs. Canada*[62]. The dispute took its beginnings in the invalidation by Canadian courts of two of Eli Lilly's patents for ADHD and anti-psychotic drugs. Eli Lilly argued that Canada's evolving patent law, specifically the application of the 'promise utility doctrine', breached the FET standard under chapter 11 of the North American Free Trade Agreement (NAFTA) by being arbitrary and unpredictable and depriving the company of its legitimate expectations. The tribunal in its final award of 17 July 2017 emphasized that there had been no dramatic changes to Canadian patent law, that changes in legal doctrines over time are a normal part of legal systems and that, in any case, the changes in this case did not amount to a breach of FET, as they were not arbitrary or discriminatory. It noted that Eli Lilly could not have had legitimate expectations that Canadian patent law would remain unchanged.[63] Although Eli Lilly was not successful in the investment treaty arbitration case, the Canadian Supreme Court later weakened the utility requirement, reducing the amount of evidence required for successfully defending patents and has recently recognised the need for renewed review by granting leave to appeal in two pharmaceutical cases.[64]

With respect to what may constitute reasonable expectations of the investor, in *Methanex v. United States*[65], another NAFTA chapter 11 case, the tribunal held that the regulatory and political environment may be a factor that the investor should take into account and anticipate regulatory change in areas where high levels of regulation can be foreseen, unless the host country has given assurances that no regulatory changes will take place.[66]

---

61 PUSCEDDU, (see footnote 56), p. 1055.

62 *Eli Lilly and Company v. The Government of Canada,* UNCITRAL, ICSID Case No. UNCT/14/2, award 16. March 2017, (hereinafter referred to as 'Eli Lilly v. Canada').

63 Ibid. paras 386-387.

64 See for example 'Plavix' appeal, SCC Case Number 35562 and 'Esomeprazole' appeal, SCC Case Number 36654.

65 *Methanex Corporation v. United States of America,* UNCITRAL, award 3. August 2005.

66 Ibid Part IV - Chapter D, paras. 9–10.

A case involving Gilead Sciences, Inc. and Ukraine could also have given rise to a tribunal's application of the fair and equitable treatment standard.[67] The case was settled in 2017 but, presumably, had been filed under the US-Ukraine BIT (1996). From what has been reported, Gilead had obtained official permission by the Ukrainian Ministry of Health (MoH) to market its drug Sovaldi, a hepatitis C medicine, on an exclusive basis in Ukraine for five years in mid-2015. Already by the end of 2015, however, the State Register of Medical Products listed a generic version of Sovaldi, thereby violating the exclusivity granted to Gilead for Sovaldi. Gilead initially filed a claim with local courts demanding that the government revoke and declare illegal the MoH's registration of the generic product. In 2016, the local court ruled against the claimant, refusing to revoke the generic product registration, a decision which Gilead subsequently appealed. While details of the settlement are unknown, the MoH announced that in order to comply with the agreement signed with Gilead, it was removing the generic competitor product from the State Register of Medical products.[68]

Other examples of potential violations of FET could be cases where governments grant themselves emergency powers that are normally reserved to the legislative branch and widely exceed their regular constitutional capacities or in cases of denial of justice. The latter can be invoked where the host State's courts refuse to hear a case brought by an investor, subject it to undue delay, administer justice inadequately, or clearly and maliciously misapply the law.[69] In *Merck v. Ecuador*[70] (also known as MSDIA v. Ecuador), the tribunal found that Ecuador breached several investment protection standards under the Ecuador-United States BIT of 1993. The core issue revolved around a $200 million judgment rendered against Merck in a commercial dispute with an Ecuadorian company following the failed sale of a factory in 2003. The tribunal in its award of 5 March 2020 held that Ecuador had breached the FET standard by failing to provide due process and by an egregiously wrong decision by the Ecuadorian courts. The tribunal determined that the courts had failed to follow proper judicial procedures, including inconsistencies in rulings and disregard for legal principles. The tribunal also found that Ecua-

67 As also noted by MANCIAUX, (see footnote 22), p. 104.

68 PETERSON, LUKE ERIC / WILLIAMS, ZOE, Gilead Pharma corp withdraws investment arbitration after Ukraine agrees to settlement of dispute over monopoly rights to market anti-viral drug, Investment Arbitration Reporter, 16. March, 2017.

69 HAGEMANN, TIM, Corporate Wealth Over Public Health? Assessing the Resilience of Developing Countries' COVID-19 Responses Against Investment Claims and the Implications for Future Public Health Crises, Pace International Law Review, Vol 34 Issue 1, December 2021, p. 48

70 *Merck Sharpe & Dohme (I.A.) Corporation v. The Republic of Ecuador*, PCA Case No. 2012-10, award 5. March 2020 (hereinafter referred to as '*Merck v. Ecuador*').

dor had breached its obligation to provide effective means for the investor to assert claims and enforce rights.[71]

Another example illustrating abuse of sovereign powers and violation of due process is *Diag Human SE and Mr. Josef Stava v. Czech Republic*[72]. In the early 1990s, Conneco, later Diag Human SE (Diag), and its ultimate owner, Mr. Stava, were engaged in negotiations with Czechoslovakia concerning the supply of blood plasma. While the tender process was ongoing, Diag began to supply blood plasma directly to hospitals in Czechoslovakia under certain cooperation agreements. In 1992, the Czechoslovakian Minister of Health issued a letter to Diag's third party business partner raising concerns as to Diag's ethics. The partner ceased relations with Diag and the cooperation agreements between Diag and hospitals were cancelled. Diag's claim in relation to losses allegedly suffered as a result of the letter was subject to commercial arbitration against the Czech Republic for 12 years, during which the Czech Republic interfered with the arbitration procedure by: (i) using the Czech security services to obtain information, (ii) threatening arbitrators with criminal prosecution, and (iii) meeting Diag's former lawyer to obtain information about Diag's position (ultimately leading to his disbarment). The tribunal held that the letter was a breach of Czech competition and commercial laws and criticised the Czech MoH for the undue interference in the arbitral process. To ensure the integrity of the commercial arbitration, the tribunal had seen necessary to transfer the file to a safe place abroad. The MoH initiated a second commercial arbitration to review the issued award, in which is also severely interfered. In 2017, Diag and Mr Stava initiated investment treaty arbitration under the Czech Republic - Swiss BIT from 1990. In its award of 2022, the tribunal held that the Czech Republic had breached the FET standard under the BIT by issuing the letter and abusing its sovereign powers in order to interfere with the commercial arbitration. It also held that the Czech Republic had manifestly failed to comply with the principle of due process during the review proceedings. The tribunal upheld the damages award in the commercial arbitration. The award was subsequently, to the greater part unsuccessfully, challenged by the Czech Republic before English Courts.[73]

---

71 The tribunal's awards are not public, but a summary of the case is available in the Judgement of The Hague District Court from 16. June 2016 (case nr C/09/600011 / HA ZA 20-948), dismissing the claim for annulment of the arbitral awards, paras 2.01-2.19.

72 *Diag Human SE and Mr. Josef Stava v. Czech Republic*, PCA Case No. 2018-20, award 18. May 2022 (hereinafter referred to as '*Diag v. Czech Republic*').

73 For a summary see STOTHARD, PAUL / BENTLEY, JOSEPH / JUDKINS, ANDREW / FOX, OLIVIA, Czech Republic v Diag Human SE: English Court hands down guidance on

3. *Violation of the protection against unlawful expropriation*

States may expropriate assets, but not in any way or under any conditions, as described in more detail in Chapter II B above. Most investment treaties lay down criteria for lawful expropriation. The more recent investment treaties also distinguish between direct expropriation, which involves an actual transfer of a title in the sense of an open and claimed dispossession of the property of the investor, and indirect expropriation resulting from a measure (or a series of measures) which, without dispossessing the contractor of its assets, renders them so useless that the measure is tantamount to dispossession.[74] Indirect expropriation claims may arise when State actions, such as compulsory licensing[75], confiscatory taxation, strict price regulation or a decision to invalidate patents, reduce the value of an investment (e. g. intellectual property rights or market access). The case of compulsory licensing, which would be highly relevant in the field of access to medicines and pharmaceutical investment, has not yet been assessed by an arbitral tribunal.[76]

In *Eli Lilly v. Canada*, the investor's claim that the decisions of the Canadian courts not only violated the duty of FET, but also constituted unlawful indirect expropriation was rejected by the tribunal in its final award, stating that the judicial invalidation of a patent through a lawful court process with reasonable and not arbitrary application of domestic law, did not constitute an expropriation under NAFTA.[77] The tribunal held that the Canadian courts were acting within their jurisdiction when invalidating the patents. It also recalled that it was not an appeal body for decisions taken by the judiciary of a State.[78]

Claims based on indirect expropriation feature in about 70 % of all known investment treaty arbitration proceedings (across sectors) and are thereby one

challenges to awards under Sections 67 and 68 of the Arbitration Act 1996, Norton Rose Fulbright Global Publication, April 2024.

74 Manciaux, (see footnote 22), p. 106 ff.

75 A "compulsory" or "non-voluntary" license is, in essence, an authorisation provided by a public body to a third party under national law to use the subject matter of a patent where the right holder has not agreed to such use. See WIPO Webinar For Judges: Compulsory Licenses and the Courts – Understanding Landmark Cases and New Developments, available at https://www.wipo.int/about-ip/en/judiciaries/news/2023/news_0006.html, last accessed 30. September 2024; Compulsory licensing has been standing out as a state regulatory measure held to be of particular relevance to access to medicines. For a detailed analysis, see Urias / Ramani, (see footnote 56).

76 Manciaux, (see footnote 22), p. 109 f.

77 *Eli Lilly v. Canada*, (see footnote 62), para 221.

78 *Eli Lilly v. Canada*, (see footnote 62), para 225.

of the most common claims. A breach of indirect expropriation prohibitions is the second most common finding in proceedings decided in favour of the investor, FET breaches taking the first place.[79]

4. Violation of national treatment and most favoured nation standards

National treatment or most favoured nation clauses require States to treat foreign investors no less favourably than domestic investors or investors from other nations that benefit from the protection of a bilateral investment treaty. A pharmaceutical investor could invoke these provisions for example if a State subsidizes or provides incentives to local generic manufacturers while imposing stringent price controls on foreign originator drugs or in cases of denial of access to infrastructure or necessary raw materials.[80] In *Eli Lilly v. Canada*, the investor also suggested that it was subject to discriminatory treatment in comparison to Canadian pharmaceutical companies, but the tribunal found no evidence of discrimination and maintained that the invalidation of the patents was based on the application of general Canadian patent law, which applied equally to both domestic and foreign companies.[81]

As outlined above and as evident from the research presented in Chapter VI, new generation investment treaties contain comprehensive exceptions for States' rights to regulate and clarifications on the applicability of FET and expropriation protections.

V. Investment treaty trends

A. Investment treaty reform initiatives intending to safeguard States' right to regulate

Almost all known investment treaty arbitration cases until end of 2023 were filed pursuant to old-generation investment treaties[82], generally featuring

---

79 UNCTAD IIA Reform Accelerator, (see footnote 15), p. 24, p. 20.

80 *Marvin Roy Feldman Karpa v. United Mexican States*, ICSID Case No ARB(AF)/99/1, award 16. December 2002, para 103, (hereinafter referred to as *'Marvin Roy Feldman Karpa v. United Mexican States'*).

81 *Eli Lilly v. Canada*, (see footnote 62), para 441.

82 Roughly 97 % of all investment treaty arbitration cases were filed pursuant to 'old-generation' IIAs, signed prior to 2012. At the time of writing, 85 % of all signed or

broad and unspecific formulations and including few exceptions or safeguards with respect to States' regulatory autonomy. As eluded on above, these investment treaties were concluded, for the most part, during a different era and do not reflect today's global challenges relating to public health, the environment and sustainable development goals. Arbitral tribunals have interpreted their provisions expansively, which has at times been held to reduce the capacity of host States to regulate in the public interest, contributing to so called 'regulatory chill'.[83] Critics of the investment treaty arbitration system argue that it disincentivizes State regulatory action, rendering conduct that is taken in good faith and in the public interest illegal or requiring States to compensate investors for the potential or actual implications of pursuing legitimate public policy objectives.[84] Research shows, however, that investment treaty arbitration can in fact also have a 'regulatory heating' effect, in particular in States with low regulatory capacity.[85]

The perception of a need to reform old-generation investment treaties was strengthened by the COVID-19 pandemic, as policy responses taken by governments[86] were feared to lead to significant increases in investment treaty arbitration cases.[87] To the extent known in light of the fact that arbitrations can be kept confidential, this fear did not (yet) materialise. In 2022, 46 new publicly known investment treaty arbitration cases under investment treaties were filed, which was the lowest annual number of known cases since 2010. In 2023, there were 60 new cases filed. The average number of cases between 2012 and 2021, had been 75 per year, with 79 and 77 cases respectively in the pandemic years 2020 and 2021.[88] These developments in combination with the wider criticism of the investment treaty system described above triggered

signed and in force IIAs belong to the 'old-generation', as per a search in the UNCTAD International Investment Agreements Navigator.

83 UNCTAD IIA Reform Accelerator, (see footnote 15), p. 3.

84 See for example BAKER, BROOK K. / GEDDES, KATRINA, Corporate Power Unbound: Investor-State Arbitration of IP Monopolies on Medicines - Eli Lilly v. Canada and the Trans-Pacific Partnership Agreement, Journal of Intellectual Property Law, 2015

85 BERGE LAUDAL / BERGER, (see footnote 11), p. 19.

86 States have exercised their regulatory autonomy for example by imposing export restrictions, foreign direct investment screening and nationalisation, see KPMG, Government and institution measures in response to COVID-19, 2020.

87 UNCTAD IIA Reform Accelerator, (see footnote 15), p. 2 ff.

88 As per search via the UNCTAD, Investment Dispute Settlement Navigator on 14. September 2024.

efforts of reforming the investment treaty and investment treaty arbitration system in ICSID[89], OECD[90], UNCITRAL[91], UNCTAD[92] and other fora.

Whereas the ICSID and UNCITRAL initiatives focus on the legitimacy critiques of the investment treaty arbitration system at large[93], resulting so far in several changes, including a proposal for a standing mechanism for the resolution of international investment disputes, updated ICSID and UNCITRAL arbitration rules and an ICSID and UNCITRAL Code of Conduct for Arbitrators in International Investment Disputes, UNCTAD and OECD review is specific to the reform of investment treaty provisions and concepts. UNCTAD suggests focusing on the reform of eight investment treaty provisions[94] all of which, but perhaps in particular the following, have a degree of relevance to States' right to regulate and the cases in which a claimant investor could challenge regulatory public health related measures:

- 'national treatment'; subordinating the right of national treatment to the host country's domestic laws and clarifying applicability,
- 'FET'; replacing FET with an exhaustive list of State obligations, clarifying the FET standard, reducing FET to a political commitment or entirely omitting the FET clause,
- 'indirect expropriation'; clarifying the concept or completely exclude indirect expropriation from the investment treaty scope,
- 'public policy exceptions'; including exceptions for domestic regulatory measures in pursuit of circumscribed policy objectives or prudential measures; preventing abuse of such exceptions by host States.[95]

Due to the particular relevance for regulatory measures in the field of access to medicines, the developments in post-pandemic investment treaties will be

---

89 Amendment to the ICSID arbitration rules in 2022 https://icsid.worldbank.org/sites/default/files/publications/rule_amendment_proposals_convention.pdf, last accessed 30 September 2024

90 OECD work programme on the Future of Investment Treaties, launched in March 2021

91 UNCITRAL Working Group III: Investor-State Dispute Settlement Reform; UNCITRAL Code of Conduct for Arbitrators in International Investment Dispute Resolution 2024

92 UNCTAD Multi-Stakeholder Platform on IIA Reform; UNCTAD IIA Reform Accelerator (see footnote 14).

93 For extensive comment on the investment treaty arbitration system reform, see for example: ALVAREZ, JOSÉ E., ITA Reform: The Long View, Institute for International Law and Justice, Working Paper 2021/6, International Economic Law Series, November 2021, p. 9 f.

94 UNCTAD IIA Reform Accelerator, (see footnote 15), p. 9 ff.

95 Ibid., p. 10

further investigated with regard to indirect expropriation, explicit exceptions for health policy regulatory measures, specification or omittance of the FET standard, and explicit exclusion of investment treaty arbitration in the case of health-related regulation.

B. The right to regulate in post-pandemic investment treaties

For the purpose of this section, investment treaties signed between 1. January 2022 and 31. December 2023 as well as model BITs released during that same time period[96] have been reviewed to identify trends in treaty formulations relevant to States' right to regulate. The analysis of treaty language is made against the UNCTAD reform options as outlined in the UNCTAD International Investment Agreements Reform Accelerator:[97]

Category A. Expropriation

Clarifications of the protection standard, such as criteria to be met for a finding of indirect expropriation, definition of measures that do not constitute an indirect expropriation	**68 %** (13/19) investment treaties **100 %** (3/3) model BITs

Category A. Expropriation

Exclusion of indirect expropriation from the treaty scope, such as limiting protection standard to direct expropriation	**5 %** (1/19) investment treaties **0 %** (0) model BITs

Category A. Expropriation

Exclusion of compulsory licenses from the expropriation provisions	**63 %** (12/19) investment treaties **100 %** (3/3) model BITs

[96] To the extent the texts are known and available in searchable versions in English or German language.

[97] UNCTAD IIA Reform Accelerator (see footnote 15).

Category B. Explicit health policy exceptions

Inclusion of explicit exceptions for domestic regulatory measures in pursuit of health policy objectives	**100 %** (19/19) investment treaties **100 %** (3/3) model BITs

Category B. Explicit health policy exceptions

Inclusion of language to prevent abuse of the exceptions by host States	**63 %** (12/19) investment treaties **100 %** (3/3) model BITs

Category C. FET clarification or omittance

Specification of FET standards	**42 %** (8/19) investment treaties **100 %** (3/3) model BITs

Category C. FET clarification or omittance

Omittance of the FET standards	**21 %** (4/19) investment treaties **0 %** (0) model BITs

Category D. Exclusions of investment treaty arbitration in cases of health-related regulation by the State

Exclusion of investment treaty arbitration	**0 %** (0) investment treaties **0 %** (0) model BITs

A table with the findings per investment treaty / model BIT is included in Annex A, Figure 1.

The analysis of the 2022-2023 investment treaties and the model BITs and clauses released in the same timeframe demonstrates that treaty language is constantly evolving in a direction of increased protection of States' regulatory autonomy in the field of public health in line with the investment treaty reform suggestions published by UNCTAD in 2020.[98] In particular, combinations of the above language categories A-B are frequently seen.

[98] UNCTAD IIA Reform Accelerator (see footnote 15)

Whereas only 2 % of the so called 'old generation'[99] investment treaties, signed between 1959 and 2011 explicitly exclude compulsory licensing from the expropriation provisions[100], 63 % of the investment treaties signed 2022-2023 do so. This may be a consequence of the increased scrutiny of TRIPS-plus provisions included in some investment treaties and their potential impact on access to medicines, particularly in low-income countries. About 7 % of the old-generation investment treaties contain explicit health policy exceptions to safeguard States' right to regulate, whereas such exceptions are present in all investment treaties and model BITs signed 2022-2023. 4 % of the old-generation investment treaties define indirect expropriation, whereas 68 % of the investment treaties and 100 % of the model BITs signed in 2022-2023 do so.[101]

VI. Conclusion

Access to medicines is becoming a renewed concern on a global scale due to increasingly frequent shortages in medicines supplies.[102] These developments highlight the relevance of actors other than pharmaceutical patent holders to secure access to medicines. With health systems and governments under increased pressure, the measures may become increasingly radical. As seen during the COVID-19 pandemic, during times of crisis, States may well evaluate the adoption of measures such as compulsory licensing or regulation in favour of domestic investors which could substantially reduce the value of pharmaceutical investments. Investment treaty arbitration can provide a tool to ease the tension between pharmaceutical investors trying to protect their investments and State measures taken under the umbrella of public health policy. From a general investor's perspective, investment treaty arbitration may in many cases be a better tool for investors to mitigate political and regulatory risks, compared to litigation. Suing the host State in its own courts is never appealing in light of the inherent risk of hometown justice and related fears of not being guaranteed due process. In the worst case, the host State sovereign may enjoy immunity. Likewise, suit in the investor's State courts may be precluded due to immunity of the sovereign host State. In addition,

---

99 Signed prior to the launch of UNCTAD's Investment Policy Framework for Sustainable Development in 2012.

100 UNCTAD International Investment Policies and Public Health, (see footnote 49), p. 4.

101 Research on 'old-generation' investment treaties through the UNCTAD International Investment Agreements Navigator.

102 OECD, Securing Medical Supply Chains in a Post-Pandemic World, (see footnote 36), p. 10.

enforcement of a judgment resulting from litigation may be difficult, either due to domestic restrictions on judgment execution against a foreign sovereign or to the lack of a treaty between the judgment-rendering State and the State where the offending country has assets, whereas the enforcement of awards in BIT arbitrations is subject to a very favourable regime.[103]

However, despite its potential, pharmaceutical investors so far do not seem to frequently make use of investment treaty arbitration. This may have many causes. One may be the reputational risks associated with a case against a State. In many cases, States are not only the regulator but also the main customers of the pharmaceutical investor. It is easy to see how such relationship, among other reasons, may make pharmaceutical investors hesitant to pursue full scale investment treaty arbitration, possibly in favour of alternative dispute resolution mechanisms, including mediation and settlement negotiations. It has also been held, however, that the perhaps most central value of investment treaty arbitration is not the proceedings as such, but rather the credible threat of the initiation of proceedings.[104]

With the developments in investment treaty negotiations and investment treaty language, however, investment treaty arbitration may be viewed in a different light in the future. The more detailed and specific wording on the rights of States to regulate in new-generation investment treaties as well as an increased incorporation of corporate social responsibility provisions, make many of the old concerns relating to the imbalances of investment treaty arbitration obsolete. The playing field is becoming more levelled in that investment treaties are increasingly entered into between developed economies that are both capital importing and exporting[105]. This stands in contrast to the old-generation investment treaties, which often primarily safeguarded the interests of capital exporting countries and thus the protection of investments.[106] As treaty-makers as well as treaty-takers, States are in control of the 'cost' of attracting foreign investment through investment treaties and should anticipate being tried on their promises.

---

103 RUTLEDGE, (see footnote 45), p. 157 ff.

104 Ibid. p. 163

105 See UNCTAD International Investment Agreements Navigator. Search for IIAs signed in the past 10 years.

106 BALTAG / JOSHI / DUGGAL (see footnote 23), p. 385 f.; p. 420

VII. Annex A

Figure 1

INVESTMEN TTREATY / MODEL CLAUSES	CLARIFICA TIONS TO 'INDIRECT EXPROPRIA TION' (A)	EXCLUSION OF INDIRECT EXPROPRIA TION FROM SCOPE (A)	EXCLUSION OF COMPULSO RY LICENSES FROM THE EXPROPRIA TION PROVISION S (A)	EXPLICIT EXCEPTION FOR HEALTH POLICY REGULATO RY MEASURES (B)	LANGUAGE TO PREVENT ABUSE OF THE EXCEPTION S BY HOST STATES (B)	FET STANDARD EXHAUSTI VE LIST OR FET STANDARD S OMITTED (C)	EXCLUSIO N OF ARBITRA TION IN CASES OF HEALTH RELATED REGULAT ION (D)
1. CHILE COLOMBIA MEXICO PERU SINGAPORE FTA 2022	Yes, Annex 8 (C)	No	Yes, Art. 8.13 (5)	Yes, Annex 8 (C), Art. 3(b); 8.3; 8.9.6	Yes, Art. 8.9.6	No	No
2. HUNGARY OMAN BIT 2022	Yes, Art. 6.4; 6.4(c)	No	No	Yes, Art. 2.7; Art. 3.1-2; Art. 6.4(c)	Yes, Art. 3.1	Yes, Art. 2.3	No
3. UK NEW ZEALAND FTA 2022	Yes, Annex 14B	No	Yes, Art. 14.14.5	Yes, Art. 14.1; 14.18.1; 14.8.8	No (only limited Art. 14.8.8)	No	No (no investor – state)
4. TURKEY URUGUAY BIT 2022	Yes, Annex A	No	Yes, Art. 8.4	Yes, Pream-ble; Art. 7.1	No	No	No
5. INDONESIA SWITZERLA ND BIT 2022	Yes, Anhang A	No	Yes, Art, 7.6	Yes, Anhang A 3(b); Art. 41(b)	Yes, Anhang A 3(b)	Yes, Art. 4.2	No
6. PHILIPPINES ISRAEL BIT 2022	Yes, Annex A	No	Yes, Art. 6.4	Yes, Art. .12.2	Yes, Art. 12.2	Yes, Art. 2.2	No
7. BAHRAIN JAPAN BIT 2022	No	No	Yes, Art. 11.6	Yes, Art. 18.1(a); Art. 24	Yes, Art. 18.1(a)	No	No
8. SERBIA TURKEY BIT 2022	Yes, Art. 6.2; 6.5; 6.6	No	No	Yes, Art. 6.2; Art. 10; Art. 5.1(a)	No	Yes, Art. 3.2	No
9. HUNGARY SAN MARINO BIT 2022	Yes, Art. 6.2	No	No	Yes, Art. 3; Art. 6.2(c); 16.8; Art. 2.7	Yes, Art. 6.2(c); 16.8	Yes, Art. 2.3	No
10. HUNGARY TURKMENIS TAN BIT 2023	Yes, Art. 6.2	No	No	Yes, Art. 3; 6.2(c); 2.7	Yes, Art. 6.2(c)	Yes, Art. 2.3	No
11. EFTA MOLDOVA FTA 2023	No	No	No	Yes, Art. 4.6; Art. 9.2; Art. 9.3	No	FET standard omitted	No (but no investor – state)
12. EU NEW ZEALAND FTA 2023	No	No	No	Yes, 19.2, Preamble; 7.5; 10.1; 12.3; Art. 22	No	FET standard omitted	No (but no investor – state)
13. TURKEY UAE BIT 2023	Yes, Annex; Art. 7.2; 7.3	No	Yes	Yes, Art. 8	Yes, Art. 6.3	Yes, Art. 3.3	No
14. TURKEY VENEZUELA BIT 2023	Yes, Art. 7.4	No	No	Yes, Art. 7.4; 6.1	Yes, Art. 6.4	No	No
15. ANGOLA JAPAN BIT 2023	No	No	Yes, Art. 12.6	Yes, Art. 16.1	Yes, Art. 16.1; 21	No	No

INVESTMENTTREATY / MODEL CLAUSES	CLARIFICATIONS TO 'INDIRECT EXPROPRIATION' (A)	EXCLUSION OF INDIRECT EXPROPRIATION FROM SCOPE (A)	EXCLUSION OF COMPULSORY LICENSES FROM THE EXPROPRIATION PROVISIONS (A)	EXPLICIT EXCEPTION FOR HEALTH POLICY REGULATORY MEASURES (B)	LANGUAGE TO PREVENT ABUSE OF THE EXCEPTIONS BY HOST STATES (B)	FET STANDARD EXHAUSTIVE LIST OR FET STANDARDS OMITTED (C)	EXCLUSION OF ARBITRATION IN CASES OF HEALTH RELATED REGULATION (D)
16. CHINA NICARAGUA FTA 2023	Yes, Annex IIB Art. 4	No	Yes, Art. 11.6.5	Yes, Annex IIB Art. 4(b)	Yes, 11.8.3(d)	No	No
17. CANADA UKRAINE FTA 2023	Yes, Art. 17.10.3	No	Yes, 17.10.6; 17.12	Yes, Art. 17.10.3; 17.4; 17.5; 17.17	Yes, Art. 17.12(f)	FET standard omitted	No
18. MERCOSUR SINGAPORE FTA 2023	No	Yes	Yes, see e. g. Annex, Art. 9A-5.6	Yes, Art. 9.11ext. reservations in schedules	No	FET standard omitted	No (but no investor-State)
19. CHILE EU 2023	No	No	Yes, Art. 17.19.4	Yes, Art. 17.3; 18.3; 26.3	No	Yes, Art. 17.17	No
	Model BITs						
I. ITALY MODEL BIT 2022	Yes, Annex II	No	Yes, Art. 9.5	Yes, Art. 6; Annex II para 3	Yes, Art. 15.1-2	Yes, Art. 4	No
II. BULGARIA MODEL BIT 2023	Yes, Annex I	No	Yes, Art. 8.6	Yes, Art. 2.3; 15; Annex I para 3	Yes, Art. 2.5; 15	Yes, Art. 5	No
III. EU BIT MODEL CLAUSES 2023	Yes, Annex I	No	Yes	Yes, Annex I para 3	Yes, in General Exceptions article	Yes	No

VIII. Description of the author

Samantha Regenthal is an internationally practising lawyer and arbitration practitioner specialised in life-sciences and antitrust. She holds a Master of Law from the University of Lund (2006), an LL. M. in German Law from the University of Constance (2007), a Certificate of Advanced Studies (CAS) in Antitrust Law from the University of Constance (2006) and a graduate of the CAS programme in arbitration of the Swiss Arbitration Academy in association with the University of Lucerne and the University of Neuchâtel (2025).

Rethinking Procedural Safeguards: Artificial Intelligence and the Right to Be Heard in International Arbitration

Dr. MEHMET TANK

Table of Contents

Acknowledgments

The author is deeply grateful to Prof. Daniel Girsberger and Dr. Urs Weber-Stecher for their careful review and constructive suggestions during the revision stage, which substantially improved the clarity and quality of this paper. Any remaining shortcomings are the author's sole responsibility.

The author acknowledges the use of AI-based academic assistance tools (ChatGPT and DeepL) during the research process and in the preparation of this article. This tool was used under the author's meticulous guidance to improve the structure and coherence of the paper, ensuring full adherence to standards of academic integrity. All critical analysis, legal research, argumentation and substantive contributions are original intellectual works of the author. The use of AI support has been carried out transparently, without compromising the originality or scientific rigor of the research, both to facilitate the academic writing process and to ensure that the points conveyed in the thesis are, in a sense, put into practice.

I. Introduction

In international arbitration proceedings, the parties' *"right to be heard"* is recognized as one of the fundamental procedural safeguards. Every legal system guarantees the right to be heard, which refers to the ability of the parties to present their case effectively. The New York Convention effectively protects this right and provides that recognition of an award may be refused if a party "fails to present its case."[1] Similarly, almost all national laws protect the parties' right to be heard in arbitration proceedings. This right ensures that parties have the opportunity to present their claims and evidence, respond to the submissions of the opposing party, and participate meaningfully in the proceedings.[2]

The increasing integration of artificial intelligence (AI) technologies into arbitration proceedings creates both significant opportunities and substantial risks for the effective exercise of the right to be heard. This study critically examines the implications of AI use by party representatives, arbitral tribunals, and institutions on the protection and realization of this fundamental procedural right. The prevailing view is that AI both enhances and threatens the right to be heard.[3]

---

1 Art. V(1)(b) of the Convention on the Recognition and Enforcement of Foreign Arbitral Awards (hereinafter **"New York Convention"**) https://www.newyorkconvention.org/text, (all links in this "Research Paper" last visited on 25 September 2025).

2 GIRSBERGER/VOSER, International Arbitration – Comparative and Swiss Perspectives, Nomos, V. Edition, 2024, N. 1020-1047; BORN, International Commercial Arbitration, 3rd ed., Kluwer Law International, 2021, pp. 2338-2344, 2338; GABRIEL/SCHREGENBERGER, The New Swiss Approach to the Right to be Heard – Balancing Challenging Fairness And Efficiency Concerns; In: Indian Journal Of Arbitration Law (IJAL), Volume 8, Issue 2, 2020, p. 48 et seqq. https://www.gabriel-arbitration.ch/en/publications-and-speaking/right-to-be-heard-swiss-approach; OLIVEIRA, Access to justice and the right of a physical hearing in arbitration, in: Does a Right to a Physical Hearing Exist in International Arbitration?, The ICCA Reports no. 10, 2022, PP. 45–68.

3 SCHERER, International Arbitration 3.0 – How Artificial Intelligence Will Change Dispute Resolution in: Klausegger/Klein/Kremslehner/vd. (eds.), Austrian Yearbook of International Arbitration 2019, pp. 503-524, ISBN 978-3-214-04325-4, available at SSRN: https://ssrn.com/abstract=3377234; CHAN/GORE/JIANG, Harnessing Artificial Intelligence in International Arbitration Practice, Harnessing Artificial Intelligence in International Arbitration Practice (2023), Contemporary Asia Arbitration Journal, 2023, pp. 263-300, p. 286, <https://ssrn.com/abstract=4648246; SVAMC, Guidelines on the Use of Artificial Intelligence in Arbitration (hereinafter **SVAMC Guidelines**), 1st ed., 2024, <https://svamc.org/wp-content/uploads/SVAMC-AI-Guidelines-First-Edition.pdf>; The Chartered Institute of Arbitrators CIArb, Guideline on the Use of AI in Arbitration (hereinafter **CIArb Guideline**) 2025, https://www.ciarb.org>; Stockholm Chamber of Commerce (SCC) Arbitration Institute, Guide to the Use of

This study adopts a mixed methodology that incorporates both normative and empirical elements. The first section F outlines the aim, subject matter, scope of the study, and briefly explains the methodology employed. The second section examines the position of the right to be heard within arbitration law using a classical doctrinal approach. In this framework, the interpretation and application of this right in leading legal systems, primarily under the Swiss lex arbitri, are analysed.[4] The third section examines the normative regulations and guidelines[5] governing the use of AI in international arbitration. The fourth section provides a detailed analysis of how AI tools are utilized in arbitral proceedings and assesses the benefits and risks AI tools present in relation to the right to be heard. The final section summarizes the discussions and highlights the key findings regarding the evaluation of AI use within procedural safeguards protecting the right to be heard.

II. The Right to Be Heard in International Arbitration: Doctrinal and Comparative Foundations

A. Definition of the Right to Be Heard

The right to be heard («Rechtliches Gehör»/«droit d'être entendu») is a cornerstone of procedural fairness in international arbitration[6] and forms part of the transnational principles of due process.[7] The right to be heard provides the parties to the dispute with the right to present their evidence and legal arguments and to request evidentiary measures to be taken when necessary.[8] This includes being given the right to participate in the evidentiary proceedings, to rebut the counter allegations, examining and challenging evidence brought by the opposing party by presenting its own evidence.

Artificial Intelligence in Cases Administered Under the SCC Rules (hereinafter **SCC Guide**), 16 October 2024, <https://sccinstitute.com>

4 GIRSBERGER/VOSER, see fn.2, N. 1040-1047.

5 Such as, SVAMC Guidelines; CIArb Guideline, SCC Guide.

6 GIRSBERGER / VOSER, see fn. 2, p. 259-265, see also: BORN, International Arbitration: Law and Practice, Kluwer Law International, II. Edition, 2015, pp.155-182; BERGER/KELLERHALS, International and Domestic Arbitration in Switzerland, Stämpfli Fourth Edition, 2021, pp. 648-654; MOSES, The Principles and Practice of International Commercial Arbitration, 4th ed., Cambridge University Press, 2021, pp. 161-197.

7 SCHNEIDER/KNOLL, International Arbitration in Switzerland: A Handbook for Practitioners, 2nd ed., 2014, p. 134.

8 BORN, see fn. 2, p.159; GIRSBERGER/VOSER, see fn. 2, N. 1020.

The arbitral procedure is governed by the arbitration law of the country in which the arbitral tribunal has its seat (lex arbitri).[9] The right to be heard is recognised under most national arbitration laws and institutional rules.[10]

Art. 24(1) of the UNCITRAL Model Law[11], which deals, among others, with the general entitlement of a party to oral hearings, provides that, unless the parties have agreed that no oral hearings be held for the presentation of evidence or for oral arguments, the tribunal shall hold such hearings at an appropriate stage of the proceedings, if so requested by a party. Notably, as reflected in Art. 34(2)(a)(ii), a violation of the right to be heard may constitute grounds for setting aside an arbitral award.[12]

Although the content of this right may vary depending on the applicable procedural law, its core elements remain consistent: the right to notice, the right to be heard within a reasonable time, the right to equality of arms, and the right to have arguments duly considered.[13] Compliance with these core components is essential to ensuring legitimacy, trust, and acceptability of the arbitral award, particularly in cross-border disputes.

Various provisions of Chapter 12 of the Swiss Private International Law Act (SPILA) demonstrate that the spirit of the UNCITRAL Model Law has influ-

---

9 BERGER/KELLERHALS, see fn. 6, p. 6.

10 Art. 18 of the United Nations Commission on International Trade Law (UNCITRAL) Model Law on International Commercial Arbitration (hereinafter **UNCITRAL Model Law**): *"Equal treatment of parties: The parties shall be treated with equality and each party shall be given a full opportunity of presenting his case."*; The Arbitration Rules of the International Chamber of Commerce 2021 (hereinafter **"ICC Rules"**) Art. 22(4): *"In all cases, the arbitral tribunal shall act fairly and impartially and ensure that each party has a reasonable opportunity to present its case."*; The English Arbitration Act (2025) (Section 33(1)(a) does necessitate *"giving each party a reasonable opportunity of putting his case"*. France "Code de procédure civile" (Civil Code of Procedure) (2005), Art. 1485 stipulates that *"the arbitral tribunal shall rule after having heard the parties or having given them the opportunity to be heard."* In a similar vein, Art. 1039 of Dutch Arbitration Act (1986) mandates that the arbitral tribunal provide each party with an opportunity to substantiate their claims and present their case. In Sweden, the principle of procedural fairness is similarly enshrined, stipulating that *"the arbitrators shall afford the parties, to the extent necessary, an opportunity to present their respective cases in writing or orally."* Section 24, Swedish Arbitration Act (2018).

11 The UNCITRAL Model Law has exerted a considerable influence on the arbitration laws of numerous Arbitral institutions.

12 Art. 34 (2)(a)(ii) of UNCITRAL Model Law states: "the party making the application was not given proper notice of the appointment of an arbitrator or of the arbitral proceedings or was otherwise unable to present his case."

13 BINDER, International Commercial Arbitration and Conciliation in UNCITRAL Model Law Jurisdictions, 4th ed., 2019, p. 293–295.

enced Swiss arbitration law.[14] The right to be heard is explicitly enshrined in Art. 182(3) of SPILA, which provides that *"regardless of the chosen procedure, the arbitral tribunal shall ensure equal treatment of the parties and their right to be heard in adversarial proceedings."*[15] In addition, this fundamental procedural guarantee is reinforced by Art. 29(2) of the Swiss Federal Constitution, which ensures the right to a fair hearing before judicial authorities.

B. Application of the right to be heard in International Arbitration

The right to be heard is not merely a theoretical construct in terms of procedural rights; rather, it is an imperative that encompasses the practical rules that arbitral tribunals are obliged to follow throughout the proceedings. It delineates the regulations that must be observed during the implementation of procedural rights, encompassing the notification of arbitration and the issuance of the final award. In practice, the exercise of this right entails the assurance that each party is accorded sufficient time and opportunity to present their arguments and evidence on an equal footing. Furthermore, it is imperative that these submissions be given due consideration by the arbitral tribunal.[16]

The UNCITRAL Model Law, in alignment with all other national and international arbitration legislation, ensures the autonomy of the parties to select the applicable procedural rules, contingent upon a limited set of obligatory provisions that encompass the fundamental due process requirements.[17] The parties may tailor the proceedings by preparing their own individual set of rules or by referring to standard rules of arbitration institutions. These laws

---

14 BERGER/KELLERHALS, see fn. 6, p. 6.

15 Art. 182(3) of SPILA.

16 REDFERN/HUNTER, Law and Practice of International Commercial Arbitration, 6th ed., 2015, N. 6.83.

17 Art. 18 and Art. 19 of the UNCITRAL Model Law set out the core principles of procedural fairness, from which the parties may not derogate. Art. 24(1), addresses the general entitlement of a party to oral hearings, stipulates that, unless the parties agree otherwise, the arbitral tribunal decides whether to hold oral hearings or proceed based on documents. Art. 24(2) reads, the parties must receive sufficient advance notice of any hearing or tribunal meeting for inspecting goods, property, or documents. Art. 24(3) stipulates that all statements, documents, and other information furnished by a party to the tribunal must be communicated to the other party. Additionally, any expert report or evidentiary document on which the arbitral tribunal may rely in making its decision must be communicated to the other parties. ps://www.swissarbitration.org/wp-content/uploads/2023/08/Swiss-Rules-2021-EN.pdf>.

also empower arbitrators to conduct the arbitration in such a manner as they consider appropriate, if the parties were silent or have failed to reach an agreement.[18]

In the Swiss context, the Supreme Court has repeatedly emphasized that a party's right to be heard is violated when a tribunal fails to address a party's potentially decisive argument or evidence.[19] For example, in its decision 4A_6/2019, the Court annulled an arbitral award due to its failure to address a significant legal objection raised by the respondent. This is indicative of the Swiss judiciary's circumscribed yet substantial interpretation of the right to be heard.

The same principle is echoed in other jurisdictions applying the UNCITRAL Model Law, where awards may be set aside if a party was not given a full opportunity to present its case.[20] However, most courts adopt a deferential standard, recognizing the tribunal's discretion to manage proceedings efficiently, provided that fundamental fairness is maintained. In this regard, experts suggest that due process in arbitration, must be balanced with efficiency. While fairness is essential, excessive formality can increase costs and delay justice, potentially limiting access for financially weaker parties. Therefore, true fairness includes efficiency, and true efficiency requires fairness, both are necessary for effective dispute resolution.[21]

C. The Right to Be Heard under Swiss Rules and Other Institutional Rules

The protection of the right to be heard in institutional arbitration is not solely grounded in national arbitration laws, but also prominently reflected in procedural rules of major arbitral institutions.

For example, the Swiss Rules of International Arbitration (2021) **(Swiss Rules)** explicitly incorporate due process guarantees: "... *arbitral tribunal may conduct the arbitration in such manner as it considers appropriate, including by adopting measures for the efficiency of the arbitration proceed-*

---

18 Art. 182(3) of SPILA: "Regardless of the chosen procedure, the arbitral tribunal shall ensure equal treatment of the parties and their right to be heard in adversarial proceedings."; See FORTESE/HEMMI, Procedural Fairness and Efficiency in International Arbitration (May 29, 2015). Groningen Journal of International Law, 2015, SSRN: <https://ssrn.com/abstract=2611337> pp. 110-124, p. 113.

19 Decision by the Swiss Federal Tribunal, Decision 4A_6/2019, of 11 April 2019.

20 Art. 34(2)(a)(ii) of UNCITRAL Model Law.

21 FORTESE/HEMMI, see fn.18, p. 116.

ings, provided that it ***ensures equal treatment of the parties and their right to be heard.***"[22] Art. 19(1) of the Swiss Rules affirms these principles, closely mirroring Art. 182(3) of the SPILA.[23] These guarantees illustrate that the right to be heard remains a cornerstone of Swiss arbitration practice, embedded across statutory, constitutional, and institutional frameworks.

According to the Swiss Supreme Court case law, the right to be heard, along with the principles ensuring its effective exercise primarily pertains to the proper establishment of the factual background of a case.[24] This procedural guarantee affords each party the opportunity to:

- *"submit all statements of fact essential to a decision on the case,*
- *present legal arguments,*
- *request appropriate evidence-taking measures,*
- *participate in the proceedings, and*
- *be given access to the records"*[25].

Further, the right to be heard also includes the parties' right to be represented by legal counsel, although it does not extend to legal aid in arbitration.

This interpretation under Swiss law aligns with the broader international approach, as set out in the UNCITRAL Model Law[26] and other national frameworks. These frameworks emphasise that annulment is only justified in cases of material breaches affecting the integrity of the proceedings. Importantly, the right to be heard should not be considered violated due to minor procedural errors or controversial decisions made by the arbitral tribunal in the normal course of proceedings. Its violation must reach a threshold that affects the outcome or integrity of the process.[27]

---

22 Art. 19(1) of the Swiss Rules of International Arbitration 2021 **(«Swiss Rules»)** <https://www.swissarbitration.org/wp-content/uploads/2023/08/Swiss-Rules-2021-EN.pdf>

23 Art. 182(3) of SPILA: "Regardless of the chosen procedure, the arbitral tribunal shall ensure equal treatment of the parties and their right to be heard in adversarial proceedings."

24 GIRSBERGER/VOSER, see fn. 2, N 1040-1047: For the case law: DSC, 29 January 2019, 4A_424/2018, reason 5.2.3; DSC, 9 August 2018, 4A_525/2017, reason 3.1.

25 GIRSBERGER/VOSER, see fn. 2, N 1041.

26 Art. 34(2)(a)(ii): "the party making the application was not given proper notice of the appointment of an arbitrator or of the arbitral proceedings or was otherwise unable to present his case."

27 ORTOLANI, Art. 34, Application for Setting Aside as Exclusive Recourse against Arbitral Award, in BANTEKAS/ORTOLANI/F. ALI/GOMEZ/POLKINGHORNE, UNCITRAL

Scholars observe that the focus of evaluating infringements of the right to be heard under the Swiss *lex arbitri* has shifted over time.[28] Whereas a few decades ago a breach of the right to be heard led directly to the annulment of the award, irrespective of the impact of the breach on the final outcome of the award, the Swiss Supreme Court has, for some time now, come to require that such a breach must have had a potential effect on the substantive outcome of the case in order to justify the setting aside of the challenged award. The case law in Austria[29], the United Kingdom[30] and the 'International Center for Settlement of Investment Disputes' (ICSID)[31] has also evolved in this direction.[32]

The right to be heard encompasses the obligation of the arbitral tribunal to examine and address the relevant issues. Consequently, a tribunal violates the right to be heard if it fails to address a party's arguments that are relevant for the decision.

This alignment is deliberate, as the Swiss Rules were developed to remain consistent with Swiss arbitration law while also adhering to widely recog-

Model Law on International Commercial Arbitration: A Commentary (Cambridge University Press, 2020), pp. 858-898, p. 878.

28 GABRIEL/SCHREGENBERGER, see fn. 2, p. 48 et seqq.

29 OGH (Austria), 28 November 2012, 4 Ob 185/12b, published in: ZEILER/NUEBER, Decisions of the Austrian Supreme Court on Arbitration in 2012 and 2013, Austrian Yearbook on International Arbitration 2014, 243, at 245 *"...the right to be heard in arbitration is only violated if a party, at all stages of the proceedings, is completely deprived of any possibility to argue its case"*, https://assets.ctfassets.net/wwqh0hdhnyw9/6dftK57akDluKEJ1tEdprB/d3ad13f428786198596ada2c3ecfb0c1/Decisions_of_the_Austrian_Supreme_Court_on_Arbitration.pdf

30 Lesotho Highlands Development Authority v. Impregilo SpA [2005] UKHL 43, para. 28 ("serious irregularity means an irregularity ... which the court considers has caused or will cause substantial injustice to the applicant"), https://arbitrationlaw.com/sites/default/files/free_pdfs/lesotho_highlands_development_authority_v_impregilo_spa_and_others_2005_ukhl_43.pdf.

31 Compañía de Aguas del Aconquija SA and Vivendi Universal v. Argentina, ICSID Case No. ARB/97/3, Annulment Decision, 3 July 2002, para. 248, https://www.transnational-dispute-management.com/downloads/6329_case_report_vivendi_v_argentina_decision_on_annulment_2002.pdf.

32 E.g., DSC of 18 April 2018, (Errani), 4A_424/2018; reason 5.2.2: "Thus, in addition to the alleged violation, the party allegedly affected by the arbitrators' inadvertence must demonstrate, on the basis of the grounds set out in the challenged award, that the facts, evidence or law which it had duly presented, but which the arbitral tribunal failed to take into consideration, were of such nature as to influence the outcome of the dispute." (Translation by: GABRIEL/SCHREGENBERGER see fn. 2, p. 48).

nized international standards.[33] The emphasis on party equality and fair hearing reflects Switzerland's commitment to procedural fairness as a cornerstone of its arbitration-friendly legal environment.

Similarly, the ICC Rules (2021) and UNCITRAL Rules (2021)[34] enshrine the right to be heard as part of the general conduct of the proceedings. ICC Rules 22(4) imposes a duty on the arbitral tribunal to *"ensure that each party has a reasonable opportunity to present its case"* These provisions reinforce the universal recognition of this right and frame it as a structural element of procedural legitimacy in arbitration.

Despite textual similarities, the practical interpretation and application of these rules may vary. For instance, some institutions adopt detailed procedural guidelines or explanatory notes, such as the ICC *"Note to Parties and Arbitral Tribunals"* (2021), which elaborate how fairness and the right to be heard should be balanced with procedural efficiency and cost considerations.[35] These supplementary documents are crucial in understanding how institutional rules evolve to address contemporary procedural challenges, including those introduced by the integration of AI.

D. Comparative Analysis of Key Judicial Decisions on the Right to Be Heard

The judicial interpretation of the right to be heard in the context of arbitration plays a critical role in setting procedural standards and guiding arbitral tribunals. Swiss jurisprudence has played a significant role in shaping a body of case law that emphasizes a restrained yet impactful understanding of the right to be heard. The Swiss Supreme Court has repeatedly established that a violation of this right occurs exclusively in instances where the arbitral tribunal has disregarded arguments or evidence that could have been pivotal in determining the outcome of the case.[36] For instance, in case 4A_150/2020, the court emphasized that the failure to engage with a potentially outcome-

---

33 GIRSBERGER/VOSER, see fn. 2, N 1036-1049. And see: Swiss Rules (2021), Preamble and Art. 19(1), Swiss PILA, Art. 182(3).

34 ICC Rules 2021, Art. 22(4); Art. 17(1) of the UNCITRAL Arbitration Rules 2021: *"each party is given a reasonable opportunity of presenting its case."* Also see, ICSID, *Rules* (2022), Rule 3, https://icsid.worldbank.org/resources/rules-and-regulations.

35 ICC, Note to Parties and Arbitral Tribunals on the Conduct of the Arbitration, 2021, paras. 41, 43, 102, and 148 (for expedited procedure).

36 DUTOIT, Commentaire de la Loi fédérale sur le droit international privé, 5th ed., 2016, Art. 190 N 18.

determinative factual allegation constituted a breach of Art. 190(2)(d) of SPILA.[37]

In another point, under Swiss law, the right to be heard primarily concerns a party's opportunity to comment on the facts and evidence, while arbitral tribunals retain discretion to apply legal rules ex officio based on the principle of *jura novit curia*. However, where a tribunal intends to rely on a legal ground that has been unforeseeable to the parties, it must give them a chance to respond. In decision 4A_634/2014, the Swiss Supreme Court reiterated that surprise reliance on unexpected legal reasoning may breach Art. 190(2)(d) PILA.[38]

This standard is particularly relevant when AI tools are used to generate legal reasoning. If a court adopts AI-derived arguments or interpretations that were not discussed by the parties or arbitrators during the proceedings and whose legal basis is not clear and foreseeable, this may violate the right to be heard unless the parties to the dispute are provided with appropriate procedural safeguards, such as the opportunity to discuss and comment. This concern is echoed in the CIArb Guideline on the Use of AI in Arbitration (2025), which cautions that arbitrators should not delegate legal analysis or application of the law to AI tools and requires that parties be consulted and given an opportunity to comment before such tools are used in a way that could influence procedural or substantive decisions (paras. 8.2, 9.1).

This approach aligns with the principle of *iura novit arbiter*, as acknowledged in international arbitral guidelines, which recognises the tribunal's authority to apply legal rules not raised by the parties, so long as such reasoning remains foreseeable and does not compromise the parties' right to be heard.[39]

---

37 Decision of Swiss Federal Tribunal, 4A_150/2020 of 3 December 2020.

38 Decision of Swiss Federal Tribunal, 4A_634/2014 of 21 May 2015, consid. 4.1–4.2; ATF 130 III 35, consid. 5. 1.

39 For example, Art. 7 of the Prague Rules on the Efficient Conduct of Proceedings in International Arbitration, 2018, (hereinafter Prague Rules) empowers the tribunal to apply unpleaded legal provisions (including public policy rules) ex officio, but requires seeking parties' views first to mitigate surprises. This concern is also addressed in the **CIArb Guideline on the Use of AI in Arbitration (2025, paras. 8.2, 9.1)**, which requires arbitrators to consult the parties before using AI tools in a way that could affect the proceedings and prohibits reliance on AI-generated legal reasoning without affording the parties an opportunity to comment. Also see; SVAMC, Guidelines on the Use of Artificial Intelligence in Arbitration, 2024, Guideline 7; UNCITRAL, Notes on Organizing Arbitral Proceedings, 2016, paras.105, 115; Also see LIMOND/CALTHROP, GAR, Artificial Intelligence in Arbitration – Evidentiary Issues and Prospects, https://globalarbitrationreview.com/guide/the-guide-evidence-in-international-arbitration/3rd-edition/article/artificial-intelligence-in-arbitration-evidentiary-issues-and-prospects, 09 September 2025; ALEXANDER/BOSCARIOL, The

The *jura novit arbiter* principle is also applicable in international arbitrations seated in Switzerland, albeit with the proviso of "no-surprise" to the parties. [40] Despite the absence of an explicit provision in the SPILA, this principle is deeply embedded in the Swiss legal order and consistently upheld in Federal Supreme Court jurisprudence.[41] According to the Swiss Supreme Court, arbitral tribunals may freely assess the legal significance of the facts and may rely on legal rules not expressly invoked by the parties. However, as an important exception, the parties must be consulted whenever the tribunal intends to rely on a legal norm or consideration that was not raised during the proceedings and whose pertinence could not reasonably have been anticipated.[42]

This cautious approach is mirrored in other Model Law jurisdictions. In Singapore, the Court of Appeal in *L W Infrastructure Pte Ltd v Lim Chin San Contractors Pte Ltd* held that procedural breaches only justify annulment where they result in real prejudice to the complaining party.[43] Similarly, the German Federal Court of Justice (BGH) has ruled that only material violations affecting the party's ability to participate in the proceedings may trigger the setting aside of awards.[44] This principle reflects a general reluctance among national courts to interfere with arbitral awards, except in cases of egregious procedural errors.

Nevertheless, certain jurisdictions adopt a more interventionist stance. French courts, while supportive of arbitration, do not hesitate to annul awards where basic principles of adversarial process are disregarded. In *Kriton Berbati v. Benedetti*, the Paris Court of Appeal annulled an award on the ground that the tribunal's reliance on a legal argument not raised by the parties deprived one

---

Prague Rules and the IBA Rules on Taking of Evidence in International Arbitration: Friends or Foes?, Transnational Notes (NYU School of Law), 6 Feb 2019; and Loizou, Revisiting the "Content-of-Laws" Enquiry in International Arbitration, 78 La. L. Rev. 2018, p. 633 ff.

40 LOIZOU, Revisiting the "Content-of-Laws" Enquiry in International Arbitration, 78 Louisiana Law Review (2018), pp. 843-847, https://digitalcommons.law.lsu.edu/cgi/viewcontent.cgi?params=/context/lalrev/article/6678/&path_info=2___LOIZOU.F.pdf

41 Decisions of Swiss Federal Supreme Court, 4A_218/2015 of 28 October 2015; 4A_709/2014 of 21 May 2015; 4A_440/2010 of 7 January 2011 referenced by LOIZOU, see fn. 40, cited in LOIZOU, fn. 40.

42 Decisions of Swiss Federal Supreme Court, 4A_136/2016 of Nov. 3, 2016; 4A_202/2016 of Aug. 3, 2016, cited in LOIZOU, fn. 40.

43 Decision of Singapore Court of Appeal, *L W Infrastructure Pte Ltd v Lim Chin San Contractors Pte Ltd* [2013] SGCA 16, para. 45.

44 Decision of Germany, Federal Court of Justice (BGH), Judgment of 31 October 2012 – III ZR 190/11.

side of the opportunity to respond.[45] The analogy with AI-assisted decision-making is clear: if algorithmic reasoning remains opaque or produces outputs on the basis of factors not foreseeable to the parties, the same due process concern arises. In this sense, the 'black-box' problem in AI could mirror the unforeseeable-grounds problem. This shows how unforeseeable reasoning, whether by human tribunals or opaque algorithms, may jeopardize the right to be heard. It also illustrates why divergent judicial approaches to this principle may generate enforcement risks under the New York Convention.

III. Regulatory and Normative Frameworks for AI in Arbitration

Technological advances, especially in the field of informatics, led to changes in the rules of arbitration. In addition to this, following the COVID-19 pandemic, many arbitration institutions quickly adapted their rules and procedures. The ICC, for instance, issued guidance on conducting virtual hearings and made changes to its rules to facilitate the use of electronic documents.[46]

As the use of AI in arbitration proceedings continues to expand, new international rules are being developed to ensure that the use of AI remains consistent with fundamental procedural safeguards, including the right to be heard. AI holds considerable promise for arbitrators as a tool to enhance efficiency, offer more profound insights, and attain a level of precision that was previously unattainable.[47]

A. Understanding the Role and Functions of AI in International Arbitration

The term "AI" is often used broadly and covers a range of technologies such as machine learning, deep learning, neural networks, bots, cognitive computing such as understanding natural language processing (NLP), recognising

[45] Decision of Paris Court of Appeal, of 1 March 2011, in KRITON BERBATI v. BENEDETTI, Rev. Arb. 2011, p. 517.

[46] ICC, Leveraging Technology for Fair, Effective and Efficient International Arbitration Proceedings, ICC Publication, (2022).

[47] EVANS/ GUILLON/ LOSEY/ WASHINGTON/ YANCEY, Dispute Resolution Enhanced: How Arbitrators and Mediators Can Harness Generative AI, 2023 pp. 1-34, p. 1 <https://go.adr.org/rs/294-SFS-516/images/DRJ%20Journal%20Article%202024.pdf>.

complex semantic patterns, and generating human-like outputs.[48] It also extends to text-mining, predictive analytics, speech recognition, and Optical Character Recognition (OCR).[49]

Large language models (LLMs) represent a significant advance in the field of generative AI. These models mark a significant leap forward in the field of AI by using extensive and diverse datasets to process and generate human language. As models such as GPT, which underpins platforms such as ChatGPT and Claude, demonstrate, advanced NLP capabilities are demonstrated through the recognition of patterns, relationships and anomalies in extensive document collections. [50] The revolutionary power of GPTs is their capacity to understand, interpret and generate human language quickly and at scale[51] - in short, their potential to mimic human intelligence.

AI can learn automatically from patterns or features within data. In the digital age, nearly all information relevant to an arbitration case is stored in digital form. This applies to many elements of the process, including communications between parties, interactions with the arbitral institution, arbitrator discussions, submitted evidence (like emails), details and testimonies of expert and fact witnesses, hearing transcripts, arbitrators' internal communications, and even draft versions of awards.[52]

In the field of international arbitration, AI is expected to support a broad spectrum of functions, ranging from arbitrator selection and legal research to the drafting and refinement of written submissions. Its anticipated uses further include document translation, procedural and evidentiary organization, cost forecasting, logistical aspects of hearings, such as real-time transcription and multilingual interpretation, and the automated generation of standard components of arbitral awards, including procedural summaries.[53]

---

48 SVAMC Guidelines, see fn. 3, p. 8.

49 CHAN/GORE/JIANG, fn. 3, p. 286.

50 EVANS/ GUILLON/ LOSEY/ WASHINGTON/ YANCEY, see fn. 47, p. 2.

51 EVANS/ GUILLON/ LOSEY/ WASHINGTON/ YANCEY, see fn. 47, p. 2.

52 PAISLEY/SUSSMAN, Artificial Intelligence Challenges and Opportunities for International Arbitration, NYSBA New York Dispute Resolution Lawyer, Spring 2018, pp. 35-40, p. 35.

53 SCHERER, Artificial Intelligence and Legal Decision-Making: The Wide Open? Study on the Example of International Arbitration, Queen Mary University of London, School of Law Legal Studies Research Paper No. 318/2019, pp. 1-32, p. 3; APOSTOLOVA/KUNG, Don't Fear AI in IA, Global Arbitration Review (27 Apr. 2018); MALHOTRA/AHMAD, "Artificial Intelligence and International Arbitration," Revista Novos Estudos Jurídicos, 2022, pp. 258–281, p. 259.

B. Safeguarding the Right to Be Heard: Normative Frameworks Governing the Use of AI in International Arbitration

In the international arbitration arena, numerous guidelines, notes, standards and codes of 'best practices' for the conduct of the proceedings have been issued by groups such as the ICC, the CIArb, and SVAMC Guidelines on the Use of Artificial Intelligence in Arbitration. Other institutions such as SCC and VIAC have also issued soft law guidance notes on the use of AI and technology in arbitration[54]. Together, these efforts reflect an emerging normative consensus: while AI can enhance procedural efficiency, it must be deployed within a framework that preserves due process and the right to be heard. The implementation of soft law codification has been demonstrated to be an effective mechanism for enhancing procedural uniformity, certainty, and predictability among parties from diverse judicial traditions.[55]

In the context of AI use by arbitral institutions or alternative dispute resolution bodies, the EU Artificial Intelligence Act classifies such systems as "high-risk" when their outcomes produce legal effects for the parties. Particularly, it mandates that *"the use of AI tools can support the decision-making power of judges or judicial independence, but should not replace it: the final decision-making must remain a human-driven activity"*[56]. This address highlights the importance of preserving the human role in arbitration processes, especially in arbitration, where party autonomy and procedural fairness are paramount.

All UNESCO member states have endorsed a universal standard on AI ethics, emphasizing adherence to the rule of law, prevention of harm, and redress for affected parties. The TAP framework *"transparency, accountability, and privacy"* guides AI use across key sectors such as law, education, healthcare, and economics and strengthens data protection, empowering individuals and

---

[54] Stockholm Chamber of Commerce (SCC) Arbitration Institute, Guide to the Use of Artificial Intelligence in Cases Administered Under the SCC Rules, 16 October 2024, pp. 1–3, <https://sccinstitute.com> Vienna International Arbitral Centre (VIAC) Note on The Use of Artificial Intelligence In Arbitration Proceedings (April 2025) https://www.viac.eu/wp-content/uploads/2025/04/VIAC-Note-on-AI.pdf.

[55] KAUFMANN-KOHLER, Soft Law in International Arbitration: Codification and Normativity, 1(2) Journal of International Dispute Settlement (2010) p. 284.

[56] EU Parliament and Council, Regulation (EU), OJ L, 2024/1689, 12.7.2024, *laying down harmonised rules on artificial intelligence (Artificial Intelligence Act)*, 2024, p. 41, http://data.europa.eu/eli/reg/2024/1689/oj> under [regulation].

organizations.[57] Similarly, the Organization for Economic Co-operation and Development (OECD) has published recommendations on AI, urging members to promote and implement principles for responsible stewardship of trustworthy AI.[58]

While AI systems may enhance procedural efficiency through advanced case management, the delegation of legal decision-making to AI systems without human oversight would constitute a substantial infringement of the right to be heard. The delegation of the power to construct the judicial award is considered to reduce procedural safeguards and jeopardize the legitimacy of arbitral proceedings.[59] Consequently, in the case of the application of AI in arbitration, AI's function should be limited to auxiliary functions that do not replace the arbitrators' core competence of adjudication. This imperative, deriving from the humanity of this reasoning, provides a normative basis for setting limits to the procedural integration of AI, thus ensuring that the right to be heard remains intact even in highly digitized environments.

The non-binding report of the **ICC** Commission on Arbitration and ADR on *"Leveraging Technology for Fair, Effective and Efficient International Arbitration Proceedings"*[60] serves as a widely recognized soft law framework, outlining consensus-driven best practices for ethical AI and digital technology use in arbitration.

The increased integration of AI tools in arbitration proceedings has prompted institutions and scholars to consider new normative responses aimed at maintaining procedural fairness. **SVAMC**, for instance, published its first edition of the *Guidelines on the Use of Artificial Intelligence in Arbitration* in 2024.[61] These guidelines are among the most comprehensive instruments addressing

---

57 UNESCO, Recommendation on the Ethics of Artificial Intelligence, 2022, <https://unesdoc.unesco.org/ark:/48223/pf0000381137>.

58 OECD, Recommendation of the Council on Artificial Intelligence, OECD/LEGAL/0449 (21 May 2019, Last amended on 3 May 2024), <https://legalinstruments.oecd.org/en/instruments/OECD-LEGAL-0449.

59 MADIEGA, Artificial Intelligence Act – EU Legislation in Progress, EPRS – European Parliamentary Research Service, September 2024, p. 2, <https://www.europarl.europa.eu/thinktank/en/document/EPRS_BRI(2021)698792> under [briefing].

60 ICC Commission Report, Leveraging Technology for Fair, Effective and Efficient International Arbitration Proceedings, 2022, p. 1, <https://iccwbo.org> under [commission report]. While its recommendations lack enforceability, tribunals may adopt them as procedural guidance under their discretionary powers, especially absent party-agreed tech rules. The Report advances norms for integrating AI in arbitration, emphasizing procedural fairness, transparency, and safeguarding participants' rights through practical tech protocols.

61 SVAMC Guidelines, see fn. 3.

both the opportunities and the risks posed by AI in the arbitral context. They emphasize principles of transparency, accountability, and non-delegation of decision-making authority, cautioning against overreliance on opaque algorithms.[62]

The American Arbitration Association's International Centre for Dispute Resolution (ICDR) Principles for AI in ADR (AAA-ICDR Principles)[63], and the CIArb *Guideline on the Use of AI in International Arbitration* in 2025[64] are other sets of guidelines. CIArb recommends that arbitrators disclose the use of AI tools in procedural orders and maintain ultimate control over case management and decision-making processes. The guideline promotes a 'human-in-the-loop' model to ensure that AI serves as an assistive, not determinative, element in arbitration.

C. Use of AI under Swiss, ICC, and UNCITRAL Frameworks

The Swiss Arbitration Centre (SAC) has incorporated several procedural updates within the 2021 Swiss Rules, including provisions for electronic filings, digital communications, and cybersecurity protocols.[65] While these developments are not AI-specific, they provide the digital infrastructure necessary for the deployment of intelligent tools.

The Swiss Rules form a foundational reference for the normative use of AI in arbitration, particularly within Switzerland's arbitration-friendly legal environment. While the Swiss Rules do not mention AI explicitly, their emphasis on efficiency, flexibility, and technological adaptation sets a procedural framework conducive to AI integration.[66]

62 SVAMC Guidelines, see fn. 3; Principles 2, 3, and 5. Guideline 7, titled 'Respect for Due Process', regulates the right to be heard by stating that *"An arbitrator shall not rely on AI-generated information outside the record without making appropriate disclosures to the parties beforehand and, as far as practical, allowing the parties to comment on it"*.

63 Aaa & Icdr, Principles Supporting the Use of AI in Alternative Dispute Resolution (Nov. 2023), https://mediate.com/aaa-icdr-principles-supporting-the-use-of-ai-in-alternative-dispute-resolution/.

64 CIARB Guideline, see fn. 3, N. 8.2, https://www.ciarb.org.

65 Arts. 16(2) and 19(2) of the Swiss Rules.

66 Art. 16(1) of the Swiss Rules states *"All participants in the arbitration proceedings shall act in good faith and make every effort to contribute to the efficient conduct of the proceedings and to avoid unnecessary costs and delays."* These provisions pro-

Turning to the ICC Arbitration Rules, the use of AI is not directly regulated but several provisions enable its adoption. Art. 22(1) entrusts tribunals with the duty to conduct arbitrations in a *"fair, expeditious and cost-effective manner,"*[67] a mandate that implicitly supports the use of technologies including AI applications, that can streamline proceedings.

In its 2022 Working Group II sessions, UNCITRAL acknowledged the challenges and prospects posed by AI in arbitration. The Secretariat emphasized the necessity of preserving core procedural guarantees, especially transparency, explainability, and non-delegation of decision-making. [68] Although UNCITRAL has not adopted a binding instrument on AI, its progressive discussions signal institutional support for responsible technological adaptation.

IV. Implications of AI Use for the Arbitral Procedure

International arbitration is built upon four key elements: the arbitration agreement, the arbitral tribunal, the seat of arbitration, and the final award. These elements derive their validity from existing legal frameworks, which are continuously updated through new conventions, treaties, and national reforms. Such developments aim both to refrain from the risks and to enhance efficiency, transparency, and accessibility, objectives that closely align with the potential benefits of AI integration[69].

Recent developments demonstrate a growing integration of specialized AI tools into international arbitration practice. Platforms such as JusMundi's JusAI[70], Everlaw, or CaseText's CoCounsel[71] Kluwer Arbitration Blog, ICCA

vide the legal and procedural elasticity necessary for AI-supported tools such as automated document processing or real-time translation during hearings.

67 Art. 22(1), also (4) of the ICC Rules. See also Art. 19 of the UNCITRAL Model Law. The ICC's 'Note to Parties and Arbitral Tribunals on the Conduct of the Arbitration' (2021) supports this approach, explicitly referencing case management and communication tools. Paragraphs 89 to 92 promote technology use for document management, remote hearings, and cost control while cautioning that fairness and equal treatment must be protected. ICC's recommendations, as a soft law, serve as a normative anchor for responsible AI integration in ICC arbitrations.

68 UNCITRAL, Report of Working Group II (Dispute Settlement) on the Work of its 75th Session, UN Doc. A/CN.9/1089, 2022, paras. 41–45.

69 RAUCH, AI in IA: To What Extent and Capacity Can Artificial Intelligence Assist in International Arbitration Procedures and Proceedings?, 1 April 2024, https://ssrn.com/abstract=5100706.

70 JUSMUNDI, JusAI Platform Overview, https://jusmundi.com/en.

71 CASETEXT, Introducing CoCounsel: the AI Legal Assistant, <https://casetext.com/cocounsel.

Blog, Westlaw, SSRN facilitate targeted legal research by providing access to a comprehensive database of arbitral awards and international legal materials. They also assist parties, counsel and tribunals in drafting procedural documents, including procedural orders and Redfern schedules. In addition, such tools can be used to support case management conferences, generate procedural timetables, streamline document production requests, produce transcripts and translations, draft standard procedural directions, calculate institutional fees and party costs, and even develop cybersecurity or confidentiality protocols, thereby enhancing procedural efficiency and consistency. Moreover, arbitral institutions and their nomination committees tasked with proposing arbitrators for institutional appointments, may employ AI in identifying suitable candidates for appointments, taking into account the specific requirements of a case.

Predictive analytics platforms like Arbilex provide insights into the potential success rates and enforcement risks of arbitral awards, supporting early case evaluation strategies.[72] Other AI-enhanced tools relevant to arbitration include Relativity, Kira Systems, DeepL Pro, DISCO E-Discovery, Opus 2, and TransPerfect Legal Solutions; they are used for applications ranging from e-discovery and contract analysis to translation and court reporting.[73]

A. Implications for Parties and Counsel

1. *Procedural Benefits: Legal Research, Drafting, and Argument Structuring*

The landscape of AI in international arbitration has evolved significantly. While earlier concerns centered on the lack of AI tools tailored for arbitration and the challenges posed by confidentiality due to limited access to arbitral awards, recent developments have addressed these issues through the introduction of specialized guidelines and frameworks.[74]

Today, artificial intelligence tools have made it possible for parties and lawyers to navigate complex legal databases at a very high speed and depth. NLP is a field of artificial intelligence that focuses on analysing the interaction between computers and humans through natural language. With the develop-

---

72 ARBILEX, Predictive Analytics for Arbitration Outcomes, https://www.arbilex.co.

73 These examples were identified through a ChatGPT-based inquiry conducted for the purpose of this research, and they reflect tools frequently and discussed in practitioner reports and industry commentary.

74 See Chapter III/B.

ment of NLP, complex tasks such as summarizing legal documents and developing legal arguments have been simplified, and it has become possible to develop solutions on legal issues even for non-lawyers.[75] NLP enhances search capabilities by comprehending the underlying meaning, synonyms- antonyms, and even the context of the entered search query.[76] It can identify specific data from texts, such as names, dates, obligations, and more. This is especially valuable in legal scenarios where specific clauses, terms, patterns, and trends can be identified.[77]

Advanced NLP-based search engines retrieve precedents and legal commentaries that support a party's position and enable sophisticated comparative legal reasoning. AI also helps clarify patterns of reasoning across jurisdictions, giving counsel a sharper lens for persuasive argumentation.[78] Adequately trained legal research tools that can process multilingual and diverse forms of data strengthen parties' ability to present their claims and defences more clearly, thereby reinforcing their effective participation in legal proceedings.[79]

Beyond streamlining legal research, AI helps democratize expertise in international arbitration. While experienced parties have traditionally held advantages in strategy and arbitrator selection, integrating their insights into large datasets and analysing them with advanced algorithms makes such knowledge accessible to a broader range of users. This promotes greater equality and informed participation across all users, regardless of prior experience, and supports procedural fairness by diffusing strategic expertise more widely.[80]

AI is now widely used to prepare first drafts of pleadings, motions and other legal documents that can be refined by lawyers, who can focus more on strategy and less on the rote aspects of the drafting process.[81] Predictive analytics and generative AI models also help counsel conduct risk assessments and simulate counterarguments. This strengthens a party's procedural engagement, especially in the early phases. In-house GPT- powered copilots con-

---

75 ARIAI/DEMARTINI, Natural Language Processing for the Legal Domain: A Survey of Tasks, Datasets, Models, and Challenges, ACM Computing Surveys, last revised 25 March 2025. <https://arxiv.org/pdf>/2410.21306>.

76 WILKINSON / TSAI / CURLE, How natural language processing can improve legal search results, Kira Systems, 202[AD], as cited in: RAUCH, see fn. 69, p. 16.

77 RAUCH, see fn. 69, p. 16.

78 CHAN/GORE/JIANG, see fn. 3, p. 288.

79 SCHERER, fn. 3, p. 507, https://ssrn.com/abstract=3377234.

80 PAISLEY, SUSSMAN, see fn. 52, p. 37.

81 KIRBY, International Arbitration and Artificial Intelligence: Ideas to Improve the Written Phase of Arbitral Proceedings, Journal of International Arbitration 2023 (no. 6), pp. 657 – 666, p. 660.

nected to the law firm's legal precedents data bank and legal research databases could generate the first draft of pleadings. These copilots are capable of establishing legal tests and generating supporting authorities based on specific factual matrices, while adhering to the firm's established drafting style.[82]

The use of AI to generate case chronologies offers the prospect of considerable procedural efficiencies. Arbitrators often reasonably require a detailed chronology of key documents and events, yet compiling and updating such records can be highly time-consuming, particularly as the volume of evidence grows and the demand for precision increases. This burden affects both parties and tribunals as proceedings advance.[83] These technologies, like ChatGPT, streamline and expedite the creation and maintenance of these chronologies.

2. *Case Management and Document Analysis*

AI-enhanced document review platforms are now central to modern arbitration. They identify relevant evidence, suggest thematic clusters, and flag inconsistencies or duplications. AI has a wide range of potential applications for discovering and evaluating evidence, especially considering its expanding analytical and manipulative abilities.[84] A number of legal tech platforms are currently employing automation to facilitate the preliminary evaluation of documentation for production. These platforms utilize low-code and no-code tools to establish rule-based automation processes, including the identification and organization of all pertinent documents into a centralized repository.[85]

These tools may help uncover concealed or overlooked information, thereby supporting the fact-finding process. However, their opaque logic necessitates ongoing human supervision. Relying too heavily on algorithmic anticipations, can unintentionally push lawyers toward more rigid and uniform thinking, reducing creativity in legal reasoning. These tools are most valuable when they assist human judgment, not when they replace it. It assists arbitrators to make decisions by analysing and drafting evidence such as expert reports[86] on

---

82 CHAN/GORE/JIANG, see fn. 3, p. 290.

83 KIRBY, see fn. 81, p. 665.

84 MAGAL et al., Artificial Intelligence in Arbitration: Evidentiary Issues and Prospects, A&O SHEARMAN (Jan. 12, 2024), https://www.aoshearman.com/en/insights/artificial-intelligence-in-arbit ration-evidentiary-issues-and-prospects>.

85 CHAN/GORE/JIANG, see fn. 3, p. 290.

86 CHATTERJEE/SINGHANIA/SHARMA, Technology and Artificial Intelligence: Reengineering Arbitration in the New World, International Bar Association (Dec. 20, 2023) https://www.ibanet.org/tchnology-and-artificial-intelligence-reengineering-arbitration-in-the-new-world#notes>.

quantum calculations, predict delays and damages in construction arbitration cases.[87]

The application of AI technologies has expanded to encompass the analysis of arbitration clauses and the provision of drafting guidance.[88] The AAA's **"Clause-Builder"** is a tool that assists users in creating customized and effective arbitration agreements that are tailored to the specific circumstances of their disputes. Furthermore, software such as "Lex Machina" and "Premonition" is already employed by legal professionals to estimate the likelihood of case outcomes.[89]

The integration of AI into arbitration proceedings may significantly assist parties and counsel in case management and the preparation of submissions. By frontloading factual and legal analysis, AI can help claimants prepare more comprehensive Statements of Claim and respondents more complete Statements of Defense, including counterclaims and prayers for relief, thereby ensuring that key issues are comprehensively addressed at an early stage of the proceedings. This reduces reliance on rejoinders, prevents the late introduction of new claims that might otherwise prolong the arbitration, or even trigger separate proceedings, and mitigates unnecessary costs.

AI can also expedite the drafting of subsequent submissions and post-hearing briefs, and more ambitiously, even draft awards, thereby further accelerating the overall procedure. A notable example is the adaptation of the Scott Schedule[90] for broader application with AI support.[91] Through AI-generated schedules, parties may swiftly consolidate the material points of contention along with references to the underlying evidence and legal authorities. This process enables arbitrators to focus more directly on the pivotal issues of the case, thereby promoting procedural efficiency without compromising the

---

87 CRESPO, A.I. in ADR: Fundamentals, CHARTERED INST. OF ARB. (Apr. 11, 2024) https://www.ciarb.org/media/qzzn2xxk/ai-in-adr-fundamentals-transcript.pdf>

88 REDDY/SINGH, Soft Law, Hard Justice: Regulating Artificial Intelligence in Arbitration, Contemporary Asia Arbitration Journal 2024 (no. 2), 191–236 p. 197.

89 ALETRAS et al., Predicting Judicial Decisions of the European Court of Human Rights: A Natural Language Processing Perspective, PeerJ Computer Science (2016) https://peerj.com/articles/cs-93/>.

90 WITTMANN, Using a 'Scott Schedule' in Arbitration, ADR Perspectives (2018), https://adric.ca/using-a- scott-schedule-in-arbitration/>.The Scott Schedule was originally developed by the Official Referee George Alexander Scott (1862–1933) for use in construction disputes, but it is now used in a wide variety of other cases.

91 ICC Commission on Arbitration and ADR Report, Construction Industry Arbitrations – Recommended Tools and Techniques for Effective Management (2019), paras 11.3–11.11.

parties' right to be heard.[92] The notion of parties submitting draft awards following hearings remains a subject of considerable controversy. However, it serves to illustrate the capacity of AI to transform procedural timelines and the framework of arbitral proceedings.[93]

AI tools have the capacity to meticulously analyse memorials, systematically identifying the disputed and undisputed facts pleaded by the parties involved. These tools can then organize the facts into concise tables and assess their legal strength, taking into account existing case law or witness statements.[94]

The utilization of AI in memorial scanning and fact classification primarily affects a party's internal case preparation. While this does not in itself amount to a violation of the opposing party's right to be heard, it may undermine the party's own ability to present its case effectively if relevant evidence or arguments are omitted or misclassified by the AI tool. In such instances, the risk is not one of external due process infringement, but rather of self-inflicted procedural disadvantage.

3. Communication and Language Assistance

International arbitration, by its very nature, is inherently cross-border. Consequently, it often involves parties from diverse cultural and linguistic backgrounds. This characteristic necessitates the handling of evidence and testimony in multiple languages. To ensure equitable dispute resolution, effective communication and understanding of legal content are essential. In this context, AI-enhanced machine translation technologies, such as DeepL[95] and Google Translate[96], have become indispensable tools. These platforms leverage artificial neural networks and deep learning algorithms to provide precise and context-aware translations of legal documents and communications. This

---

92 KIRBY, see fn. 81, p. 664. As discussed by the ICC Special Commission, the Scott Schedule is useful for a schedule to be prepared (by the parties or the tribunal, or both) after the first exchange of evidence or before the hearing takes place, so as to find out what needs investigating and deciding. It is particularly helpful on matters of valuation and quantification.

93 KIRBY, see fn. 81, p. 662.

94 EFSTATHIOU / APOSTOL, Arbitration Tech Toolbox: Will ChatGPT Change International Arbitration As We Know It? In: Kluwer Arbitration Blog, 26 February 2023, https://arbitrationblog.kluwerarbitration.com/2023/02/26/arbitration-tech-toolbox-will-chatgpt-change-international-arbitration-as-we-know-it/>.

95 DEEPL, https://www.deepl.com/en/translator>.

96 GOOGLE Translate, https://translate.google.com.

capability enables participants to engage meaningfully in proceedings and promotes fairness and impartiality across language barriers.[97]

These tools also enable non-native speakers, elderly individuals, and persons with disabilities, who might otherwise be unable or unwilling to pursue valid claims of low monetary value due to the need to travel, testify in person against brokers or corporate representatives, or directly present their case to professional arbitrators, to communicate their positions with greater clarity and confidence. AI-based simplification engines have the potential to further mitigate the rhetorical disadvantages experienced by counsel who are linguistically disadvantaged. In this manner, AI technologies contribute to ensuring equality of arms and help prevent any party from being procedurally sidelined due to linguistic complexity.[98]

Lastly, as the cost of AI-enhanced technologies decreases, specialized hearing and evidence presentation platforms will become more affordable for medium, boutique, and independent practitioners. This development has the potential to enhance accessibility to arbitration services for a wider range of parties.[99]

B. Implications for Arbitrators

1. Procedural Efficiency and Tribunal Management

AI tools offer arbitrators valuable support in procedural management. Automated transcription, summarization, and case clustering streamline administrative tasks. As envisaged by legal futurist Richard Susskind, systematisation of workflows, empowers arbitration practitioners to create structured and repeatable processes for handling cases, ensuring consistency, and reducing the risk of errors.[100]

In document-intensive proceedings like arbitration AI tools enhance efficiency and decision-making. AI can assist in searching and indexing large document sets based on semantic meaning, enabling arbitrators to quickly locate relevant facts or sections even during hearings. They are also able to compare content across documents, expert reports, revealing evidentiary inconsistencies or overlapping interests. Beside this, some specialized platforms allow

97 CHAN/GORE/JIANG, see fn. 3, p. 271.
98 BROYDE/MEI, Don't Kill the Baby: The Case for AI in Arbitration (August 25, 2024), p. 25. <https://ssrn.com/abstract=4936638 or http://dx.doi.org/10.2139/ssrn.4936638>.
99 CHAN/GORE/JIANG, see fn. 3, p .289.
100 SUSSKIND, Tomorrow's Lawyers: An Introduction To Your Future 47 (3d ed. 2023) as cited by CHAN/GORE/JIANG, see fn. 3, p. 290.

contract analysis by identifying dispute resolution clauses dispersed throughout complex agreements. Furthermore, AI can generate detailed document summaries to guide neutrals efficiently through extensive records, and even produce chronological timelines by extracting and organizing key dates from the document set.[101]

By expediting document review and filtering repetitive filings, AI allows arbitrators to concentrate on substantive analysis. AI-generated hearing summaries, when used carefully, may assist arbitrators in structuring orders or drafting procedural directions. These tools can improve efficiency, reduce delays, and lower costs,[102] thus indirectly reinforcing the right to be heard through timely justice.[103]

Some commentators[104] have observed shortcomings in the way arbitrators engage with written submissions, which may raise due process concerns. For example, Lucy Reed's "Reed Retreat"[105] and Kirby's commentary suggest that certain arbitrators read submissions only shortly before the hearing or

---

101 EVANS/ GUILLON/ LOSEY/ WASHINGTON/ YANCEY, see fn. 47, p. 2. For the results of an empirical study comparing different AI instruments (Casetext's CoCounsel, Anthropic's Claude Pro, and OpenAI's ChatGPT-4) according to their functions and outputs, see pages: 2-15. 1. These capabilities streamline preparatory work, real-time case management, and evidence analysis, offering substantial procedural benefits when used with appropriate oversight.

102 MALHOUTRA/AHMAD, Artificial Intelligence and International Arbitration, Revista Novos Estudos Jurídicos 2022 (no. 2), pp. 258-281, p. 268-271.

103 CIHANOVÁ, The Role of Artificial Intelligence in Alternative Dispute Resolution, Acta Facultatis Iuridicae Universitatis Comenianae 2023, p. 65.

104 LEGUM, The Ten Commandments of Written Advocacy in International Arbitration, 29 Arb. Int'l1 (2013), doi: 10.1093/arbint/29.1.1; RISSE, An Inconvenient Truth: The Complexity Problem and Limits to Justice, 35 Arb. Int'l 292–293 (2019), doi: 10.1093/arbint/aiz017; GEISINGER, President's Message: A 'Clarion Call' Seconded, 33 ASA Bull. 731, 735–737 (2015); RIVKIN, Keynote Address: A New Contract between Arbitrators and Parties, 18 Asian Disp. Rev. 4, 10 (2016), all as cited by KIRBY, International Arbitration and Artificial Intelligence: Ideas to Improve the Written Phase of Arbitral Proceedings, Journal of International Arbitration 2023 (no. 6), p. 658, 659.

105 REED, Tribunal Decision-Making: Art, Science, Sport, Kaplan Lecture (2012) as cited by KIRBY, see fn. 81, p. 657, 658. As to "Reed Retreat", KIRBY states: *"Lucy Reed has proposed the Reed Retreat where the arbitrators gather in advance of the hearing to discuss the issues they'd like the parties to address. The Retreat serves to prod the arbitrator's conscience and encourages every member of the tribunal to read the written submissions in anticipation of the conversation with the other members of the tribunal."*

scan them selectively, potentially leading to procedural inefficiencies and undermining informed decision-making.[106]

2. Decision Support and Predictive Analysis

AI systems can assist arbitrators by generating draft procedural orders, cost allocation scenarios, or timelines based on similar past cases. Pattern recognition algorithms are utilized to analyse individual cases, with the objective of detecting similarities and differences in data patterns concerning court decisions and arbitral awards. These tools facilitate the identification of pertinent case law, the detection of conflicts of interest among arbitrators, and the evaluation of the consistency of awards and decisions. Some other tools integrate statistical models to predict settlement windows or likely outcomes by employing historical data to forecast future outcomes.[107]

On the other hand, studies on decision outcome prediction have achieved remarkable accuracy rates of 70–80 percent; however, these studies are encumbered by significant limitations. A thorough examination of the methodology and assumptions employed reveals concerns regarding the assertion that these models have the capacity to facilitate ex ante outcome predictions.[108]

With the assistance of such tools, AI may enable arbitrators to prescience the possible factual outcomes of their awards, based on historical cases and jurisprudential data. In other words, AI can be used to predict the chances of an award being annulled, denied enforcement or voluntarily complied with. This may allow arbitrators to draft their awards in ways that ensure their longevity and compliance.[109] However, the use of such decision support tools must be carefully constrained[110] as it risks undermining the individualization of justice. Arbitrators must retain full discretion, and any automated input must remain contestable to avoid AI-driven biases.

---

106 KIRBY, see fn. 81, p. 658.

107 CHAN/GORE/JIANG, see fn. 43, p .268.

108 SCHERER, see fn. 53, p. 31

109 LEONARDO/MCMURTRIE, Arbitration Tech Toolbox: Will ChatGPT Change International Arbitration as We Know It?, Kluwer Arbitration Blog, February 26, 2023, https://arbitrationblog.kluwerarbitration.com/2023/02/26/arbitration-tech-toolbox-will-chatgpt-change-international-arbitration-as-we-know-it/>.

110 GICQUELLO, Artificial Intelligence in International Arbitration, Oxford Handbook of International Arbitration, 2020, pp. 591-616, https://doi.org/10.1093/law/9780198796190.003.0025>.

The use of AI tools carries the risk of overlooking the unique evidential and factual circumstances of each case. While every dispute requires an individualized assessment, AI systems may generalize on the basis of algorithmic patterns, thereby focusing on certain elements while disregarding others. Such omissions could ultimately affect the outcome of the proceedings and risk encroaching upon the parties' right to be heard.

A further concern arises when AI is used to analyse and predict the outcome of an arbitration based on the information, documents, and arguments within the case. In such instances, the risk exists that the AI may develop a bias depending on how the prompts are framed by the arbitrators. Instead of uncovering an objective truth, the AI might align with the perspective it has been most frequently directed to process, for example, the claimant's arguments. This could result in AI inadvertently shaping the case outcome in a way that favours one side, not because of the merits of the dispute but due to the way the queries were posed during the fact-evidence checking process. These risks underscore the importance of ensuring that AI-assisted analysis remains as neutral as possible and that arbitrators remain vigilant to such potential biases in order to preserve fairness and impartiality in their final decisions. A recent article suggests that *"AI models are also able to learn based on feedback given by human reviewers and while it may seem that ChatGPT is merely predicting, rather than reasoning, this may be incorrect. Microsoft's researchers*[111] *considered that ChatGPT's exam performances indicated core mental capabilities such as reasoning, creativity and deduction"*[112].

This observation underscores that AI tools do not merely generate neutral predictions but are shaped by the prompts and feedback provided during their use. In the arbitral context, this means that an AI tool analyzing a case file may adapt its output to the specific way questions are framed by the arbitrators or counsel, thereby influencing the result. As commentators note, research has suggested that systems such as ChatGPT exhibit capabilities akin to reasoning and deduction. This further illustrates the considerable risk that AI-assisted analysis may replicate prompt-driven biases, thereby undermining the expectation of objective assessment.

---

111 BUBECK, et al., 'Sparks of Artificial General Intelligence: Early experiments with GPT-4', Microsoft, March 2023, http://www.microsoft.com/en-us/research/publication/sparks-of-artificial-general-intelligence-early-experiments-with-gpt-4/, quoted in LIMOND/CALTHROP, see fn. 39.

112 LIMOND/CALTHROP, see fn. 39.

3. *Bias Detection and Conflict Checks*

AI tools are increasingly being deployed to detect potential arbitrator bias based on past awards, language patterns, or party appointments. For example, an AI system may flag an arbitrator who consistently rules in favour of claimants in investment disputes or who exhibits repeated language patterns suggesting predispositions toward certain procedural arguments.[113] These technologies can enhance transparency in tribunal constitution by identifying previously undisclosed affiliations, repeat appointments, or systemic preferences that may otherwise go unnoticed through manual checks.

However, it is imperative to exercise discernment when interpreting these insights derived from AI. An overreliance on the presumed neutrality of algorithms may obscure underlying biases embedded in the training data. To illustrate this point, consider a dataset comprising past awards that predominantly reflects systemic inequalities, such as outcomes historically biased in favour of certain types of parties. In such cases, AI predictions are likely to replicate and reinforce these patterns. Therefore, although AI can function as a beneficial instrument in the processes of conflict checking and bias detection, the presence of human oversight remains indispensable for the critical evaluation of the relevance and credibility of findings generated by AI in the context of the appointment process.

The IBA Guidelines on Conflicts of Interest in International Arbitration provide a well-recognized framework for disclosure and impartiality, which AI tools may complement by extending the scope and speed of conflict checks. In practice, AI can scan vast datasets, including prior appointments, academic publications, and professional affiliations, to uncover potential conflicts that might escape traditional manual review. AI use may reinforce the disclosure obligations embedded in the Guidelines by making conflict checks both more comprehensive and more efficient. However, in line with the Guidelines' emphasis on fairness and transparency, any AI-derived findings should be disclosed to the parties and remain subject to adversarial scrutiny. In addition to this, cognitive biases inherent in human decision-making pose a significant threat to the integrity of fact-finding in international arbitration. Arbitrators, like all individuals, are prone to unconscious cognitive distortions that can affect their evaluation of evidence, potentially leading to decisions that appear reasoned but are in fact skewed by subjective influ-

113 Malhoutra/Ahmad, see fn. 106, p. 271.

ences.[114] If these risks are not addressed, the fundamental guarantees[115] underpinning the parties' right to be heard may be compromised.

In order to address the dangers posed by such cognitive biases, procedural safeguards must be rigorously applied, particularly in response to the challenges posed by the growing influence of AI in arbitration. Because human arbitrators are prone to unconscious cognitive biases when assessing evidence, there is an increased risk that some arguments or evidence may not be objectively or fully considered. Rigorous application of existing evidentiary standards helps ensure that each party's submissions are fairly examined and weighed. These measures aim to reinforce impartial fact-finding and preserve the integrity of the decision-making process in international arbitration.

In addition to stricter procedural safeguards, AI tools themselves can assist in promoting neutrality in the evaluation of written submissions. The cautious use of AI by arbitral tribunals to organize, categorize, and summarize evidence may help reduce the influence of cognitive biases, such as confirmation and framing effects.[116] By providing a more objective structuring of the case file, AI can help arbitrators avoid premature formation of views based on selectively persuasive narratives. However, while AI can serve as a valuable support in enhancing procedural neutrality, it cannot replace the arbitrators' obligation to independently assess the evidence.

4. *Virtual Hearings and Remote Management*

Particularly during and following the COVID-19 pandemic and lockdown, AI technologies have emerged as pivotal components, amplifying the efficacy, security, and accessibility of virtual arbitration processes, thereby revealing newfound potentials in the realm of dispute resolution. SAC[117], ICC[118] and

---

114 HORNIKX, Cultural Differences in Perceptions of Strong and Weak Arguments, in COLE (Ed.), The Roles of Psychology in International Arbitration (Kluwer Law International 2017); SCHAUER, The Role of Rules in the Law of Evidence, in DAHLMAN/STEIN/TUZET, (eds), Philosophical Foundations of Evidence Law (Virginia Public Law and Legal Theory Paper Series, OUP 2021), as cited by BARTKUS, AI v. Arbitrator: How can the Exclusion of Evidence Increase the Appointments of the Arbitrators?, 2023 1(18) Access to Justice in Eastern Europe, pp. 111-124, p. 113-115, https://doi.org/10.33327/ AJEE-18-6.1-a000114>.

115 See Chapter III/B.

116 BARTKUS, see fn. 120, p. 111-124.

117 Art. 27 (2) of the Swiss Rules (2021). The previous Rules had also allowed witness examination by videoconference Art. 25(4) but the 2021 amendment clarified that any hearings may be held in person or remotely by videoconference or other appropriate

many other institutions[119] provided further guidance on the use of technologies for virtual hearings.

To illustrate this, Art. 26(1) of the 2021 ICC Rules expressly authorizes tribunals to conduct hearings not only in person but also by videoconference or *"other appropriate means of communication."* That provision also clarifies that the arbitral tribunal, after consulting the parties, may decide on the format of the hearing, taking into account the relevant circumstances, fairness of the proceedings, and equal treatment of the parties. It expressly allows hearings not only by videoconference but also by telephone or "other appropriate means of communication," thereby ensuring flexibility and avoiding prejudice against parties with limited access to costly technologies or high-speed internet. Notably, the Rule does not presume in-person hearings as the default, reflecting a broader shift towards virtual hearings even in the post-pandemic context.[120]

In practice, parties and counsel are now expected to address logistical issues such as videoconferencing capabilities for witnesses, secure channels of communication, and adaptations to hearing strategy, thereby reflecting the increased flexibility and procedural efficiency afforded by virtual hearings.[121] The procedural objections made by the parties against holding the hearing via video conferencing were also rejected by the Courts and the set aside requests were rejected.[122] As Born states: *"A 'remote hearing' is, in every meaningful*

---

means, as decided by the arbitral tribunal after consultation with the parties Art. 27(2). See further amendments in 2021: RUSCH/MÖHLER/CHEVALLEY, Swiss arbitration revamped: new Swiss Arbitration Centre, revised Swiss Rules of International Arbitration 2021, and launch of Swiss arbitration platform, https://pestalozzilaw.com/en/insights/news/legal-insights/swiss-arbitration-revamped-new-swiss-arbitration-centre-revised-swiss-rules-international-arbitration-2021-and-launch-swiss-arbitration-platform/.

118 ICC Commission Report, see fn. 60, R 6.2.2, p. 36

119 ICC, WIPO Center, JAMS, AAA-ICDR, and the International Institute for Conflict Prevention & Resolution (CPR) are some of the institutions that allow hearings via videoconference.

120 Leoveanu/Giosan, The 2021 ICC Arbitration Rules: Changes to the Arbitral Tribunal's Powers, January 4, 2021, https://legalblogs.wolterskluwer.com/arbitration-blog/the-2021-icc-arbitration-rules-changes-to-the-arbitral-tribunals-powers/.

121 TAN/BETANELI, The 2021 ICC Rules: reflections on key changes and the ICC Secretariat's guidance note, 29 January, 2021, https://blog.freshfields.us/post/102gpss/the-2021-icc-rules-reflections-on-key-changes-and-the-icc-secretariats-guidance.

122 Decision by Oberster Gerichtshof [OGH] (Supreme Court) 23 July 2020, ONc 3/20s No. 18 (Austria). The Supreme Court heard a challenge to an arbitral award because the tribunal had decided to conduct a remote hearing via videoconference over the respondents' objection. Although the respondents claimed the conduct of a remote hearing had violated their right to be treated equally and fairly, the Austrian Supreme Court rejected the challenge because using videoconference does not violate Art. 6 of

sense, a 'hearing'"[123]. AI-driven platforms like Zoom and Microsoft Teams, or specialized legal conference tools, offer intelligent scheduling, speech and face recognition, enhanced security features, and advanced interaction capabilities, ensuring a smooth and secure environment for conducting hearings.[124]

While virtual hearings supported by AI-driven platforms enhance accessibility and efficiency, their legitimacy ultimately depends on safeguarding the parties' right to be heard. By ensuring that parties can effectively present their case, examine witnesses, and respond to opposing arguments in a technologically mediated environment, tribunals and institutions prove that remote hearings, assisted by AI, do not diminish but may rather strengthen the procedural guarantees central to arbitration.

5. Evidentiary Processes and Disclosure Enhanced through AI

AI technologies, particularly machine learning and natural language processing, offer tools for faster case analysis by handling large volumes of information, and detecting patterns. The ICC, therefore, introduced revisions to its Arbitration Rules effective from 1 January 2021. ICC emphasized improved case management and more efficient dispute resolution processes. The rules also granted greater flexibility and transparency in evidentiary matters, empowering tribunals to determine the appropriate level of scrutiny for each

the ECHR even if one of the parties does not agree to the remote hearing as cited by OLIVEIRA see fn. 2, p. 65; In "Sky Power v Iraero" (HKCFI, 2023) *"The Hong Kong Court of First Instance determined that an objection to a fully virtual hearing is insubstantial grounds to resist the enforcement of an arbitration award. The court underscored the pandemic-induced acceptability of remote hearings and upheld that arbitrators hold discretion in case management, unbounded by prior agreements on semi-virtual hearings."* as cited by RAUCH, see fn. 69, p. 28.

123 BORN, see fn.2: further states "in most cases, the essential attributes of a traditional in-person hearing – real time interaction with the tribunal, witnesses and parties, with both visual and audio connections – are provided by a remote hearing."

124 ZOOM AI Companion, <https://explore.zoom.us/en/ai-assistant/>. Of note, the recently released Zoom AI Companion can enhance the efficiency and clarity of virtual arbitration hearings by enabling participants to create summarizations of hearings in real-time and streamline communication with intelligent chat and email composition. Additionally, with Smart Recording, parties can easily revisit critical parts of hearings through organized chapters and highlighted segments.

piece of evidence.[125] AI-enhanced document review tools are well-positioned to support these developments by automating document/evidence analysis and accelerating the identification of relevant information.[126]

Such an extensive use of AI tools has also led to a broader application of the IBA Rules on the Taking of Evidence in International Arbitration. By enabling the processing and organization of substantial evidentiary records, AI assists tribunals in giving proper consideration to each party's submissions.[127] In practice, AI can support document production (for example by organizing and refining Redfern Schedules), privilege review, multilingual translations and transcriptions, and even fraud detection by identifying suspicious patterns across financial documents. These applications can significantly strengthen evidentiary processes and contribute to safeguarding the parties' right to be heard. However, important concerns are raised: excessive reliance on automated classifications may obscure relevant evidence, unequal access to advanced AI may undermine equality of arms, and inaccuracies in translation or privilege review may prejudice a party's case. Therefore, AI must be used with caution, and tribunals must ensure transparency, adversarial scrutiny and procedural safeguards.

AI's integration into evidentiary processes also raises the prospect of AI-generated evidence. While tribunals are unlikely for now to treat ChatGPT outputs as probative, examples such as AI-generated minutes or even testimony before a UK parliamentary inquiry demonstrate that parties may increasingly seek to rely on such material.[128] This development highlights difficult questions regarding evidential weight, accuracy and reliability, particularly in light of the well-documented risk of hallucinations, fabricated sources, and cultural or

---

[125] See further information: BSG Resources Limited, Vale S. A. v Republic of Guinea (ICSID, [2022]), "The case is an example of how AI-powered e-discovery tools were significantly leveraged to handle a substantial volume of evidence and disclosure documents. The case revolved around a dispute concerning a mining concession in Guinea, involving allegations of corruption related to the acquisition of mining rights. This arbitration procedure required the examination of an extensive amount of documents and electronic data, which led the tribunal and the parties involved to adopt sophisticated e-discovery software. These tools were instrumental in searching, filtering, and organizing the extensive digital data and documentation, which were disclosed by the parties, allowing the tribunal to manage the evidentiary material efficiently." as cited by RAUCH, see fn. 69, p. 29.

[126] RAUCH, see fn. 69, p. 28.

[127] INTERNATIONAL BAR ASSOCIATION, Rules on the Taking of Evidence in International Arbitration (17 December 2020).

[128] LANDI, 'Ai-Da robot makes history by giving evidence to parliamentary inquiry', The Independent, 11 October 2022, http://www.independent.co.uk/news/uk/politics/house-of-lords-technology-liberal-democrat-b2200496.html.

data-driven biases. As the GAR commentary notes, generative AI tends to produce outputs that are only as reliable as the underlying data and the prompts provided, which underscores the need for verification and adversarial scrutiny.[129] These accuracy concerns are compounded by broader risks of confidentiality, privacy and authenticity, discussed below.

Evidentiary risks in AI use also extend to confidentiality, privacy and authenticity. Uploading sensitive arbitration records to AI platforms may endanger client confidentiality and expose proceedings to cyberattacks, as demonstrated by past breaches of arbitral institutions. Regulatory initiatives such as the European Union's Artificial Intelligence Act (EU AI Act)[130], as well as soft law instruments including the CIArb and SVAMC Guidelines, stress the importance of human oversight and disclosure of AI use. Equally pressing is the risk of AI-generated forgeries and deepfakes, which could undermine the integrity of witness evidence and remote hearings. To counter these threats, commentators suggest procedural safeguards such as requiring expert authentication of digital evidence or mandating disclosure of AI involvement, thereby preserving the parties' right to be heard and the overall legitimacy of arbitral proceedings.[131]

A further dimension arises from regulatory frameworks such as the EU AI Act. The Act explicitly classifies AI systems used in the administration of justice and democratic processes as "high-risk," thereby subjecting them to stringent requirements, including reliance on high-quality datasets, human oversight, and demonstrable robustness, security, and accuracy.[132] In the arbitral evidentiary context, these safeguards are particularly significant: disclosure platforms or AI tools used to organise, translate, or classify evidence must comply with such standards to avoid reinforcing systemic biases or compromising the equality of arms, as highlighted in the broader concerns of evidentiary fairness. While these obligations may initially slow the deployment of advanced AI tools, they ultimately aim to bolster confidence in the reliability of AI-assisted evidentiary processes and thereby reinforce the parties' right to be heard.[133]

---

129 LIMOND/CALTHROP, see fn. 39.

130 EU AI Act entered into force on 1 August 2024 as the world's first comprehensive regulation on AI

131 LIMOND/CALTHROP, see fn. 39; SCHİLKE/REİMANN, The transparency dilemma: How AI disclosure erodes trust, Organizational Behavior and Human Decision Processes, Volume 188, May 2025, 104405 https://www.sciencedirect.com/science/article/pii/S0749597825000172. And also see, Such as, SVAMC, Guidelines, Guides 3 and 7; CIArb Guideline Guides 4 and 7, SCC Guide

132 LIMOND/CALTHROP, see fn. 39.

133 LIMOND/CALTHROP, see fn. 39.

C. Implications for Arbitral Institutions

1. Arbitrator Selection and Case Allocation

The existence of a technological tool that can assist in identifying arbitrators with the necessary skills and relevant qualifications for a given case is of growing importance. While institutional use to support the nomination process remains at an exploratory stage, commentators have suggested that algorithmic tools could one day assist in arbitrator selection by analyzing factors such as prior appointments, reasoned awards, subject-matter expertise, and language proficiency.[134] When applied responsibly, such tools may enhance party confidence and reduce implicit bias. However, the risk of data bias and systemic exclusion remains, as algorithmic outputs are ultimately dependent on the quality and neutrality of the underlying data. [135]

Nomination committees within arbitral institutions- such as the Swiss National Committee of the ICC- may benefit from AI-supported platforms in establishing candidate lists for institutional appointments. By taking into account criteria such as subject-matter expertise, prior case experience, linguistic skills, availability, potential conflicts of interest, and diversity considerations, AI could help committees generate balanced rosters that reflect the demands of each case. Such applications would promote transparency and efficiency, while also addressing concerns about repeat appointments and unconscious bias.

At the same time, the appointment process is not purely technical. Nomination committee members consistently emphasize the importance of trust and distinctive qualifications- often referred to colloquially as *"unique selling propositions" (USPs)*- such as foreign legal degrees, multiple bar admissions, international practice experience, or sector-specific expertise.[136] While AI can systematize such information, it cannot substitute the relational and reputational dynamics that underpin committee decision-making. In practice, plat-

---

[134] JOHNS, Artificial Intelligence in the Selection of Arbitrators: Whether to Trust the Machine, ITA in Review 2024, Vol. 6 Issue 3, 1 et seq, et seq, https://www.itainreview.org/articles/2024/vol6/Issue3/artificial-intelligence-in-the-selection-of-arbitrators-whether-to-trust-the-machine.html.

[135] ONYEFULU/KINGSTON, AI-Based Technologies in International Arbitration: An Exploratory Study on the Practicability of Applying AI Tools on International Arbitration, World Academy of Science, Engineering and Technology International Journal of Computer and Information Engineering, 2024, pp, 651-656, p. 652. https://www.researchgate.net/publication/385586785>.

[136] Remarks delivered at the Introduction Event of the ICC Swiss National Committee Nomination Members, Zurich, 21 August 2025.

forms such as ASA Profiles[137] already serve as valuable repositories of arbitrator experience and qualifications, enabling parties and institutions to access structured information on expertise, prior appointments, and language skills. These platforms illustrate how digital tools can enhance transparency and accessibility in arbitrator selection, and they may eventually provide the empirical basis for more advanced AI-supported case allocation. Nonetheless, responsiveness, professional reputation, and visibility within the arbitral community remain decisive factors in appointments.

Accordingly, AI has the potential to complement but not replace the work of nomination committees. Technological tools may enhance fairness and consistency, particularly by reducing information asymmetry and improving conflict checks. Yet human supervision remains indispensable to ensure that institutional appointments reflect not only efficiency and transparency but also the relational aspects of reputation, trust, and professional engagement that safeguard the legitimacy of arbitral proceedings.

Monitoring Timelines and Ensuring Compliance

AI can create interactive timelines, charts, and graphs that illustrate the progression of events or the significance of certain data points.[138] Timeline tracking systems powered by AI can issue automated alerts and assist case managers in ensuring timely administration. By reducing delays and missed deadlines, this contributes to procedural efficiency and supports the parties' right to be heard without undue delay. Arbitrators and parties can access exhibits in real-time during hearings, facilitating a deeper understanding of the evidence presented.

During hearings, real-time transcription and translation powered by AI will enable seamless communication among parties from different linguistic backgrounds. This approach is expected to expedite proceedings and ensure that all participants have equal access to the arbitration process, regardless of language barriers.[139]

---

137 See Swiss Arbitration Association (ASA) Profiles Database, https://profiles.swissarbitration.org/

138 CHAN/GORE/JIANG, see fn. 47, p. 289.

139 CHAN/GORE/JIANG, see fn. 47, p. 289.

2. *Adoption of AI Platforms by Arbitral Institutions and Service Providers*

A growing number of arbitral institutions and service providers are developing AI-supported platforms tailored for dispute resolution. In Switzerland, the Swiss Arbitration Association (ASA), which provides professional support and resources to the SAC, the core institutional body of the Swiss arbitration framework[140], has developed two important digital resources. First is the Arbitration Toolbox[141] which is designed to enhance efficiency while preserving procedural fairness, particularly safeguarding the parties' right to be heard. Secondly, in collaboration with Jus Connect,[142] ASA also launched the world's first "Global Tribunal Secretary Platform", providing an AI-assisted, verified directory of tribunal secretaries.[143]

As part of the broader effort to uphold fundamental procedural rights in arbitration proceedings, this Platform fosters transparency, promotes diversity, and supports procedural integrity by enabling arbitral tribunals to select qualified tribunal secretaries through objective and accessible processes.[144] Jus Connect automates minute-taking, facilitates scheduling, and ensures procedural transparency for tribunal secretaries.

Similarly, the ICC has introduced in 2022 '*Case Connect*', a digital case management platform enabling secure document exchange, timeline monitoring, and streamlined communication between parties, tribunals, and the ICC Secretariat. By integrating automated organization and oversight features, this

---

[140] SAC established in 2021 as the successor to the Swiss Chambers' Arbitration Institution (SCAI), administers cases under the Swiss Rules. It operates as a Swiss limited company, with the ASA as majority shareholder and the Swiss Chambers of Commerce as further shareholders. For further information, see: Swiss Rules of International Arbitration, Introduction.

[141] https://toolbox.swissarbitration.org/toolbox/case-overview>.The Arbitration Toolbox provides a structured decision-tree framework offering practical checklists, templates, and procedural guidance to users across all stages of arbitration.

[142] https://jusconnect.com/en/directory/arbitrators/all>.

[143] https://www.swissarbitration.org/asa-announces-strategic-partnership-with-jus-connect-to-launch-tribunal-secretary-platform/.

[144] JUS CONNECT, Tribunal Secretary Platform, https://jusconnect.com/en/tribunal secretaryplatform>. This platform offers a glimpse into the future of institutional AI usage, where procedural coordination and secretarial functions are supported by intelligent interfaces.

platform strengthens procedural efficiency and transparency, thereby indirectly safeguarding the parties' right to be heard.[145]

On the other hand, in respect to the data security and privacy, parties must be assured that their confidential data under prevailing data privacy regulations, such as the right to access, rectify, and delete their data, are maintained.[146] AI has the potential to bolster the security of sensitive information employed in arbitration proceedings. This can be achieved through the implementation of AI-driven systems that are capable of detecting and preventing data breaches, as well as unauthorized access. Additionally, the integration of AI into arbitration processes can ensure compliance with pertinent data protection regulations.[147]

Jus Mundi's *Jus AI* suite provides legal research and drafting tools designed specifically for arbitration professionals, leveraging multilingual NLP capabilities, and its proprietary arbitration database.[148] Similarly JAMS *Next* initiative includes AI-enhanced tools for conflict checks and automated transcription services.[149]

Such AI-enabled platforms provide a secure, centralized, cloud-based environment in which parties, tribunals, and arbitral institutions can collaborate seamlessly from anywhere in the world. By integrating enhanced e-filing, secure digital document management, customized user portals, and financial oversight tools into a more intuitive interface, these systems significantly refine case management processes and reinforce transparency and efficiency in international arbitration.

D. Specific Procedural Risks and Challenges in AI-Assisted Arbitration

Integrating AI into arbitral proceedings introduces distinct procedural risks and challenges that extend beyond traditional due process concerns such as

---

145 ICC, Case Connect – Secure Online Case Management, https://iccwbo.org/news-publications/news/icc-launches-icc-case-connect-secure-online-case-management-made-easy. See also Opus 2, *The International Chamber of Commerce launches next-generation digital case management platform for dispute resolution services*, 1 April 2025, https://www.opus2.com/news/icc-launches-icc-case-connect-powered-by-opus2/ .

146 RAUCH, see fn. 69, p. 24, p. 46

147 Chatterjee/Singhania/Sharma, see fn. 77.

148 JUS MUNDI, Jus AI, https://jusmundi.com/en/jus-ai.

149 JAMS, JAMS Next: AI-Powered ADR Services, https://www.jamsadr.com/news/2024/jams-leads-adr-into-ai-age-with-launch-of-jams-next-ai-powered-services.

impartiality, fairness, and equal treatment of the parties.[150] While AI can enhance efficiency and even support impartiality, its use also raises fundamental questions about procedural legitimacy and perceived neutrality, the risks of delegation and non-human decision-making, and the so-called “black box” problem of explainability and reasoned decision-making. In addition, information asymmetry and unequal access to AI tools, as well as linguistic and cultural misrepresentation, may undermine equality of arms between the parties.[151] Concerns regarding the lack of contestability and transparency further complicate parties’ ability to scrutinize or challenge AI-assisted outputs. Finally, ethical and legal challenges underscore the need for robust safeguards. The following sub-chapters explore each of these seven categories of risks and assess their implications for parties, counsel, arbitrators, and arbitral institutions.

1. Procedural Legitimacy and Perceived Neutrality

The perception of fairness is as critical as fairness itself. Use of AI tools must be disclosed to parties to maintain confidence in the proceedings. A tribunal’s legitimacy depends not only on formal neutrality but on transparent methods. Parties must be assured that no invisible digital force is substituting human deliberation. To preserve the integrity of arbitral proceedings, they must remain explainable, auditable, and contestable.

The effectiveness and reliability of an AI system are contingent upon the accessibility of substantial data sets for training purposes. In the context of arbitration, unlike in litigation,. the pool of available awards remains limited because most arbitral awards are confidential and decentralized.[152] While certain data sets are accessible, such as investment arbitration awards[153], insti-

---

150 RIVKIN, Towards a New Paradigm in International Arbitration: The Town Elder Model Revisited, (2008) 24(3) Arbitration International, p. 375, 377: According to Rivkin, the legitimacy of international arbitration rests on (i) a fair and neutral process, (ii) conducted by intelligent and experienced arbitrators, (iii) resulting in a timely and well-reasoned decision, and (iv) benefiting from an effective enforcement mechanism.

151 FORTESE/HEMMI, see fn. 17, p. 111-112.

152 PAISLEY/SUSSMAN, see fn. 50, p. 37: The ICC, ICDR, SIAC, Stockholm Chamber, and Milan Chamber publish selected redacted awards with party consent, while the LCIA and Stockholm Chamber publish anonymized challenge decisions. HKIAC and SCAI do not proactively publish awards but allow publication upon request.

153 PRAŠTALO, Arbitration Tech Toolbox: AI as an Arbitrator – Overcoming the “Black Box” Challenge?, Kluwer Arbitration Blog, 23 August 2024, http://arbitrationblog.kluwerarbitration.com/2024/08/23/arbitration-tech-toolbox-ai-as-an-arbitrator-overcoming-the-black-box-challenge under [blog] >.

tutional summaries, or court judgments on setting-aside or enforcement proceedings, the majority of commercial arbitral awards remain confidential and fragmented. This scarcity of comprehensive data poses challenges for developing reliable AI training sets, particularly for predictive models. Furthermore, erroneous or inconsistent data can distort algorithmic outcomes, potentially leading to unfair adjudication.[154]

The implementation of data protection legislation, particularly the General Data Protection Regulation (GDPR), has further complicated this process by requiring the redaction of personal information.[155] Furthermore, the decentralized nature of arbitral awards, dispersed across various jurisdictions, contributes to the augmentation of costs and complexity in the process of assembling a data set that is suitable for AI training. In addition, because arbitral awards are often issued collectively by three-member tribunals, it is difficult to identify the individual contribution of each arbitrator. This lack of attribution limits the reliability of AI models that attempt to predict how a specific arbitrator might decide.[156]

Training AI arbitration tools exclusively on national laws and court judgments presents significant limitations, particularly regarding procedural issues such as the admissibility of evidence. The discrepancy between arbitration rules and court procedures in this regard is a notable concern. Moreover, this approach entails the potential for accelerating the judicialization of arbitration, a process in which arbitral proceedings increasingly mirror those of court litigation. Historically, arbitrators have exhibited a greater degree of procedural flexibility, particularly when granted the authority to determine matters *ex aequo et bono*. Excessive reliance on court-based training data has the potential to compromise the flexibility that is integral to arbitration, thereby diminishing its effectiveness.[157]

While the right to be heard is primarily invoked during the conduct of arbitral proceedings, concerns over procedural fairness may also arise at the enforcement stage, particularly where AI-generated financial assessments (e. g., interest calculations) are relied upon without adequate party involvement or verification. This underscores the necessity of ensuring that any AI-assisted

---

154 ONYEFULU/KINGSTON, see fn. 138, p. 654-655.

155 RYAN/BRINSON, "Putting the Artificial Intelligence in Alternative Dispute Resolution: How AI Rules Will Become ADR Rules," Amicus Curiae, Series 2 (Spring 2023), pp. 685–706, p. 696 ff. RYAN/BRINSON extensively discuss use of AI with regard to the EU GDPR which allows persons *"to refuse to be the subject of a decision based exclusively on automated processing..."*

156 PAISLEY/SUSSMAN, see fn. 50, p. 38.

157 PRAŠTALO, see fn. 131.

determination of interest, penalties, or enforcement parameters is explicitly disclosed and subject to input from the relevant parties. Such safeguards are especially important where the resulting figures could be contested as excessive, unforeseeable, or inconsistent with national enforcement regulations. Swiss case law, for example, illustrates how contested financial determinations can raise fairness concerns: the Federal Tribunal has held that the awarding of compound interest does not, in itself, breach public policy under Art. 190(2)(e) SPILA. In a 2023 case, the Geneva Surveillance Chamber upheld an attachment order based on a foreign arbitral award despite objections to compound interest, reiterating the Federal Tribunal's stance in 4A_634/2014.[158] This jurisprudence demonstrates that even traditional financial determinations can generate controversy at the enforcement stage, suggesting that AI-generated calculations could face similar scrutiny if not subject to disclosure and transparent party involvement.

2. Delegation and Non-Human Decision-Making

Generative AI tools such as ChatGPT and Claude, offer arbitrators significant support in drafting and document creation tasks. These tools can swiftly generate, summarize, and refine legal texts, enhancing time and resource efficiency, fostering creativity, and improving consistency in written outputs. Their potential applications in arbitration include drafting arbitration agreements, mediation clauses, pleadings, procedural orders, settlement agreements, and standard correspondence.[159] However, reliance on LLMs raises critical challenges regarding the accuracy and reliability of generated content, compliance with ethical and professional standards, and the necessity of maintaining human oversight. Arbitrators must carefully review AI-generated drafts, ensure alignment with legal and ethical norms, and remain fully responsible for the content and quality of all procedural documents.

While AI-generated consolidated lists of disputed issues could greatly assist arbitral tribunals in focusing their attention on the core matters requiring resolution, they should not replace the tribunal's obligation to engage fully with the parties' submissions. By enabling tribunals to identify and prioritize the most material issues, AI tools may enhance procedural efficiency; however,

---

158 Decision by Cour de Justice de Genève, DCSO/251/2023, 8 June 2023, consid. 2.2; referring to Swiss Federal Tribunal, Decision 4A_634/2014 of 21 May 2015, consid. 5.2.2.

159 EVANS/ GUILLON/ LOSEY/ WASHINGTON/ YANCEY, see fn. 47, p. 23-24.

arbitrators must continue to review the entire record to ensure that no substantive argument is overlooked.[160]

Current AI models can elevate probabilistic inferences to serve as the normative basis for legal decision-making. This raises critical concerns about determining future outcomes solely based on past data.[161] Particularly in today's context, where commercial relationships evolve rapidly and disputes increasingly arise from new types of evidence and facts, reliance on probabilistic reasoning may impair the appropriate analysis of novel circumstances. Such shortcomings risk undermining the parties' right to be heard by failing to adequately consider unique evidentiary material.

Using AI to pre-draft findings or procedural rulings also raises concern over whether the tribunal is truly 'hearing' the parties. If decisions are partially shaped by automated logic, but not manifestly disclosed by the arbitrators, the guarantee of human judgment is diluted.

With the assistance of AI tools, counsels can also generate post-hearing draft awards. Each side might prepare an award draft it wishes the tribunal to render. While such drafts could expedite the tribunal's deliberations and the preparation of its final award, they also risk tempting arbitrators to abdicate their responsibility to independently analyse and decide the case. Such a development would pose serious challenges to procedural integrity.[162]

3. *The Black Box Problem: Explainability and Reasoned Decision-Making*

If AI tools influence decision-making, parties must be able to understand how and why conclusions were reached. The effective participation of parties in arbitration depends on their ability to understand the reasoning behind decisions and to respond appropriately. For instance, if AI is used to support calculations of damages or to filter relevant evidence, parties must be given a transparent explanation of how these outputs were generated. [163]

---

160 KIRBY, see fn. 81, p. 664. Thus, while the use of AI in this context supports procedural economy, it must be carefully integrated so as not to compromise the fundamental guarantees embedded in the right to be heard.

161 SCHERER, see fn. 53, p. 31.

162 KIRBY, see fn. 81, p. 663.

163 SCHERER, see fn. 53, p. 31: "The need for reasoned decisions is likely to be an important barrier for AI-based legal decision-making. At least at the current technological level, it may be difficult to identify the factors that have led to a certain outcome prediction in case of black-boxed models"; Also see ALHASAN, Integrating AI Into

AI systems often operate through opaque decision-making processes, where it is difficult, even for developers, to explain the rationale behind a given output. This is widely referred to as a “black-box” problem, and is especially prevalent in Deep Learning models. The concern is heightened in arbitration because most national arbitration laws *(leges arbitri)* restrict courts from reviewing the merits of an award or the tribunal’s assessment of evidence. Parties therefore cannot rely on post-award judicial review to uncover or challenge opaque algorithmic reasoning.[164]

The opacity of algorithmic reasoning threatens the principle that decisions must be reasoned and understandable. A lack of transparency and clarity in reasoned awards could prevent a losing party from identifying possible grounds for annulment, or could even lead to refusal of enforcement under Art. V(1)(b) of the New York Convention, where violation of the right to be heard is invoked. To mitigate these risks, it is crucial to implement standards that promote explainability, accountability, and transparency in AI-assisted arbitration. The tribunal’s duty to articulate its reasoning cannot be delegated to a black-box model.[165]

4. *Information Asymmetry and Access Disparities*

Access to sophisticated AI tools is often conditioned by financial resources. When one party enjoys algorithmic advantages, such as faster data processing, superior document review, or advanced outcome prediction, this imbalance threatens the principle of equal treatment. Technology-rich counsel may outpace opponents not through legal skill or persuasive advocacy, but through computational capacity. Such disparities risk creating a digitally driven due process gap.

The utilization of a predictive algorithm in international arbitration further illustrates this concern. While these tools may enhance strategic case assessment, they also carry the risk of discouraging a weaker party from pursuing or fully engaging in arbitration if the algorithm suggests that defeat is inevitable. This is problematic because it undermines meaningful access to justice, erodes the right to be heard of the technologically weaker party, and distorts

Arbitration: Balancing Efficiency With Fairness and Legal Compliance Conflict Resolution Quarterly, 09 Jan. 2025,1-12, pp, 1-12, p. 4, <https://onlinelibrary.wiley.com/doi/10.1002/crq.21470.

164 REDDY/SINGH, see fn. 85, p. 206, https://papers.ssrn.com/sol3/papers.cfm?abstract_id=5038334.

165 ALHASAN, see fn. 179, p. 4.

equality of arms. If only one side has access to advanced predictive capabilities, arbitration risks degenerating into a contest of technological resources rather than legal merit.[166]

5. *Linguistic and Cultural Misrepresentation*

Linguistic and cultural diversity lies at the heart of international arbitration, where parties, counsel, and arbitrators frequently come from different legal traditions and backgrounds. Yet Natural Language Processing (NLP) systems, trained predominantly on Western legal corpora, often fail to interpret -or may misinterpret- non-standard argumentation styles, idiomatic expressions, metaphors, or culturally embedded references. This can lead to subtle distortions of meaning and mischaracterization of party submissions. Such algorithmic misreadings often risk reinforcing epistemic marginalization, whereby arguments from non-dominant linguistic or cultural contexts are systematically undervalued.[167] Ensuring diverse and representative training data and allowing human intervention are therefore indispensable to safeguarding equality of arms and the parties' right to be heard.

Empirical studies highlight these limitations. For example, a recent experimental comparison between AI tools and human referees revealed that while AI systems can efficiently tailor questions based on available information, they lack the capacity to exercise human judgment in context.[168] Unlike human arbitrators, AI currently remains limited in its ability to discern nuances, interpret non-verbal cues such as tone, demeanor, or body language, and make context-sensitive decisions. [169] In practice, these shortcomings underscore the necessity for sustained human oversight and discretion in arbitration proceedings. Without such safeguards, reliance on AI-generated documents or analyses risks undermining procedural fairness and eroding party confidence in the arbitral process.

---

166 ONYEFULU/KINGSTON, see fn. 138, p. 652.

167 HOWEIL et al., Reflective Design for Informal Participatory Algorithm Auditing, A Case Study with Emotion AI. In Nordic Conference on Human-Computer Interaction (NordiCHI) 2024, pp. 1-13, p. 6, https://doi.org/10.1145/3679318.3685411.

168 CARDOSO/CHAN/QUINTÃO/PEREIRA, Generative Artificial Intelligence and Legal Decision-Making, Global Trade and Customs Journal 2024, pp. 710–730, p. 719 https://justen.com.br/wp-content/uploads/2024/11/IE-231-Generative-Artificial-Intelligence-and-Legal-Decision-making.pdf.

169 RAUCH, see fn. 69, p. 24.

6. *Lack of Contestability and Transparency*

A major difficulty in using AI in international arbitration is the lack of interpretability and transparency behind AI-generated decisions. Although machine learning models can produce outcomes, they often fail to clearly explain their reasoning. When the reasonings for procedural or substantive decisions are not sufficiently clear, it becomes difficult, if not impossible, for parties to mount challenges.[170] Such opacity undermines contestability, breeds distrust among users, and slows the broader acceptance of AI technologies.

For AI to be trustworthy, any use by a tribunal must be disclosed to the parties. Arbitral institutions increasingly recognize this requirement. To illustrate, it is advised in the SVAMC Guidelines that *"decisions regarding disclosure of the use of AI tools shall be made on a case-by-case basis taking account of the relevant circumstances, including due process and any applicable privilege"*[171]. While acknowledging that some AI uses may be uncontroversial and may not require disclosure, the Guidelines also empower tribunals, parties, and institutions to demand disclosure or certification when appropriate. Relevant circumstances include the reliability of the technology, the accuracy of the specific tool, and its potential impact on the integrity of proceedings or evidence.[172] To preserve the integrity of arbitral proceedings, they must remain explainable, auditable, and contestable.[173]

Confidentiality and data usage policies should be clearly defined. Automated summaries and system-generated recommendations should remain subject to human control and parties ought to be informed of such uses. Data used in arbitration proceedings should be anonymized to protect confidentiality and fairness. Transparency in data handling is also a prerequisite for contestability: if parties cannot see how their information was processed, they cannot meaningfully challenge the outputs. Without adequate confidentiality and transparency safeguards, parties may hesitate to fully present their case, fear-

---

170 RAUCH, see fn. 69, p. 34.

171 SVAMC Guidelines, see fn. 3, Guideline 3.

172 CARDOSO/CHAN/QUINTÃO/PEREIRA, see fn. 188, p. 730.

173 While electronic submissions and cybersecurity protocols facilitate a more efficient workflow, they do not inherently ensure procedural fairness. If AI-assisted tools are used, without appropriate party disclosure, to analyse, categorize, or respond to evidence or submissions, this may impair a party's ability to effectively engage with the proceedings. Therefore, use of AI must be balanced with fundamental principles such as the right to be heard and equal treatment of the parties. AI's institutional use must also reflect the same principles of transparency, accountability, and due process that bind tribunals and counsels.

ing that disclosure of sensitive information or trade secrets could compromise their interests.

7. *Ethical and Legal Challenges*

In international arbitration, AI ethics refers to the application of widely accepted standards of fairness, transparency and accountability to the development, deployment, and use of AI technologies.[174] Adherence to these principles is crucial to ensure that AI use preserves human agency and respect for the parties' fundamental procedural rights.

As emphasized by the EU High-Level Expert Group Guidelines[175], the development and use of AI systems must guarantee human agency, technical robustness, data confidentiality, transparency, non-discrimination, societal well-being, and accountability throughout their entire lifecycle.[176] In arbitration, this implies that any use of AI by tribunals should be disclosed to the parties. Such disclosure is essential not only for safeguarding procedural fairness but also for upholding the legitimacy of the tribunal and preserving the integrity of the arbitral process.[177]

A detailed analysis of the use of AI in arbitration highlights some important ethical and legal challenges. One of the most pressing concerns relates to the opacity and limited interpretability of AI algorithms, which can lead to deci-

---

174 RAUCH, see fn. 69, p. 38.

175 Independent High-Level Expert Group on Artificial Intelligence, Ethics Guidelines for Trustworthy AI, (EU Ethics Guidelines) European Commission, (8 April 2019), pp. 1-39, <https://ec.europa.eu/futurium/en/ai-alliance-consultation.1.html.

176 EU Ethics Guidelines, see fn. 196, p. 14. Similarly the European Commission for the Efficiency of Justice (CEPEJ) adopted in 2018 five ethical principles for the use of AI in judicial systems, including ODR: respect for fundamental rights, non-discrimination, quality and security, transparency, impartiality and fairness, and user control. While CEPEJ recognized the potential of AI-assisted dispute resolution (AIDR) to enhance access to justice, it emphasized that users and deployers must assess the appropriateness and extent of AI integration to ensure that transparency, neutrality, and loyalty standards are maintained.

177 Ethical principles are especially more important today, when the line between truth and manufactured truth (post truth) has almost completely disappeared, and truth can change color, shape and form depending on who has the power to determine or impose what truth is. Moreover, the humanitarian realities of those who code AI algorithms, as well as the contributions of large segments of the public that feed into AI systems, are inevitably reflected in the development of AI itself. Consequently, the uncontrolled and unregulated use of AI is untenable.

sions being made without full transparency about the influencing factors.[178] This undermines fairness and accountability, especially where biases embedded in educational data are reproduced in outputs. Furthermore, the adoption of AI in arbitration raises sensitive issues of confidentiality and privacy, requiring strict safeguards to protect party information and maintain trust in the arbitral process.[179]

V. Conclusion

This research has explored how the increasing adoption of artificial intelligence (AI) in international arbitration is reshaping the parties' right to be heard and the procedural safeguards that underpin fair proceedings. The findings indicate that arbitral institutions, arbitrators, and counsel alike have begun to integrate AI-driven technologies into their practices. Institutions have issued guidelines and updated rules to enable greater efficiency; arbitrators increasingly rely on AI tools for case management and evidence organization; and counsel use AI for legal research, predictive analytics, and drafting. These developments bring tangible benefits such as accelerating case processing, improving access to legal information, and supporting the identification and examination of evidence. However, the study also highlights persistent and serious challenges, particularly regarding disclosure, transparency, data protection issues and the protection of trade secrets.

Given the restricted public access to arbitral awards and the divergent methodologies adopted by institutions and arbitrators, it is unlikely that AI systems will, in the foreseeable future, develop the consistent legal reasoning power required to establish uniform standards across the field of arbitration. While the idea of fully autonomous AI arbitrators has been discussed in academic literature and policy debates, its relevance will likely remain limited to narrow categories of disputes, such as small-volume consumer claims or standardized contractual relationships. For international commercial and investment arbitration, there is currently little reason to expect that AI will dominate the market or replace human arbitrators. The legitimacy of arbitration continues to depend not only on just and fair outcomes but also on foundational elements such as party equality, human judgment, and transparent procedures.

The analysis reveals a broad consensus that AI will function as a powerful tool assisting human reasoning especially for tribunals and counsel, rather

178 SCHERER see fn. 3, p. 503.

179 PAISLEY/SUSSMAN, see fn. 52, p. 35.

than acting as an autonomous decision-maker. In an increasingly digital arbitration environment, the role of experienced human arbitrators remains essential to ensure that AI outputs are auditable and that the right to be heard is fully protected. Although institutions have made important strides through updated rules and guidelines, efforts to develop a comprehensive and coherent framework for the ethical use of AI in arbitration are still ongoing. In parallel with rapid technological developments, safeguards are being actively designed and refined, reflecting the urgency and importance of this task.

It is important to recognize the limitations of this study. This research has adopted a mixed methodology, combining normative/doctrinal analysis with selective empirical references, such as recent institutional guidelines, arbitrator-facing tools for case management and drafting support, and counsel-oriented applications. While both elements have informed the analysis, the empirical component has remained illustrative rather than comprehensive. These empirical references have been considered not only as illustrations of technological innovation but also as relevant to safeguarding the right to be heard. A full empirical assessment of AI's impact on arbitral practice exceeds the scope of this work. Furthermore, the rapid pace of technological development risks outstripping current regulatory and soft-law responses. Addressing these challenges will require interdisciplinary collaboration among AI specialists, procedural lawyers, and arbitration practitioners.

In parallel, academic institutions and arbitration academies can play a proactive role by offering dedicated seminars on the use of digital technologies and AI in arbitration. Such training initiatives would equip new practitioners with both practical knowledge of AI-supported tools and a critical awareness of the procedural and ethical safeguards they require. Several avenues are recommended for future research:

- Conducting empirical studies to evaluate the actual impact of AI tools on party equality and the quality of arbitral decision-making;
- Examining how explainable AI models can be designed to support fair and transparent proceedings.

In sum, the integration of AI into arbitration must remain guided by a commitment to human-centred justice. However transformative technology may become, the right to be heard will continue to stand as the unshakable foundation of dispute resolution.

VI. Description of the author

Dr. Mehmet Tank is an independent practitioner in international arbitration and dispute resolution based in Bern, Switzerland. He holds the Certificate of Advanced Studies (CAS) in International Arbitration from the Swiss Arbitration Academy (in collaboration with the Universities of Lucerne and Neuchâtel).

Before establishing his practice in Switzerland, Dr. Tank served for twelve years as an administrative judge in Türkiye, most notably at the Istanbul Tax Court, following three years as a tax auditor at the Ministry of Finance. He earned his PhD in Public Law from Istanbul University with a dissertation on the evaluation of evidence. During his doctoral studies he undertook a one-year Visiting Scholar appointment at Pennsylvania State University Dickinson School of Law.

Specialising in procedural law, evidence evaluation, interpretation doctrines, and dispute resolution, he focuses on complex commercial, tax, and cross-border disputes. He regularly acts as counsel in high-stakes litigation, international arbitration, and regulatory proceedings, and advises on overall dispute resolution strategy, case management and regulatory compliance.

Dr. Tank is a member of the Swiss Arbitration Association (ASA) and the International Association of Tax Judges (IATJ) and holds observer status with the Association of European Administrative Judges (AEAJ). He previously served as Vice-President of the First Study Commission of International Association of Judges First Study Commission (2012-2018).

Consent Beyond Signature: Extending Arbitration Agreements in Finnish and Swedish Law

LAURI MARKUS HEISKANEN

Table of Contents

I. Introduction

Around 40 or so years ago, a partial award was rendered in the ICC Case No. 4131, worldwide known as the Dow Chemical.[1] In the case, the claimants, four companies of the Dow Chemical group commenced the arbitration while only two of the companies were formal parties to the arbitration agreement. The arbitral tribunal ruled that it had jurisdiction over the non-signatories Dow Chemical France and Dow Chemical Company, despite them not being formal parties to the arbitration agreements. In reaching its conclusion, the tribunal examined the role of the non-signatories in the negotiation, performance, and termination of the agreements.[2]

The award has become associated with the so-called 'group of companies doctrine', although the term itself was not used in the decision.[3] The award and the doctrine have been widely discussed, especially in the international context[4], and also in Sweden[5] and Finland[6]. One of the reasons for the interest can be derived from the fact that the award is sometimes understood as a non-consensual theory which allows the arbitrators to bind non-signatories to the arbitration agreement despite their lack of consent.[7] The name of the doctrine itself is to give understanding that non-signatories might be bound to an arbitration agreement signed by other parties based solely on the existence of a corporate link between them.[8]

---

1 ICC Case No. 4131, Interim Award of 23 September 1982.

2 Ibid.

3 Ibid.

4 HANOTIAU/OHLROGGE, 40th Year Anniversary of the Dow Chemical Award, in: 40 Asa Bulletin 2/2022, p. 300 ff.; BREKOULAKIS, Parties in International Arbitration: Consent v. Commercial Reality, in: Brekoulakis/Lew, et al. (ed.), The Evolution and Future of International Arbitration, International Arbitration Law Library, 2016, ¶8.68; BORN, International Commercial Arbitration, (3rd ed), Kluwer Law International, 2021 (updated 2024), ¶5.01[C].

5 HOBÉR, International Commercial Arbitration in Sweden, Oxford University Press, New York 2011, ¶3.149.

6 HEMMO, Välimiesmenettely, Alma Talent, Helsinki 2022, p. 211; KAISTINEN, Reach of the ICC and the FAI to Non-Signatory Parties in Prima Facie Jurisdictional Decisions, in: Liikejuridiikka 2/2017, Vantaa 2017, p. 116.

7 HOBÉR, see fn. 5, ¶3.149; Partial Award in ICC Case no. 10818 of 2001, as referenced in ICC International Court of Arbitration Bulletin Vol. 16(2). On the criticism see, HANOTIAU /OHLROGGE, see fn. 4, p. 300 ff.

8 GIRSBERGER/VOSER, International Arbitration – Comparative and Swiss perspectives, 5th edition, Zurich 2024, p. 87; MADSEN, Commercial Arbitration in Sweden – A Commentary on the Arbitration Act (1999:116) and the Arbitration Rules of the Arbitration Institute of the Stockholm Chamber of Commerce, Jure Förlag Ab, Stockholm 2016, p. 55 f.

The controversial nature of the Dow Chemical award stems from its prima facie departure from the consensual foundation of arbitration. Arbitration, whether international or domestic, is fundamentally consensual in nature. The parties' consent to arbitrate – and thus to derogate from the jurisdiction of domestic courts – derives from their agreement to submit disputes arising from their underlying legal relationship to arbitration. A strong presumption exists, which is true in most cases, that the formal signatories to an arbitration agreement are the only parties with rights or obligations under that agreement. This principle reflects the doctrine of privity, which confines the rights and obligations of an arbitration agreement to its formal parties.[9]

Consistent with this principle, Article II(1) of the New York Convention (hereinafter "NYC") implicitly affirms the subjective limits on arbitration agreements, requiring Contracting States to "recognize an agreement in writing under which the parties undertake to submit [their disputes] to arbitration." This identification of the parties to an arbitration agreement is often described as its "subjective scope" or scope ratione personae. [10] For clarity, this paper will adopt the term "subjective scope" throughout.

The limited subjective scope of arbitration agreements is similarly reflected in domestic arbitration laws. For instance, Article 7(1) of the UNCITRAL Model Law – which has served as a model for numerous national arbitration laws – defines an arbitration agreement as *"an agreement by the parties to submit to arbitration all or certain disputes which have arisen or which may arise between them."*

National arbitration laws in both Sweden and Finland follow the same principle. Section 1 of the Swedish Arbitration Act and Section 2 of the Finnish Arbitration Act similarly restrict arbitration agreements to identifiable parties. For clarity, Section 2 of the Finnish Arbitration Act provides that:

"Any dispute in a civil or commercial matter which can be settled by agreement <u>between the parties</u> may be referred for final decision to be made by one or more arbitrators. It may also be agreed that disputes which arise in the future from a particular legal relationship specified in the agreement shall be finally decided by one or more arbitrators, unless otherwise provided in statutory law." (emphasis added)

While the scope of arbitrable disputes may vary, the requirement for identifiable parties to an arbitration agreement remains universal. But what entities qualify as parties to an arbitration agreement? While this requirement is uni-

---

9 BORN, see fn. 4, ¶10.01; Judgment of the Supreme Court of Finland of 1 December 2020, KKO 2020:89.

10 BORN, see fn.4, ¶10.01.

versal, international arbitration conventions and national arbitration laws provide little explicit guidance on identifying the parties to an arbitration agreement.[11] One exception is the Peruvian Arbitration Act, which uniquely provides in Article 14 that:

"[t]he arbitration agreement extends to those who consent to submit to arbitration, in good faith, as determined by their active and decisive participation in the negotiation, execution, performance or termination of the contract that contains the arbitration agreement or to which the agreement is related. It also extends to those who seek to attain any rights or benefits from the contract, according to its terms."[12]

Such provisions are rare, however, and absent from Finnish and Swedish legislation.[13] If they existed, the analysis in this paper would be significantly simplified. Consequently, in Finland and Sweden – as in many other jurisdictions – the determination of parties to an arbitration agreement instead relies on the generally accepted doctrines concerning the extension of arbitration agreements.

In regard to examining both Sweden and Finland, a few things need to be said. The Nordic countries share significant legal similarities, with key contract law statutes – such as the Contracts Act and the Sale of Goods Act – arising from joint Nordic legislative efforts.[14] Finland's historical ties to Sweden, having been part of Sweden until the early 19th century, further contribute to these similarities. As a result, Finland's legal system has Swedish roots, and the Supreme Court of Finland has referred to Supreme Court of Sweden decisions.[15] Swedish legal literature is also frequently cited in Finnish legal literature underscoring the practical relevance of examining both jurisdictions.

Unsurprisingly, both jurisdictions are civil law countries, where both case law and legal literature (both domestic and to an extent foreign) provide useful secondary source of law. Additionally, neither jurisdiction follows the con-

11 BORN, see fn. 4, ¶10.01[c].

12 Peruvian Arbitration Law (Legislative Decree No. 1071); BORN, see footnote 4, ¶10.01[c].

13 Finnish Arbitration Act; Swedish Arbitration Act.

14 SANDVIK/SISULA–TULOKAS, Kansainvälinen kauppalaki, Lakimiesliiton kustannus, Helsinki 2013, p. 16 f.; TAMMINEN, Arbitration Agreement in: Ehrström/Timonen/Turunen (ed.): Arbitration in Finland, Helsinki 2017, p. 31.

15 See e. g. Judgment of the Supreme Court of Finland of 18 July 2019, KKO 2019:64 and Judgment of the Supreme Court of Finland of 28 October 1996, KKO 1996:129.

cept of the stare decisis although lower courts tend to follow the rulings of the Supreme Court.[16]

This paper examines the conditions under which arbitration agreements can be extended to non-signatories under Finnish and Swedish law, with particular focus on the influence of international case law and transnational principles. First, the subjective and also briefly the objective scope of arbitration agreements is assessed, as this forms the foundation for the subsequent sections **(II)**. Second, international case law is analysed to identify the main grounds on which non-signatories may be bound by arbitration agreements **(III)**. Third, Finnish and Swedish law are examined in greater detail, with particular focus on determining whether they align with transnational principles and whether such principles can serve as additional support **(IV)**. Finally, the paper concludes with a summary of key findings **(V)**.

II. Scope of the Arbitration Agreements and Privity of Contract

The interplay between arbitration agreements and the doctrine of privity is crucial in determining who can be bound by or invoke arbitration **(A)**. While the privity doctrine traditionally holds that only parties to a contract are subject to its terms, this does not mean that non-signatories can never be bound by arbitration agreements.

Determining which parties are bound by an arbitration agreement requires an assessment of its subjective scope – the identity of the parties bound by the agreement. This must be distinguished from the objective scope, which defines the range of disputes covered. Although both relate to the reach of the arbitration agreement, they address distinct issues **(B)**.

A. Privity of Contract and Consent to Arbitrate

The principle that the rights and obligations flowing from an arbitration agreement are binding only on its parties is a clear reflection of the privity of

---

[16] HOBÉR, see fn. 5, ¶¶1.18–1.19; LINNA, Linjamuutos korkeimmassa oikeudessa - vai erilainen tapaus?, in: Defensor Legis 1/1989, Helsinki 1989, p. 479. Interestingly, several Finnish lower courts have declined to follow a recent Supreme Court decision concerning the legal aid rate paid to lawyers. In contrast, no comparable instances of such "resistance" have emerged in other areas of law.

contract doctrine, upheld in both civil and common law systems.[17] The origin of the doctrine dates back at least over 140 years in English contract law.[18] To put it simply the doctrine establishes that only those who are parties to a contract can enforce its rights, assume its obligations, and initiate or face legal action under it.[19]

In relation to arbitration agreements, the scope of an arbitration agreement is tied to its voluntary nature, ensuring that no one can be compelled to arbitrate without their consent. Likewise, a third party cannot invoke arbitration based on an agreement to which they are not a party. This principle of privity is further strengthened in arbitration, as third parties cannot intervene in the arbitration process without the consent of the contracting parties.[20] This contrasts with, for example, Finnish litigation, which allows certain exceptions for third-party intervention in support of one of the parties under national procedural law.[21]

The Supreme Court of Switzerland decision 4A_636/2018 illustrates the application of privity in non-signatory cases. The dispute arose from a contract between a Turkish joint venture and a Libyan state-owned entity for a water pipeline project. Following disruptions caused by the 2011 Libyan revolution, the joint-venture initiated ICC arbitration against both the state-owned entity and the Libyan state. The tribunal upheld jurisdiction over the entity but not the state. The Supreme Court confirmed this, holding that Libya was not bound by the arbitration clause, as the claimants failed to show it was a party to the agreement or that it had interfered in the contract's negotiation or execution.[22]

In line with the doctrine of privity, a party's decision not to sign a contract is generally interpreted as a conscious choice not to be bound by its terms, including the arbitration clause. At the very least, it creates a strong presumption against any intention to arbitrate. In ICC Case No. 10758 of 2000, the tribunal emphasized this point, ruling that:

---

17 BORN, see fn. 4, ¶10.01[a].

18 Judgment of High Court of Justice of England and Wales of 7 June 1861, Tweddle v Atkinson [1861] EWHC J57 (QB).

19 Ibid; MAGNARELLI/ZIEGLER, Irreconcilable perspectives like in an Escher's drawing? Extension of an arbitration agreement to a non-signatory state and attribution of state entities' conduct: privity of contract in Swiss and investment arbitral tribunals' case law, in: Arbitration International 2020(36), p. 510, fn. 2.

20 HEMMO, see fn. 6, p. 179.

21 Chapter 18, Sections 8-10 of the Finnish Code of Judicial Procedure.

22 Judgment of the Supreme Court of Switzerland of 24 September 2019, 4 A_636/2018.

"By not signing the Contract, [the non-signatory] intended to respect the legal independence of [its affiliate signatory]'s legal personality and to be in harmony with the privity of contract principle, that is to say precisely not to become a party to the Contract nor to its arbitration clause."[23]

However, an overly rigid application of privity can lead to incorrect or poorly reasoned outcomes. In ICC Case No. 10818 (2001), the sole arbitrator referenced the Dow Chemical Award and rejected the extension of the arbitration clause to non-signatories. The arbitrator misunderstood the Dow Chemical Award as relying solely on the 'group of companies' doctrine and concluded that such an approach violated the privity principle under Swiss law.[24]

As Hanotiau correctly observes, Dow Chemical Award does not support extending arbitration clauses merely because parties belong to the same corporate group. Rather, the tribunal in Dow Chemical focused on the conduct and involvement of the non-signatory companies – issues of implied consent, not group affiliation alone. The arbitrator in ICC Case No. 10818 thus mischaracterized the doctrine and failed to assess the existence of implied consent, resulting in a questionable reasoning.[25]

Importantly, privity of contract is not a legal barrier to extending arbitration agreements to non-signatories. Courts and tribunals have recognized that entities who have not formally signed an arbitration agreement may nevertheless be bound by it. Whether they are depends on the application of relevant principles of contract, agency, and corporate law to assess whether actual or implied consent to arbitrate exists.[26] In exceptional cases, even constructed or fictitious consent may suffice.[27]

In conclusion, the extension of arbitration agreements to non-signatories hinges on two central principles: consent – whether express, implied, or constructed – and the principle of privity, which maintains that each legal entity is not bound by another's contractual obligations absent clear justification.

---

23 Partial award ICC case no 10758 of 2000, as referenced in ICC International Court of Arbitration Bulletin Vol. 16(2).

24 Partial Award in ICC Case no. 10818 of 2001, as referenced in ICC International Court of Arbitration Bulletin Vol. 16(2).

25 HANOTIAU, May an Arbitration Clause Be Extended to Non-signatories: Individuals, States or Other Companies of the Group?, in: Hanotiau (ed.): Complex Arbitrations: Multi-party, Multi-contract, Multi-issue – A comparative Study (2nd ed), 2020, ¶329; Partial Award in ICC Case no. 10818 of 2001, as referenced in ICC International Court of Arbitration Bulletin Vol. 16(2).

26 BORN, see fn. 4, ¶10.01[B].

27 LANDBRECHT/WEHOWSKY, Determining the Law Applicable to the Personal Scope of Arbitration Agreements and its "Extension", in Scherer (ed.), ASA Bulletin, 35(4), 2017, p. 837

B. Subjective and Objective Scope of Arbitration Agreements

The subjective scope concerns who are bound by the arbitration agreement, while the objective scope addresses what disputes it covers (1). Though distinct, the boundaries between them can blur in cases involving guarantors who have not signed the contract containing the arbitration agreement (2). The following sections examine each in turn.

1. What are the Subjective and Objective Scope of Arbitration Agreements

The subjective scope of an arbitration agreement refers to the identity of the parties bound by it.[28] In Finnish and Swedish legal literature, the term is used to address the applicability of arbitration agreements to non-signatories.[29] Since neither the Finnish nor the Swedish Arbitration Act explicitly regulates the subjective scope, the issue is governed by general contract law principles.[30]

Briefly on the form requirements of arbitration agreements. While most jurisdictions require arbitration agreements to be in writing, Sweden does not impose this requirement,[31] whereas the Finnish Arbitration Act mandates that an *"arbitration agreement must be in writing."*[32] This raises the question: does the formal requirement preclude extension of the agreement to non-signatories?

The short answer is no. The *in writing r*equirement applies only to the original parties. In a 2019 judgment, the Supreme Court of Switzerland clarified that Article II(2) NYC and Article 178(1) of the Swiss PILA require the written form only for the declarations of intent by the contracting parties (however, there is no requirement of a hand-written signature, thus the arbitration agreement can be concluded by an email). Whether third parties are bound is

---

28 Supra ¶4.

29 LINDSKOG, Skiljeförfarande – En kommentar, JUNO Version 3/2020, ¶I.0–5.1.4.; HEMMO, see fn. 6, p. 180

30 LINDSKOG, see fn. 29, ¶I.0–1.1.2.

31 HOBÉR, see fn. 5, ¶3.12; MADSEN, see fn. 8, p. 42; Swedish Arbitration Act.

32 Section 3 of the Finnish Arbitration Act; see also MÖLLER, Välimiesmenettelyn perusteet, Helsinki, 1997, p. 18.

a matter of substantive law, assessed by interpreting the contract and the parties' shared intent.[33]

In Finland, such a clear position has not been taken by the Supreme Court so expressly but the logic is apparent from a recent precedent.[34] In legal literature, it has been argued that the "relaxation" of the formal requirement – especially when the agreement exists in writing – makes the subjective scope of the agreement a separate issue from its formal validity.[35] While the author's view on the "relaxation" of the form requirement may be open to debate, the practical conclusion is clear: a non-signatory cannot rely on the form requirement alone to avoid arbitration under Finnish law.

The objective scope of an arbitration agreement refers to the types of disputes it covers. It addresses whether an arbitration clause extends to tort claims, related contracts, or subsequent agreements.[36] As this concerns the *content* of disputes rather than the *parties* bound by the agreement, it is a distinct issue from the extension of arbitration agreements to non-signatories. Accordingly, this section addresses objective scope only briefly, to provide contextual background on how courts interpret the reach of arbitration clauses.

In KKO 1990:106, the Supreme Court of Finland held that a hire-purchase agreement was not subject to an arbitration clause in a marketing agreement concluded previously between the parties. The contracts were treated as independent, and the dispute fell outside the arbitration clause's scope.[37]

In contrast, the Supreme Court of Sweden in NJA 2019 p. 171 upheld arbitral jurisdiction over additional work contracts concluded after the main contract containing the arbitration clause. The Court held that the phrase "has the right to petition" a court in the additional works contract did not create an obligation to litigate, and relied on general principles favouring a single forum to

---

33 Judgment of the Supreme Court of Switzerland of 24 September 2019, 4A_636/2018

34 Judgment of the Supreme Court of Finland of 1 December 2020, KKO 2020:89,. Especially, the referred Court of Appeal's reasoning *"The Court of Appeal noted that Section 3 of the Arbitration Act requires the arbitration agreement to be in writing. The statutory formal requirement is fulfilled if the agency agreement, or at least its arbitration clause, is deemed to have been transferred from M to B when the agency agreement is concluded in writing between the original parties."*

35 HEMMO, see fn. 6, p. 180. This is in contrast to earlier position taken in the Finnish legal literature where it was argued that the form requirement could not "set aside" with implied consent by the non-signatory, see KOULU, Välityssopimus välimiesmenettelyn perustana, Edilex 2008, p. 109.

36 E.g. LANDBRECHT/WEHOWSKY, see fn. 27, footnote. 13; BORN, see fn. 4 ¶9.01[D]; Judgment of the Supreme Court of Sweden of 14 November 1972, NJA 1972 p. 458.

37 Judgment of the Supreme Court of Finland of 12 September 1990, KKO 1990:106.

avoid fragmented dispute resolution.[38] The Swedish decision has been criticized in Finnish literature for overextending the arbitration clause without clear contractual language – and rightly so. While process efficiency is important, it should not justify interpretations that deviate significantly from the parties' agreed contractual framework.[39]

While cases on objective scope offer insights into how arbitration clauses are interpreted, they have limited relevance for questions concerning non-signatories. Objective scope doctrine deals with the substantive reach of the arbitration clause, not with who is bound. Accordingly, objective scope jurisprudence provides limited guidance when evaluating the binding effect of arbitration agreements on non-signatory parties.

2. *Non-Signatory Guarantors; Matter of Subjective Scope with Similarities to the Objective Scope*

The question of whether a non-signatory guarantor can be bound by an arbitration agreement in the underlying contract has attracted considerable attention in both Finnish and Swedish case law and commentary. Although guarantors are not automatically bound by such clauses, courts have recognized that the close commercial and contractual connection between the guarantee and the principal agreement may justify their inclusion. This section examines how courts in both jurisdictions have approached this issue and considers the broader implications for extending arbitration agreements to non-signatory guarantors.

A guarantor is not automatically bound by an arbitration agreement in the principal contract.[40] Whether the arbitration clause applies to the guarantor often depends on the national law governing the guarantee relationship. Factors such as scope of the guarantor's performance obligation under the guaranteed contract and its commercial role in the transaction are typically relevant.[41]

This reflects the prevailing approach in both Finnish and Swedish law.

In its ruling KKO 2019:111, the Supreme Court of Finland held that a company providing a loan guarantee was bound by the arbitration clause in the loan agreement, despite the guarantee containing a separate forum clause. The

---

38 Judgment of the Supreme Court of Sweden of 20 March 2019, NJA 2019 p. 171.

39 HEMMO, see fn. 6, p. 463 f.

40 GIRSBERGER/VOSER, see fn. 8, p. 121; BORN, see fn. 4, ¶10.01[G].

41 BORN, see fn. 4, ¶10.01[G].

Court treated the loan and guarantee as forming a contractual whole, closely tied to the same financial arrangement.

The Court emphasized that the jurisdiction clause (referring to Finnish state courts) in the guarantee was non-exclusive – a point the author finds somewhat "novel" and strikingly reminiscent of the NJA 2019 p. 171 ruling – and noted the significance of both agreements being signed by the same individual acting for both companies. The absence of special grounds for protecting the guarantor and the shared commercial context supported the conclusion that arbitration remained a valid forum.[42]

A similar conclusion was reached in a 2002 judgment by the Svea Court of Appeal. There, the Republic of Kazakhstan, acting as guarantor, was found bound by the arbitration clause in the underlying delivery agreement. Although the guarantee lacked an arbitration clause, it referred to the main contract and was part of the same commercial relationship. The guarantor's awareness and acceptance of the arbitration clause indicated implicit consent.[43]

Additionally, a Swedish legal precedent played a crucial role in supporting the view that the guarantor could be bound by the arbitration clause. Case law affirmed that a guarantor could invoke an arbitration clause as a defence and, in this instance, extended that principle to compel the guarantor to arbitrate if the creditor requested it. The Court further emphasized the need to avoid creating an unequal legal position between the parties, as exempting the guarantor from the arbitration clause would allow for strategic manipulation of the dispute resolution process. The guarantor was therefore compelled to arbitrate.[44]

However, in a 2011 judgment by the Svea Court of Appeal, a parent company that had assumed its subsidiary's debt through a new agreement with the creditor was not found to be bound by the arbitration agreement between the subsidiary and the creditor. The Court distinguished this from guarantor cases, noting that the assumption of debt did not create the same type of legal or contractual connection.[45]

Before KKO 2019:111, Finnish legal literature had already accepted that non-signatory guarantors may be bound by arbitration agreements.[46] The same

---

42 Judgment of the Supreme Court of Finland of 19 December 2019; KKO 2019:111.

43 Judgment of the Svea Court of Appeal of 15 May 2002, T4496-01 (RH 2003:61).

44 Ibid.

45 Judgment of the Svea Court of Appeal of 22 December 2011, Ö5009-11 (RH 2012:3).

46 MÖLLER, see fn. 32, p. 24 f.

view prevails in a Swedish commentary.[47] While a Swedish legislative committee once proposed including guarantors explicitly in the Arbitration Act, the idea was ultimately rejected, leaving the matter to case law.[48] This reflects the difficulty of codifying a uniform rule, given the diversity of guarantee arrangements.[49]

Case law on guarantors often mirrors objective scope disputes: courts interpret contracts in light of commercial context, interconnectedness, and party intent, prioritizing coherent dispute resolution over rigid formalism.

However, caution is warranted in applying guarantor case law to other non-signatory scenarios. Guarantee agreements are typically tightly linked to the principal obligation, and the guarantor is often aware of the relevant terms. These unique features may not exist in other non-signatory contexts, limiting the broader applicability of guarantor case law.

III. Binding Non-Signatories to Arbitration Agreements

Roughly, the doctrine concerning the extension of arbitration agreements to non-signatories can be categorized under consent-based and abuse-based theories, with the former further encompassing sub-categories such as the third-party beneficiary doctrine[50]. While this broad division into two categories can be criticised for being somewhat artificial. Somewhat artificial, it is descriptive as the abuse-based theories rely on “fictitious consent”.[51]

Accordingly, in legal literature the consent criterion has been divided into the following four categories:

i) Explicit Consent: Consent is clearly given either when the agreement is made or afterwards. This can involve adding a new party to the arbitration

---

47 HOBÉR, see fn. 4, ¶3.142.

48 Swedish Government Bill 1998/99:35, p. 63 ff.

49 SCC cases 38/1997 and 39/1997 as reported in SMIT, Jurisdictional Award rendered in 1998 in SCC cases 38/1997 and 39/1997 & Judgment of the Stockholm District Court rendered in 2001 in case T 1510-99 & Judgment of the Svea Court of Appeal rendered in 2002 in case T 4496-01 – The Government Guarantee case, in: Stockholm Arbitration Reporter 2003(1), p. 273 ff. In SCC Case 39/1999, the guarantor’s obligations differed from those of the debtor, as it had merely undertaken to assist the debtor in securing funds to repay the creditor. As a result, the tribunal declined to extend the arbitration agreement to the guarantor.

50 See infra III.A.1.

51 LANDBRECHT/WEHOWSKY, see fn. 27, p. 840 f.

agreement or replacing an original party. A signature on the agreement is typically strong evidence of explicit consent and satisfies formal requirements.

ii) Implied Consent: Consent may also be inferred from conduct, even without a formal declaration or signature. For example, if a party initiates arbitration based on an agreement that benefits a third party, this behaviour may imply consent.

iii) Presumed Consent: In some cases, legal provisions presume consent if a person agrees to a related transaction. This often applies in scenarios like succession, assignment, or joint liability, where the arbitration agreement is treated as part of the broader legal relationship. In such cases, whether the party originally signed the agreement is irrelevant.

iv) Fictitious Consent: In rare cases, a tribunal's authority may rely on concepts like equity and good faith rather than actual consent. This is often linked to doctrines such as piercing the corporate veil.[52]

Nevertheless, legal scholars have observed that the so-called "group of companies" doctrine may, depending on how it is framed, fall under either implied consent or fictitious consent.[53] Indicating that the categorisation is difficult. For the purposes of this paper, abuse-based theories or fictitious consent refer to situations where a non-signatory is bound by doctrines such as piercing the corporate veil.

The primary distinction is thus between two main categories: **(A)** consent-based theories and **(B)** abuse-based theories. Building on this framework, the analysis then considers whether the applicable choice of law to the arbitration agreement differs between these two categories **(C)**.

A. Consent based theories

In this paper, the focus is on the third-party beneficiary doctrine **(1)** and implied consent **(2)** as they have been recognized in the doctrine in both Finland and Sweden.

52 LANDBRECHT/WEHOWSKY, see fn. 27, p. 839 ff.

53 LANDBRECHT/WEHOWSKY, see fn. 27, p. 839 f.; BORN, see fn. 4, ¶10.05[C].

1. Third-Party Beneficiary Doctrine

Internationally, courts and arbitral tribunals have often held that a third-party beneficiary claiming rights under a contract is both entitled to invoke and bound by the arbitration clause contained within it. While some jurisdictions address this through statutory provisions, others rely on legal doctrine and arbitral practice.[54] Again, the third-party beneficiary doctrine can be seen as a manifestation of the implied consent.[55] It is generally uncontroversial in Finland and Sweden that a non-signatory relying on a contract is also bound by its arbitration clause – a point elaborated further below in **IV.B.1**.[56]

The key issue is whether a third-party beneficiary must show that the contracting parties intended to extend the arbitration clause specifically to them, or whether it suffices that the contract confers substantive rights. Most jurisdictions adopt the latter view: if the parties intended to benefit the third party substantively, the arbitration clause applies, even absent explicit reference.[57]

BORN argues that third-party beneficiary status should not be subject to a heightened standard of proof in international arbitration. Instead, considerations of efficiency and the goal of resolving disputes in a single forum support a more flexible standard, particularly in cross-border settings.[58]

This approach is widely followed. Courts including in England, France, and Austria have confirmed that third-party beneficiaries may rely on and be bound by arbitration clauses when substantive rights are conferred. In Nisshin Shipping v. Cleaves, the English High Court held that under Section 8 (Rights

---

[54] BORN, see fn. 4, ¶10.01[F].

[55] LANDBRECHT/WEHOWSKY, see fn. 27, p. 840.

[56] Regarding Finland, see Judgment of the Supreme Court of Finland of 6 March 2007, KKO 2007:18 and Judgment of the Supreme Court of Finland of 13 November 2013, KKO 2013:84. For Sweden, see HOBÉR, see fn. 5, ¶¶3.161–3.163. The Supreme Court of Sweden has not ruled on this issue. In the Judgment of the Supreme Court of Sweden of 5 April 2012, NJA 2012, p. 183 the issue was raised and in the published "suggested" ruling by the Secretary of Justice, the arbitration agreement was held to extend to non-signatory third-party beneficiary. However, the Supreme Court ultimately held that since the "third-party beneficiary" was seeking repayment under a loan agreement that predated the sales and cooperation agreement, the Supreme Court only needed to assess whether the later agreement, including its arbitration clause, overrode the dispute resolution mechanism in the loan agreement. The Supreme Court concluded that it did not.

[57] BREKOULAKIS, The Various Forms of 'Consent' in International Arbitration', in: Kröll et al. (ed.), Cambridge Compendium of International Commercial and Investment Arbitration, Cambridge 2023, ¶24.2.2.

[58] BORN, see fn. 4, ¶10.01[F].

of Third Parties) of the Contracts Act 1999, a third party entitled to a contractual benefit must also adhere to the arbitration clause, even if not explicitly named.[59] Similarly, the Supreme Courts of France and Austria have upheld this approach, recognizing that a third-party beneficiary enforcing a contract's substantive rights may also be subject to its arbitration clause.[60]

In conclusion, the principle that third-party beneficiaries may be bound by and invoke arbitration clauses is firmly established in international arbitration. Even without express inclusion, courts consistently recognize that granting of substantive rights is sufficient to extend the arbitration clause.

2. *Implied Consent and Group of Companies Doctrine*

In most developed legal systems, an entity can become a party to a contract, including an arbitration agreement, not only through explicit agreement or formal execution but also implicitly through conduct or non-explicit declarations.[61] In this regard, the so-called group of companies doctrine has gained particular prominence in international arbitration, where it is primarily invoked by tribunals to extend arbitration agreements signed by one or more entities within a corporate group to non-signatory affiliates in the same group. As stated in the introduction, the origin of the doctrine can be traced to the Dow Chemical Award.[62]

In legal literature and case law, the doctrine is understood in two different main ways. One perspective supports the group of companies doctrine as a significant theoretical framework in international arbitration. This view emphasizes that the doctrine plays a crucial role in highlighting specific patterns (i. e. group structure) that indicate consent to arbitration.[63] This is partly the reason why the fictitious consent has also been connected to the group of companies doctrine.[64]

Critics of the group of companies doctrine argue that the Dow Chemical Award did not establish a general rule for extending arbitration agreements to third parties without their consent. On the contrary, the arbitrators empha-

59 Judgment of the High Court of Justice England and Wales of 7 November 2003, Nisshin Shipping Co Ltd v. Cleaves & Co Ltd 2, EWHC 2602.

60 Judgment of the Supreme Court of France of 11 July 2006, 05-18.681; Judgment of the Supreme Court of Austria of 30 March 2009, 7 Ob 266/08 f.

61 BORN, see fn. 4, ¶10.01[C].

62 ICC Case No. 4131, Interim Award of 23 September 1982.

63 BREKOULAKIS, see fn. 56, ¶24.2.6.

64 LANDBRECHT/WEHOWSKY, see fn. 27, p. 841.

sized that a non-signatory can only be bound by an arbitration clause if this aligns with the parties' mutual intentions. According to this view, simply belonging to the same corporate group is insufficient to extend an arbitration agreement. Instead, the decisive factor is consent, which must be assessed on a case-by-case basis based on factual evidence. While a company's affiliation with a corporate group may be relevant to determining intent, it is not determinative on its own. Therefore, the references to the group of companies doctrine are unhelpful and should be abandoned, as they risk distracting from the crucial inquiry into whether consent exists.[65]

Regardless of how the doctrine is categorized, tribunals have consistently emphasized that the mere existence of a corporate group is insufficient for the application of the group of companies doctrine. Therefore, the requirement is that the non-signatory company must have played an active role in the negotiation, performance, or termination of the contract containing the arbitration agreement.[66]

An important question is whether (implied) consent to the substantive terms of a contract also extends to the arbitration clause, given the principle of separability.

BORN highlights the importance of considering the separability presumption when evaluating implied consent to an arbitration agreement. Under this principle, the arbitration clause is treated as an independent contract from the main agreement. Consequently, implied consent to the arbitration clause must be assessed separately from consent to the broader commercial contract. While a party's consent to the underlying contract will typically extend to the arbitration clause, this is not automatic; it depends on whether the party's conduct demonstrates consent specifically to arbitration. Extensive involvement in key contractual matters is more likely to imply consent to arbitrate, whereas limited participation in isolated aspects of the contract may not suffice.[67]

The Supreme Court of Finland which has dealt with this question did not do such detailed analysis as suggested by BORN. The Supreme Court of Finland noted that the principle of separability is relevant and thus it cannot be automatically deduced that the consent on the other contractual provisions extends to the arbitration agreement.[68] This judgement is discussed in detail in Section **IV.B.2**.

---

65 HANOTIAU/OHLROGGE, see fn. 4, p. 308.
66 BREKOULAKIS, see fn. 4, footnote 93; BORN, see fn. 4, ¶10.01[C].
67 BORN, see fn. 4, ¶10.01[C].
68 Judgment of the Supreme Court of Finland of 1 December 2020, KKO 2020:89.

In conclusion, the concept of implied consent plays a significant role in determining whether a non-signatory can be bound by or invoke an arbitration agreement. While most legal systems recognize that consent may be given implicitly through conduct or non-explicit declarations, such consent must be assessed carefully.

The group of companies doctrine has been a focal point in this context, particularly in international arbitration. The author's opinion aligns with the criticism put forward especially by Hanotiau, the reference to the doctrine is flawed and inconsistent with core principles of contractual consent. Mere affiliation within a corporate group is insufficient; rather, meaningful involvement in key contractual matters – such as negotiation, performance, or termination – is typically required to establish implied consent.

B. Abuse Based Theories – Piercing the Corporate Veil

The doctrine of piercing the corporate veil allows courts or tribunals to disregard a corporation's separate legal personality, holding its shareholders, directors, or parent company (i. e., its "alter ego") personally liable for the corporation's actions or debts. While the precise definition and application of this doctrine vary significantly across legal systems, the core principle remains consistent: when one entity exerts extensive control over another and misuses that control, their separate legal identities may be disregarded, treating them as a single entity. In the context of arbitration agreements, establishing an "alter ego" relationship typically requires strong evidence that one entity dominated the other's daily operations and/or used this control to commit fraud or evade statutory or other legal obligations.[69]

The piercing the corporate veil doctrine was originally developed to determine whether a parent company or individual could be held accountable for a subsidiary's debts (a substantive liability matter). Consequently, some argue that the doctrine was not designed to address whether a non-signatory parent company should be bound by an arbitration agreement concluded by its subsidiary (a jurisdictional matter).[70]

Nevertheless, tribunals in various jurisdictions have extended arbitration agreements to non-signatories under this doctrine, albeit using different criteria. There is a compelling argument that establishing alter ego status may be

---

69 BORN, see fn. 4, ¶10.01[D]; GIRSBERGER/VOSER, see fn. 8, p. 122.

70 BREKOULAKIS, see fn. 4, ¶24.3.3; MÜLLER/KEILMANN, Beteiligung am Schiedsverfahren Wider Willen?, in: SchiedsVZ: Zeitschrift für Schiedsverfahren, München 2007, p. 116 f.

easier in the context of international arbitration agreements than in cases involving substantive liability under other types of contracts.[71] For instance, the Supreme Courts of Switzerland and, more recently, Lithuania have upheld the possibility of establishing jurisdiction over a non-signatory under this doctrine.[72]

Piercing the corporate veil is based on the concept of fictitious consent.[73] Unlike agency principles or implied consent, it does not rely on the parties' intentions but rather on broader considerations of equity and fairness.[74]

International arbitral tribunals have generally adopted a cautious approach when applying alter ego theories. Most decisions have required persuasive evidence of overlapping ownership, management, and active participation in the negotiation and performance of the contract. In some instances, explicit statements confirming the affiliated company's involvement in relevant transactions have been considered. However, certain factors – such as shared logos, brands, trademarks, or overlapping management structures – are generally not decisive in determining an alter ego relationship. Conversely, strong indicators of an alter ego relationship include fraudulent or abusive misconduct, undercapitalization, deliberate tortious actions, or siphoning of assets that results in financial instability.[75]

In conclusion, while the piercing the corporate veil doctrine has traditionally been applied in matters of substantive liability, its use in extending arbitration agreements to non-signatories has gained some recognition in international practice. Although the criteria for applying this doctrine vary across jurisdictions, arbitral tribunals have consistently required clear evidence of extensive control and misuse of that control.

C. Choice of Law Governing the Extension of Arbitration Agreements to Non-Signatories

The question arises as to whether the law governing the arbitration agreement always determines the subjective scope of that agreement. While some case law has suggested that this issue can be resolved under international princi-

71 BORN, see fn. 4, ¶10.01[D].

72 Judgment of the Supreme Court of Switzerland of 25 August 2009, 4A_160/2009; Judgment of the Supreme Court of Lithuania of 8 February 2023, No. 3K-3-41-823/2024.

73 LANDBRECHT/WEHOWSKY, see fn. 27, p. 841 and p. 853.

74 BORN, see fn. 4, ¶10.01[D].

75 BORN, see fn. 4, ¶10.01[D]; HANOTIAU, see fn. 25, ¶261.

ples[76], the prevailing view appears to be that identifying the parties to an arbitration agreement is a matter of substantive, rather than procedural, law.[77] Consequently, the law applicable to the arbitration agreement would generally apply.[78] Nonetheless, it has been acknowledged that different governing laws may apply depending on whether the theory for extending the arbitration agreement is based on consensual or non-consensual principles.[79]

When an arbitration agreement is extended to a non-signatory based on implied consent, the law governing the arbitration agreement should apply. Since implied consent relies on principles of contract interpretation and formation, this approach aligns with the expectations of reasonable commercial parties.[80] Similarly, where an arbitration agreement is extended under the concept of a third-party beneficiary, the prevailing view is that the law governing the arbitration agreement should determine the issue.[81]

The most contentious scenario arises when an arbitration agreement is extended to a non-signatory through the doctrine of piercing the corporate veil. BORN observes that authorities are divided on whether the governing law should be that of the main contract, the arbitration agreement, or transnational principles. Ultimately, BORN argues that *"uniform international principles better achieve the purposes of the veil-piercing doctrine, without materially interfering with the parties' expectations"*.[82]

Some scholars have rejected this view, asserting that piercing the corporate veil relates to actions involving the abuse of rights by a non-signatory in connection with the agreement containing the arbitration clause. Accordingly, such actions create a sufficient "connection" to the arbitration agreement,

76 Award in ICC Case No. 8385, reported in ARNALDEZ/DERAINS/HASCHER, Collection of ICC Arbitral Awards 1996-2000, p. 474 ff.

77 Judgment of the High Court of Justice of England and Wales of 4 Feb 2004, EWHC 121; BORN, see fn. 4, ¶10.05[B].

78 Ibid; Judgment of the Supreme Court of Germany of 8 May 2014, BGH, III ZR 371/12.

79 BORN, see fn. 4, ¶10.05[C]

80 BORN, see fn. 4, ¶10.01[C]; LANDBRECHT/WEHOWSKY, see fn. 27, p. 848 f. The latter authors have analysed the topic in detail in their article.

81 BORN, see fn. 4, ¶10.01[F]; LANDBRECHT/WEHOWSKY, see fn. 27, p. 848 f.

82 BORN, see fn. 4, ¶10.01[D]. Born bases his conclusions mainly on the Judgment by the Supreme Court of the United States of 17 June 1983, FNC Bank v. Banco Para el Comercio, 462 U.S. 611. Cf. LANDBRECHT/WEHOWSKY, see fn. 27, p. 853, who argue that *"A conflict of (national) laws analysis determining the substantive law governing scope and validity, as outlined above, is always necessary."*

making the law governing that agreement the appropriate starting point for determining the applicable law in matters of validity and subjective scope.[83]

This author takes the view that while transnational principles may offer coherence in theory, they should not override the law applicable to the arbitration agreement. Using transnational principles as a substitute risks introducing unpredictability and undermining the legal expectations of both signatories and non-signatories. That said, in exceptional circumstances where national law fails to provide adequate guidance or conflicts with international public policy, limited reliance on transnational principles may be justified as a gap-filling tool.

In conclusion, while there is some debate regarding which law should govern the extension of an arbitration agreement to a non-signatory, the prevailing view favours applying the law governing the arbitration agreement, particularly in cases involving implied consent or third-party beneficiary principles. The more complex question arises in situations where the corporate veil is pierced to bind a non-signatories.

IV. Extension of Arbitration Agreements in Finnish and Swedish Law

This section forms the fourth main part of the paper, with a stronger focus on Finnish and Swedish law compared to the preceding sections.

Section **(A)** explores the influence of transnational principles on arbitration practices in Finland and Sweden. If such principles have little to no impact, the findings from the third main part become less significant.

Section **(B)** examines consent-based theories, including third-party beneficiaries and implied consent, while Section **(C)** addresses abuse-based theories, particularly the piercing of the corporate veil. Building on these discussions, Section **(D)** analyses the choice of law for determining whether an arbitration agreement can extend to non-signatories.

A. Influence of Transnational Principles

As stated in Finnish legal literature, arbitration practices that initially appear to be purely national are likely influenced by international elements. In arbi-

---

[83] LANDBRECHT/WEHOWSKY, see fn. 27, p. 853.

tration, cases and the surrounding community are inherently international, making it unlikely for practices to be entirely domestic.[84] Thus the commonly held view is that the study of arbitration requires a comparative legal approach, even for domestic arbitration, due to the strong trend toward harmonization both globally and in the Nordic countries.[85] That being said, due to the similarity of the Finnish and Swedish legal systems, the Swedish and other Nordic case law can provide more suitable guidance than other foreign legals systems.[86]

In Sweden, the Supreme Court has itself expressly relied on the works of BORN and others when interpreting the (objective) scope of the arbitration agreement.[87] Additionally, in legal literature prominent Swedish legal scholars have accepted that developments on an international level should be taken into consideration when deciding on the position under Swedish law.[88]

Given the international nature of arbitration and the trend toward harmonization, transnational principles – such as foreign case law and commentaries – are highly relevant in interpreting arbitration agreements. While Finnish and Swedish legal systems provide useful guidance, international sources remain crucial for addressing complex issues that are relevant in various jurisdictions.

B. Consent-Based Theories in Finnish and Swedish Case Law

Consent-based theories provide the primary legal framework for extending arbitration agreements to non-signatories in both Finnish and Swedish law. Two key categories are particularly relevant: first, cases involving third-party beneficiaries, where a non-signatory seeks to enforce or is affected by rights granted under a contract **(1)**; and second, instances of implied consent, where a non-signatory's conduct is argued to reflect acceptance of the arbitration agreement **(2)**.

---

84 KURKELA/TURUNEN, Due Process in International Commercial Arbitration, Oxford University Press, New York 2010, p. 8.

85 KOULU, see fn. 35, p. 2; HEMMO, see fn. 6, p. 5.

86 Judgment of the Supreme Court of Finland of 18 July 2019, KKO 2019:64; KOULU, see fn. 35, p. 2; TAMMINEN, see fn. 14, p. 31. However, I note that is more common in Finland to rely on Swedish case law or legal principles than vice versa.

87 Judgment of the Supreme Court of Sweden of 20 March 2019, NJA 2019, p. 171.

88 MADSEN, Multi-tiered dispute resolution clauses in arbitration, SvJT 2021, p. 203; HEUMAN, Har det skett en omsvängning eller omläggning av praxis från restriktiv till extensiv tillämpning av skiljeavtal?, in: SvJT 2019, p. 534.

1. Third-Party Beneficiaries

Both Finnish and Swedish law recognize that two parties can contract for the benefit of a third party. For example, A may agree with B to sell an object to C. In such cases, the contract between A and B can create an independent right for C, allowing C to sue A if A fails to fulfil the promise.[89] The Supreme Court of Finland has expressly upheld this principle concerning third-party beneficiaries acting as claimants.[90] While the Supreme Court of Sweden has only addressed the matter in a suggested ruling by the Secretary of Justice[91], it is widely accepted in Swedish legal literature that arbitration agreements can extend to non-signatory third-party beneficiaries.[92]

However, in a Helsinki Court of Appeal judgement given in 2020, the non-signatory beneficiary was not bound by the arbitration agreement. In the case, the managing director (A) of a bankrupt limited liability company brought a claim for damages against X Oy, the company that had provided accounting services to the bankrupt entity. The two companies had concluded a client agreement containing an arbitration clause. However, A initiated proceedings in court in his personal capacity, arguing that the claim did not fall within the scope of the arbitration agreement. The claim was based on alleged unjust shareholder loan entries, which had led to payment and tax liabilities and other financial harm to A personally. According to A, the accountants had

89 HOBÉR, see fn. 5, ¶3.157; PÖNKÄ, Oikeustapauskommentti Korkeimman oikeuden ratkaisusta 2013:84 – osakassopimukseen sisältyvän välityslausekkeen sivullissitovuus, in: Liikejuridiikka 1/2016, Vantaa 2016, p. 107; Hemmo, see fn. 6, p. 192: *"There is no basis for a person relying on an agreement between others to have discretion to avoid the binding nature of an arbitration clause"*.

90 Judgment of the Supreme Court of Finland of 6 March 2007, KKO 2007:18; Judgment of the Supreme Court of Finland of 13 November 2013, KKO 2013:84. In KO 2013:84, the Supreme Court of Finland addressed a situation where A, a third party to a contract between J Oy and M Oy, had been granted a contractual right to redeem shares held by J Oy in M Oy. When A believed this right had been violated, he initiated a damages claim in court against J Oy. J Oy challenged the court's jurisdiction, invoking the arbitration clause in its agreement with M Oy. The Supreme Court upheld the jurisdictional objection, holding that the dispute fell within the scope of the arbitration clause. It reasoned that A's claim was based on a right arising from the contract between J Oy and M Oy, and on an alleged breach of that contract, making it a contractual dispute subject to arbitration.

91 Judgment of the Supreme Court of Sweden of 5 April 2012, NJA 2012, p. 183. As stated in fn. 56, the Supreme Court reached its conclusion on different legal grounds.

92 LINDSKOG, see fn. 29, ¶I.0–5.5.1–5.5.2; HOBÉR, see fn. 5, ¶3.161–3.162.

acted negligently and in breach of good accounting practice both at the company's formation and during its operations, thereby causing him damage.[93]

The District Court, following the precedent set in Supreme Court decision KKO 2013:84[94], accepted X Oy's jurisdictional objection and dismissed the case as inadmissible. The Court of Appeal, however, reached a different conclusion, holding that the dispute did not fall within the subjective scope of the arbitration clause. It distinguished the case from KKO 2013:84 on the basis that the Supreme Court's decision concerned a dispute arising from a contract that required interpretation of a specific contractual clause. In contrast, A's claim was based on harm suffered personally as a result of X Oy's conduct. According to the Court of Appeal, resolving such a claim did not involve interpreting the companies' client agreement or any of its individual clauses, nor was the claim based on an alleged breach of any contractual term. Therefore, the arbitration clause did not preclude A's claim from being heard by the court.[95]

The approach adopted in the case has been subject to criticism. It has been pointed out that X Oy would not have had any obligations relating to bookkeeping or the proper handling of shareholder loans toward any party in the absence of the client agreement. Accordingly, any limitations on liability or responsibility contained within the agreement would likely have applied equally to any liability X Oy might have had toward A. The core of the critique is that the nature or complexity of the interpretative questions concerning the agreement – or the clarity of the agreement's legal effects – is irrelevant when determining whether a claim falls within the scope of a dispute resolution clause. What matters is that the basis of the claim is inseparable from the contractual relationship governed by the agreement.[96]

Finnish case law has thus far involved situations where non-signatory beneficiaries have sought to bring claims in state courts, meaning they acted as claimants. This raises the question of whether non-signatory third-party beneficiaries can also be bound to arbitration as respondents.

Naturally, contracting parties cannot simply grant a third party a right and automatically compel it to arbitrate. In Sweden, legal literature has addressed this issue by considering whether the third party has accepted or utilized the

---

93 Decision of the Helsinki Court of Appeal 9 September 2020, S 19/1287.

94 See fn. 90.

95 Decision of the Helsinki Court of Appeal 9 September 2020, S 19/1287.

96 HEMMO, see fn. 6, p. 195. According to Hemmo, the jurisdiction of the arbitral tribunal also generally covers claims and objections based mainly on the law applicable to non-contractual relations if the claims are based on contractual obligations or otherwise on contractual cooperation (p. 457).

benefits of the main contract. If so, it is argued that the third party should also be bound to the arbitration agreement.[97] This corresponds to the views expressed internationally.[98]

In conclusion, both Finnish and Swedish law recognize that third-party beneficiaries may acquire independent rights under a contract, including potentially being bound by or entitled to invoke an arbitration agreement. The Supreme Court of Finland has expressly affirmed this for claimants, while the Supreme Court of Sweden has not addressed the issue directly, though it is accepted in Swedish legal literature. However, Finnish case law – particularly the 2020 Helsinki Court of Appeal judgment – demonstrates that courts may adopt a narrow interpretation of arbitration clauses, even when the claim appears closely linked to the underlying contract. This highlights an ongoing tension between the theoretical acceptance of extending arbitration agreements to third-party beneficiaries and the cautious, sometimes inconsistent, approach taken in practice. Nevertheless, where the beneficiary has accepted or relied on the contract's terms, the prevailing view in both jurisdictions – consistent with international principles – is that the arbitration clause should apply.

2. Implied Consent and Group of Companies Doctrine

Both jurisdictions recognize generally that contracts may be concluded implicitly.[99] However, in the words of the Supreme Court of Finland: *"There has been a cautious approach to the creation of a contract without explicit expressions of will, so that no one is bound by an agreement to which they have not consented or to which they have not otherwise expressed their will to be bound."*[100] This statement was made in a case concerning whether an arbitration agreement had been concluded implicitly. Consequently, the standard for concluding contracts implicitly in general should also apply to arbitration agreements.

A further question is whether a higher threshold should apply to arbitration agreements, given that they involve a waiver of the right to access state courts. In Sweden, this issue has been briefly addressed by former Supreme Court President Stefan Lindskog, who – in line with the Finnish Supreme

97 HOBÉR, see fn. 5, ¶3.161.

98 BORN, see fn. 4, ¶10.01[F]; GIRSBERGER/VOSER, see fn. 8, p. 122.

99 Judgment of the Supreme Court of Sweden of 21 April 1982, NJA 1982 p. 244; Judgment of the Supreme Court of Finland of 3 May 2018, KKO 2018:37 .

100 Judgment of the Supreme Court of Finland 1 December 2020., KKO 2020:89.

Court – affirms that general principles of contract law should apply when assessing the formation of arbitration agreements.[101]

Nonetheless, Lindskog adds that arbitration clauses – due to their cost implications and their effect on access to justice – should be regarded as burdensome terms. While this does not imply a stricter evidentiary standard, it does call for a more careful assessment of consent. He notes that this threshold is context-dependent: in situations involving a weaker party with limited understanding or financial means, the threshold should be higher.[102]

Internationally, this issue has prompted differing views. For example, the Supreme Court of Switzerland has held that *"[s]ince the derogation from a constitutional guarantee, it should not too readily be admitted that an arbitration agreement has been concluded if that point is contested."*[103] However, according to BORN the rationale for applying a heightened proof standard to arbitration agreements has been largely discredited in the context of international arbitration. Unlike domestic cases, international arbitration is the preferred method for resolving cross-border business disputes, precisely because it avoids conflicting national jurisdictions and potential bias. Therefore, there is no justified basis for requiring a stricter evidentiary threshold to establish the existence of an international arbitration agreement.[104]

This author agrees with the position that no categorically higher evidentiary threshold should apply to arbitration agreements, particularly in international settings. However, a case-sensitive approach is justified. In circumstances where an arbitration clause significantly limits a party's access to public courts – especially for weaker or less-informed parties – a higher degree of clarity regarding consent may be warranted. This nuanced approach aligns with both Lindskog's view and the generally stringent standards already applied to the implicit formation of contracts.

This nuance can become relevant when assessing whether an arbitration agreement can be extended to a non-signatory based on conduct. In Finnish and Swedish legal literature, it is accepted that an arbitration agreement may be extended to a non-signatory based on its conduct.[105] Relevant factors include whether the non-signatory participated in negotiations or performed substantial parts of the contract.[106] Mere interference in the contractual rela-

---

101 LINDSKOG, see fn. 29, ¶I.0–2.1.3.

102 Ibid.

103 Judgment of the Supreme Court of Switzerland of 16 October 2001, DFT 128 III 50.

104 BORN, see fn. 4, ¶5.04[C].

105 HEMMO, see fn. 6, p. 209 f.; BOMAN, Privity of contract and multi-party arbitration, Edilex, 2016, p. 15; HOBÉR, see fn. 5, ¶3.14–3.16; MADSEN, see fn. 8, p.41.

106 Ibid.

tionship does not suffice and is unlikely to establish implied consent to arbitrate.[107]

Importantly, both jurisdictions reject the "group of companies" doctrine if understood to mean that an arbitration agreement can be extended solely on the basis of group structure.[108] Accordingly, this paper has adopted the view that the so-called group of companies doctrine is not a standalone legal theory, but rather a mischaracterization of implied consent principles. In both Finnish and Swedish law, as well as in leading international commentary, consent – not corporate structure – remains the decisive factor.

There is limited case law on this issue in both Sweden and Finland. However, the Supreme Court of Finland has implicitly recognized that a non-signatory may be bound by an arbitration agreement through its conduct.

The Supreme Court of Finland held in judgment KKO 2020:89 that a non-signatory buyer of a business was not bound by an arbitration agreement between the seller and a sales agent. In this case, a Finnish company (M) sold part of its business to a Belgian company (B). A Serbian company (A), which had been M's sales agent, continued working with B for over four years. However, B had not expressly agreed to the continuance of the original agency agreement or the arbitration agreement. Rather, B had merely indicated its intention to follow the procedures in the agreement between M and A until a contract was concluded with B.[109]

The Supreme Court emphasized that arbitration clauses are treated as independent contracts and their binding effect must be assessed separately from other contractual terms. Even though B followed some procedures outlined in the original agency agreement and agreed to pay commissions temporarily, this did not indicate acceptance of the arbitration clause. The Supreme Court concluded that for a buyer to be bound by an arbitration clause in a prior contract, it must have either expressly agreed to it or demonstrated acceptance through clear conduct. In this case, B's actions, including references to future agreements and the temporary continuation of certain terms, were insufficient to establish such acceptance.[110]

---

[107] HEMMO, see fn. 6, p. 204.

[108] Hemmo, see fn. 6, p. 213.; HOBÉR, see fn.5, ¶3.154; MADSEN, see fn. 8, p. 55 f. In Finnish or Swedish literature, there has not been discussion on how the Dow Chemical Award should be understood cf. internationally HANOTIAU/OHLROGGE, see fn. 4, p. 300 ff. See supra paras 54–55 on the categorisation of the doctrine.

[109] Judgment of the Supreme Court of Finland of 1 December 2020., KKO 2020:89.

[110] Ibid.

The ruling (or at least the reasoning) has been criticized in Finnish legal literature:

"The case did not explain why the conduct of the parties would have given rise to a separate assessment of the transfer of the main contract and the arbitration agreement, since no explanation was given that the parties had intended to keep these contracts separate. The principle of separability does not mean that the main contract and the arbitration agreement should explicitly be assessed in a way that leads to a different binding effect, but that such a difference in legal effects is possible where appropriate."[111] (emphasis added)

The author agrees with this criticism. As BORN has stated, while separability is undoubtedly relevant in the assessment, extensive involvement in key contractual matters likely implies consent to arbitrate.[112] No such detailed analysis appears in the reasoning of the Supreme Court. The author considers that the decision's reasoning should be understood in the context of the case's specific facts: the non-signatory party had explicitly expressed its intention to negotiate a future contract, which had not yet been finalized. This limits the broader implications of the case regarding commitment by conduct in more typical situations.

Regarding Sweden, this issue has not been assessed by the Supreme Court or any court of appeals. However, a frequently cited case is the SCC Case 108/1997.[113] In this case, a contract was negotiated between Company X and Company Y, which included an arbitration clause. Although Company Z, the parent company of Company X, participated in the negotiations, it explicitly refused to be a party to the contract. Despite this, the arbitral tribunal determined that Company Z was bound by the arbitration agreement due to its active involvement in the contract's performance including making payments thereunder.

Notably, the arbitral tribunal did not distinguish between the arbitration clause and the rest of the contract: *"The conduct of [Z] must be considered to constitute acceptance of the full contract with all [X's] obligations including the obligation to arbitrate any dispute with [Y.]There is no ground for ex-*

111 HEMMO, see fn. 6, p. 186. See also the discussion in paras 88–91 regarding whether a different standard of proof should apply to arbitration agreements.

112 BORN, see fn. 4, ¶10.01[C]. Somewhat similarly in Sweden HEUMAN, Skiljemannarätt, Norstedts juridik 1999, p. 97.

113 SCC Case 108/1997, award given on 21 March 2000.

cluding any specific parts of the contract obligations."[114] This aligns with views expressed in Swedish legal literature.[115]

However, the award in SCC Case 108/1997 was later set aside by agreement of the parties, limiting its precedential value.[116]

In conclusion, while the Finnish and Swedish legal systems acknowledge the possibility of binding non-signatories to arbitration agreements through conduct, the threshold for such commitment remains high. The Supreme Court of Finland's ruling in KKO 2020:89 highlights the cautious approach taken in Finland, where clear evidence of acceptance or substantial involvement in contract performance is required. In contrast, the tribunal's approach in SCC Case 108/1997 demonstrates a broader interpretation in Sweden, though its legal impact is limited. Ultimately, these cases underscore the importance of clear and consistent contractual conduct when determining whether an arbitration agreement can bind a non-signatory.

C. Abuse-Based Theories in Finnish and Swedish Case Law

Both the Swedish and Finnish Supreme Courts have addressed the doctrine of piercing the corporate veil.[117] Key factors considered when determining grounds for piercing the corporate veil include: (a) lack of administrative or financial independence; (b) the parent company conducting business in the name of the subsidiary; and (c) the owner's disloyal or abusive conduct toward third parties, causing harm to creditors.[118]

In general, piercing the corporate veil has primarily been applied in statutory liability contexts opposed to contractual liability. A case from the Court of Appeal of Eastern Finland illustrates this distinction, stating: *"The fact that piercing the corporate veil is not applicable in a contractual relationship is based on the fact that in a contractual relationship, a party is in a position to*

---

114 Ibid.

115 HEUMAN, see fn. 112, p. 97. See also the discussion in paras 88–91 regarding whether a different standard of proof should apply to arbitration agreements.

116 Judgment of the District Court of Stockholm of 25 April 2003, T 7898-00.

117 Judgment of the Supreme Court of Finland of 9 March 2015, KKO 2015:17; Judgment of the Supreme Court of Finland of 21 December 2017, KKO 2017:94; Judgment of the Supreme Court of Sweden of 20 January 1975; NJA 1975 p. 45; Judgment of the Supreme Court of Sweden of 12 November 2014, NJA 2014 p. 877.

118 Ibid.

assess the will and ability of the counterparty to fulfil its obligations and the risks involved in entering into the contract."[119]

The author questions this view. While piercing the corporate veil is understandably more common in statutory liability cases, contractual contexts may also justify its application. Factors such as bargaining power, information asymmetry, and the parties' ability to manage contractual risks may warrant closer scrutiny.[120] Unsurprisingly, piercing the corporate veil has been more readily accepted in employment relationships, despite their clear foundation in (employment) contract law.[121]

Neither Supreme Court has ruled on piercing the corporate veil in the context of arbitration agreements, but the Svea Court of Appeal has examined a related case involving two company directors.

The case concerned an arbitration clause in a purchase agreement between two companies, Icon and DS Company. When DS Company went bankrupt, Icon pursued DS Company's directors, Göran W and Björn H, for interest payments due under the agreement. Icon claimed the directors were personally liable because they had failed to fulfil obligations under Chapter 13, Section 2 of the Swedish Limited Liability Companies Act, which requires directors to take specific actions if the company's capital falls below a certain threshold. The directors argued that the arbitration clause barred the court's jurisdiction.[122]

The Court of Appeal ruled that while the arbitration clause applied to disputes directly related to the agreement, the directors' potential liability under the Companies Act was not automatically covered by that clause. However, since the directors had knowledge of the arbitration clause when signing the agreement and could foresee potential personal liability linked to the agreement's terms, they were still required to participate in arbitration proceedings to resolve disputes tied to the contract.[123]

Although the factual circumstances in the Svea Court of Appeal ruling were unique, the decision has been cited as an indication that Swedish law may

---

119 Judgment of the Court of Appeal of Eastern Finland of 29 January 2016, S 15/593.

120 KÄRKI, Piercing the Corporate Veil in Finland – A Multijurisdictional Study Aimed at Developing the Finnish Piercing Doctrine, Acta electronica Universitatis Lapponiensis, 2020, p. 239 ff.; SAVELA, Vahingonkorvaus osakeyhtiössä, Talentum, Helsinki 2015, p. 414.

121 Judgment of the Vaasa Court of Appeal of 16 November 2022, S 21/40.

122 Judgment of the Svea Court of Appeal of December 27, 1990, Ö 1855/90 (RH 1991:16).

123 Ibid.

permit binding non-signatories under the piercing the corporate veil doctrine.[124] However, MADSEN appears to disagree with this characterization, noting that there is no Swedish case law in which an arbitration agreement has been extended on this basis.[125] In the only known case where a Stockholm-seated tribunal was clearly presented with the issue of extending an arbitration agreement through piercing the corporate veil, the tribunal rejected the request on procedural grounds – specifically, that the Republic in question had not been properly named as a respondent. As a result, the tribunal did not address whether such an extension would be permissible in principle.[126]

Legal literature in both jurisdictions supports this possibility.[127] HEMMO, however, argues that veil-piercing claims often rest on conduct external to the contract and may fall outside the arbitration clause. Still, where the claim is closely linked to the agreement, arbitration may remain the proper forum despite the non-contractual label.[128]

In conclusion, while piercing the corporate veil in relation to arbitration agreements appears to align with international principles, the primary challenge lies in determining whether the threshold for piercing is met. Since piercing the corporate veil has traditionally been applied in cases involving statutory liability rather than contractual obligations, its application to arbitration agreements is likely to remain rare.

D. Choice of Law for the Extension of Arbitration Agreement to Non-signatories

In both Finland and Sweden, the prevailing view is that the law applicable to the arbitration agreement is determined by the *lex arbitri*. While the Supreme Court of Finland has not definitively ruled on this issue, statements in its judgments, along with commentary in legal literature, strongly support this position.[129] In Sweden, this view is even less contentious, as the Swedish

---

124 HOBÉR, see fn. 5, ¶3.154.

125 MADSEN, see fn. 8, p. 56.

126 SCC Case 143/2003, as reported in BERGMAN/BOND, SCC Arbitral Awards: 2004-2009, Juris, 2011, p. 175 f.

127 KOULU, see fn. 35, p. 116; TURUNEN/KOULU, Prosessioikeus, Alma Talent, Helsinki 2021, p. 1297; KAISTINEN, see fn. 6, p. 115; HOBÉR, see fn. 5, ¶3.154.

128 HEMMO, see fn. 6, p. 214. On somewhat similar logic, see Judgment of the Svea Court of Appeal of December 27, 1990, Ö 1855/90 (RH 1991:16).

129 Judgment of the Supreme Court of Finland of 24 April 2007, KKO 2007:39; Judgment of the Supreme Court of Finland of 1 December 2020, KKO 2020:89; HEMMO,

Arbitration Act explicitly states that unless the parties have agreed otherwise, the law of the seat shall apply to the arbitration agreement.[130]

The question of whether the law governing the subjective scope of the arbitration agreement could differ from the law governing its validity has received limited attention in Finland. A former Justice of the Finnish Supreme Court has opined that it is inconceivable for different laws to apply to these issues.[131] On the other hand, it has also been argued that *"it is not obvious that the general conditions for contractual validity, such as whether an arbitration agreement has been concluded or has expired, are determined by the law of the place [of arbitration]. It is more logical to assume that these questions follow the general contractual status, i. e. the law which, according to the ordinary rules of private international law, governs contracts."*[132]

In Sweden, legal commentary by MADSEN does not suggest that certain issues, such as the scope of an arbitration agreement, would fall outside the law applicable to the arbitration agreement itself.[133] On the contrary, MADSEN refers to a Svea Court of Appeal case involving the succession of a party to an arbitration agreement, where the Court applied the law governing the arbitration agreement to resolve the issue.[134] Based on this and related authority, it appears that the prevailing view in Sweden is that the law applicable to the arbitration agreement also governs its subjective scope.

As noted earlier[135], the prevailing international consensus is that the law governing the arbitration agreement also determines its subjective scope, particularly when the extension is based on consent theories. Given that the requirements for piercing the corporate veil are well established in both Swedish and Finnish law, it seems unlikely that courts or tribunals in either jurisdiction would, in the absence of clear authority, rely on international principles as the governing law rather than the law applicable to the arbitration agreement itself.

---

see fn. 6, p. 222 f.; MÖLLER, Om tillämplig lag på skiljeavtal, in: JFT (Juridiska Föreningen i Finland) 6/2020, Helsinki 2020, p. 644.

130 Section 48 of the Swedish Arbitration Act. See also Judgment of the Supreme Court of Sweden of 27 October 2000, NJA 2000 p. 538. In the said case, the agreement in which the applicable arbitration clause was included stipulated that the agreement shall be governed by the law of Austria. The Supreme Court ruled that did not constitute a choice of law for the arbitration agreement and applied the *lex arbitri* i. e. the Swedish Arbitration Act.

131 MÖLLER, see fn. 129, p. 647. This author notes that the passage does not concern non-signatory issues.

132 KOULU, see fn. 35, p. 64. Koulu does not further clarify his view.

133 MADSEN, see fn. 8, p. 437.

134 Ibid; Judgment of the Svea Court of Appeal of 25 May 2004, T 1361-02.

135 Supra III.C (paras 67–72).

V. Conclusion

This paper has examined the extension of arbitration agreements to non-signatories under Finnish and Swedish law, drawing on comparative international practice and transnational principles. The analysis confirms that while both jurisdictions maintain a strong commitment to the consensual foundation of arbitration, they also recognize that non-signatories may, under certain circumstances, be bound by or entitled to invoke arbitration agreements.

Consent remains the central criterion. Both Finnish and Swedish law accept the extension of arbitration agreements based on explicit or implied consent, particularly in cases involving third-party beneficiaries and guarantors.

The so-called group of companies doctrine is not formally accepted in either jurisdiction if understood as allowing an automatic extension of arbitration agreements based solely (or mainly) on corporate affiliation. Instead, the decisive factor is the role of the non-signatory in the negotiation, performance, or termination of the relevant contract. In this regard, Finnish and Swedish positions align closely with prevailing international standards.

Abuse-based theories, particularly the doctrine of piercing the corporate veil, have received limited attention in the context of arbitration in Finland and Sweden. While both jurisdictions recognize the possibility of piercing the corporate veil – especially in statutory liability contexts – its application in general contractual relationships remains rare and subject to stringent conditions. This paper takes the view that, in principle, there is no categorical obstacle to extending an arbitration agreement to a non-signatory on this basis. However, the threshold for such an extension is exceptionally high and is unlikely to be met in most cases.

Regarding the applicable law, the prevailing view in both jurisdictions is that the law governing the arbitration agreement also governs its subjective scope, especially in cases involving consent-based theories. For abuse-based extensions, some uncertainty remains, though courts are likely to apply the law governing the arbitration agreement rather than international principles.

Ultimately, Finnish and Swedish law reflect a cautious yet flexible approach to extending arbitration agreements beyond formal signatories. Consent – whether explicit, implied, or constructed – remains the cornerstone of this analysis. While abuse-based theories such as piercing the corporate veil remain exceptional, legal doctrine in both jurisdictions has shown a degree of openness to their application where corporate manipulation or manifest unfairness is clearly demonstrated.

VI. Description of the author

Lauri Markus Heiskanen is a Finnish Attorney-at-Law at Attorneys at Law Ratiolex in Helsinki. Since his graduation, he has practiced in the areas of domestic and international arbitration, litigation, and criminal law. He holds a Master of Law from the University of Turku (2020) and a CAS in Arbitration (2025). He was admitted to the Finnish Bar Association in 2025.